Sharon Varney
Leadership in Complexity and Change

De Gruyter Transformative Thinking and Practice of Leadership and Its Development

Edited by Bernd Vogel

Volume 1

Sharon Varney

Leadership in Complexity and Change

—

For a World in Constant Motion

DE GRUYTER

ISBN 978-3-11-071306-0
e-ISBN (PDF) 978-3-11-071334-3
e-ISBN (EPUB) 978-3-11-071342-8
ISSN 2701-4002

Library of Congress Control Number: 2021942027

Bibliographic information published by the Deutsche Nationalbibliothek
The Deutsche Nationalbibliothek lists this publication in the Deutsche Nationalbibliografie;
detailed bibliographic data are available on the internet at http://dnb.dnb.de.

© 2021 Walter de Gruyter GmbH, Berlin/Boston
Cover image: Topaz777 / iStock / Getty Images Plus Marek Trawczynski / iStock / Getty Images
Plus (juggler)
Typesetting: Integra Software Services Pvt. Ltd.
Printing and binding: CPI books GmbH, Leck

www.degruyter.com

Acknowledgements

I would like to thank the many people who made this book possible, including:
- Professor Bernd Vogel for your energy and for giving me this opportunity to share my work
- Professor Jane McKenzie for inspiring and challenging me
- Dr Mandy Bromley for reading drafts and offering encouragement
- Paul Stranks for your invaluable help with the graphics
- Steve Hardman and Jaya Dalal at De Gruyter for helping me navigate the publishing process
- The wonderful complexity community for being so open and inclusive
- The many people I have worked with over the years in my consulting, research, and teaching work for broadening my horizons across so many different contexts and cultures

This book is dedicated to Nathan. Your belief and practical support made it possible. Thank you.

https://doi.org/10.1515/9783110713343-202

Foreword

All that is solid, all that is gloriously ordered, having a home, being sheltered: absolutely neces-
sary! But the fact that there is this other, the infinity of the ocean – that liberates us.
—Karl Jaspers in a radio series in 1967–68, cited in Sarah Bakewell (2016, p. 302), At the Existen-
tialist Café: Freedom, Being and Apricot Cocktails

When I was asked . . .

. . . if I wanted to develop and edit a book series on leadership and its development
I hesitated. Some voices see only the relevance of short, science-focussed papers on
the subject while at the other end of the spectrum many push for not more than
bite-sized, micro-insights for managers. Others in my network bluntly asked why I
would waste my time for other people's insights and making them shine? Finally,
we recently had an impassioned conversation amongst colleagues about: 'Do books
on leadership and leadership development today still matter?'

Against this backdrop, or better because of these voices, I sided with the generous
and generative people in my network and decided to engage with this journey. Organisations, their human members, partners and stakeholders on their paths to be healthy
and sustainable and ultimately a positive force in society, can benefit from an evolving
set of contemporary, demanding, at times provocative ideas and practices – presented
in a set of relevant, deep, and accessible books.

And, yes, books do matter. Think of books less as static objects. Instead books
can be a platform to engage. Books are processes that elicit relationships and activities, challenge assumptions of leading and developing leadership, and evolve the
thinking *and* practice of leading and developing leadership processes. However,
while these would be beneficial outcomes, this still is a place of comfortable stretch.

Ultimately activist . . .

This book series will be judged on whether it addresses, moves, and responds to those
bigger questions that matter to individuals, organisations and societies – such as the
global challenges, for instance, summarised in the United Nations Sustainable development goals and translated to people's and organisation's local lived experiences.
Some will say that this exaggerates the influence that insights and practice can have.
Point taken.

However, we can try, aspire and take an activist position. We do not have the lux-
ury any more to ignore in our day-to-day activities in practice and science how every
piece of insight and learning can shape a desirable future for our planet. There will
not be the one answer in one book or even all books of the series. Still, we can take
ideas presented here head-on and consider how smaller or bigger chunks of this expertise can make a difference to our global and local challenges. Presenting that ambition can over time help reinforce and shift the science, mindsets and practices of
people involved in leading and developing leadership.

https://doi.org/10.1515/9783110713343-203

The book series should also set an impulse for the ecosystem of leadership and development. Two of our recent pieces – a study on the future of leadership and work and a review on leadership development[1] – show that the profession and global industry of leadership and leadership development itself can be more ambitious. How about reconnecting, bridging, translating, synergising again much more amongst the expertise in science and practice?

So what is . . .

. . . the De Gruyter Transformative Thinking and Practice in Leadership and Its Development series about?

First, in each of the books the series brings ideas on leadership and on leadership development closely together instead of addressing them separately. How the practice of leading works and how we can develop our leading capabilities need to go hand in hand.

Second, we believe that there is excellence in research and excellence in practice. It is not about attaching more or less value to one or the other. Instead, each book works as a bridge builder and translator between these outstanding communities. We aim to unearth organisations' untapped practices and excellence in leadership and leadership development. Academic progress will become accessible as practical leadership and leadership development. The reader can dive deep into the ideas spaces and insights, but can also immerse into the practice of applying, experimenting, probing the insights and suggestions coming with the books. The reader can therefore switch and synergise between these areas and transform the leadership and development capabilities of themselves, their organisations and networks, and their broader environment.

Readers of the series should go away with:
- Broadened imagination, aspiration and understanding of what transformative leadership and leadership development involves and how this can positively affect, support and develop their area of responsibility and involvement
- A widened and actionable repertoire of tangible and generative insights, activities and practices of leadership and its development – in view of current and future requirements
- An urge to take action – leadership and developmental activities with others. Books are a platform and journey to creative positive change in our spheres of influence and beyond.

---

1 Vogel, B., Reichard, R. J., Batistič, S., & Černe, M. (in press). A bibliometric review of the leadership development field: How we got here, where we are, and where we are headed. *The Leadership Quarterly*; Vogel, B., Heidelberger-Nkenke, O., Moussavian, R., Kalkanis, P., Wilckens, M., Wagner, M., & Blanke, K. (2019). *Work 2028: Trends, dilemmas & choices*. Henley Centre for Leadership, Deutsche Telekom & Detecon International.

Finally, let's face it, all initiatives are only made possible through a network. So I am deeply indebted to thank Steve Hardman and Jaya Dalal at De Gruyter, numerous reviewers, Sharon Varney, colleagues at the Henley Centre for Leadership, and most importantly, Alexandra, Manouka, and Kalypso.

Our first book – Leadership in Complexity and Change . . .

Sharon, first and foremost, thanks for choosing this series. It is a privilege to have you on board.

The first book of the series should model our goals – setting an example for insights, ambition, controversy, challenging assumptions and accessible practice that help readers navigate and engage with their personal and wider organisational and societal questions. Sharon Varney's ideas and expertise, and hence this book, are an ideal platform to start. I am delighted that this book opens the series.

Leadership in Complexity and Change: For a World in Constant Motion develops nine excellent chapters as spaces for ideas, insights and leadership activities that are more current and in demand than ever.

The book takes complexity science head on and makes it digestible and accessible without losing its complexity. It then takes us on a journey into how this can enrich and lift the way we think and act while changing and leading organisations.

When you read further, you will see that the language Sharon has developed is one reason why this book is an inspiration and a source for reflecting and doing.

It is simply difficult to highlight specific ideas from the interwoven fabric of the book. The ideas are, what Sharon would call, so well 'entangled'. However, for instance, learning informed leadership or dynamic patterning and mental aperture are some of those building blocks that will gain your attention. You will reach the point where Sharon introduces the vital signs of change and the idea that people and organisations should engage in noticing, interpreting, and responding to change. Here you will dive deep into these ideas. I have seen from other learners that these insights and practices can become second nature and add to your repertoire of engaging with the complexity of organisations and of leading in the midst of changing.

We often consider books as a linear process. I rather like to borrow the idea of 'loops not lines' from the book. The manuscript engages you to read, reflect, consider, but also to probe, experiment, and plainly to engage with complexity and change.

Her way of bringing complexity, change, and leading together will be to some readers one of the unknown unknowns, as she refers to later. We need to make sure that this book evolves as a known unknown source of inspiration. In that way your curiosity will encourage you to read and reread the ideas and practices, which in turn will help grow and develop its impact over years.

Once you started reading, you are already in the midst of what Sharon is laying out in front of us. In plain words, read and do something with this platform in a world in constant motion!

Bernd Vogel
Henley-on-Thames, UK
July 2021

Contents

Part II: **Tools and techniques for leadership**

Chapter 4

Chapter 5

Chapter 6

Preface

I first came across complexity science in the early 2000s when I was studying for a masters' degree. At that time, I was the group head of learning and communications for a global engineering and construction company in the offshore oil and gas industry. Before that, I had been vice president for international learning and development at a US bank. Those senior positions gave me considerable first-hand experience of leadership in complex, international organisations.

When I came across complexity science, I was delighted. Here was a 'new' science[1] that did a much better job than anything else I had found in explaining how my working world *really* worked in practice. Finally, here was something that explained the messy and, frankly, unmanageable aspects of leadership experience that seem to spill out of the sides of the neat management models. (You know, the kinds of things that we, as managers, have been conditioned to ignore!) I was captivated and intrigued, keen to learn more about what this meant for my leadership.

I wanted to understand the implications of complexity science for organisation science and for leadership practice. I wanted to find something that busted through the unfamiliar terminology, imported from multiple disciplines, to make complexity science accessible and applicable. I searched for something that was academically robust and practically useful.

I was disappointed. I simply could not find what I was looking for. Was I looking in the wrong places, I wondered? So, when I discovered that Professor Ralph Stacey (a leading academic in organisational complexity) was in the building, I made a point of bumping into him in reception and asking; am I missing something? No, he said. That is just the kind of problem we are studying in our doctoral programme. At that moment, the seed was sown for my own doctoral journey.

He went on to explain that it was important to study the complex nature of human organisation in its own right. The problem was that the translation of complexity science to organisation science was in its infancy and the rigorous academic work required to translate insights from the physical world to the social world was embryonic. So, while complexity science provided a rich source of inspiration for writers in leadership and management, the application was often loose and ungrounded.[2]

My journey has taken me from a practical problem (how to lead change in a complex organisation), to in-depth research in real organisational contexts, and widespread application of those insights to address practical problems of leadership and change. Over the past 15 years, I have been using insights from complexity science

---

1 This is a nod to Margaret Wheatley's (1999) *Leadership and the New Science* that, along with Gareth Morgan's (1997) *Images of Organization,* fired my curiosity to discover more about complexity science.
2 See Complexity and management: Moving from fad to firm foundations (Maguire and McKelvey, 1999).

https://doi.org/10.1515/9783110713343-205

to inform leadership and change practice across a wide variety of organisations and sectors. I have used practice and theory to inform one another.

The research underpinning is important because, without that grounding, it is all too easy to get polarised into ideological camps; one that *believes* in complexity and one that does not. Without a solid research base, there is nothing to bring the opposing views of complexity converts and sceptics together and we end up in a fruitless debate. For example, if we focus on whether change should be planned or emergent, we are likely to miss how change is both planned *and* emergent.

I have now written the book that I wanted to read. It presents complexity straight-forwardly, without dumbing it down or divorcing it from the underlying science. In addition to offering you a new perspective on leadership for a complex world that is in constant motion, I am delighted to share some original tools and actionable insights with you. They started life in my doctoral research that looked deeply into some persistent leadership challenges.[3] They were then developed and refined in conjunction with several organisational partners of The Henley Forum.[4] Since then they have been used by many practising managers and professionals on the MA Leadership at Henley Business School in addressing a wide range of real-world leadership and change challenges across multiple sectors.

This book is designed to help executives, managers, and other professionals to apply complexity thinking and tools to inform and evolve their leadership and change practice. I hope you find it helpful in developing your leadership in the midst of complexity and change.

---

[3] My doctoral research, *A complexity perspective on organisational change: Making sense of emerging patterns in self-organising systems* was chosen by the editorial team of the *Leadership & Organization Development Journal* as a Highly Commended Award winner of the 2013 Emerald/EFMD Outstanding Doctoral Research Awards in the Leadership and Organization Development category.
[4] The Henley Forum is an applied research centre at Henley Business School, part of the University of Reading. The programme of research and events is designed to help the Forum's organisational partners advance their practice in developing more dynamically capable organisations, https://henley.ac.uk/henleyforum (accessed 25/08/2020).

Introduction

Experiencing complexity

Context is everything

I began writing this book in March 2020. It had been planned for some time. In late 2019, I sketched the outline, pulled together a raft of practical examples, and cleared my diary for March so I could start writing, in earnest, on return from my holiday in India.

Context is everything. Just a week after my return from India and the World Health Organisation announced that the world was officially in the grip of a pandemic: a new Coronavirus, Covid-19. Suddenly, people around the world began to experience many familiar patterns of everyday life being engulfed by a tsunami of complexity and rapid change. Disruption to on-demand access to food, medicines, and other essentials, that we normally take for granted in the developed world, dramatically revealed something of the complex web of interdependencies we rely on to enable the smooth functioning of daily life.

Information, misinformation, speculation, and wild rumours were circulating globally and changing rapidly. It was a fast-changing picture as issues of physical and mental health, financial and economic health, and societal functioning jostled for attention in our consciousness, in the headlines, and in government policies. The inherent complexity and volatility of the world was exposed to all.

Uncertainty abounded. What was known clinically and behaviourally in the early days of this pandemic was completely dwarfed by the unknown. Outcomes for populations could only be guessed at – over time, those scientific guesses *should* become more accurate – but outcomes for individuals were truly unknowable.

Action amidst uncertainty

Yet, amidst enormous uncertainty, we each had to make practical decisions about our day-to-day behaviour and how we lived our daily lives. Business leaders had to make decisions about their organisation's policies and practices. Government leaders had to make decisions about national policies and how best to gain compliance. In our personal lives and in our workplaces, we were all faced with similar questions:
- In what ways do we carry on as normal? Where, when, and how do we make small adjustments? Where do we make large adjustments and real sacrifices?
- Do we take our chances, or do we think about everyone's chances? How do we navigate between competing health, social, societal, and economic priorities? Whose needs should we prioritise?

https://doi.org/10.1515/9783110713343-206

- When should we make adjustments, how long should they last, and what is the best way to enact them? Should we go first, or wait and see what others do? Do we, as individuals, businesses, and countries, follow the official advice, move faster than the official advice, or choose to ignore it?
- Do we prioritise for the short term or the long term? What are the likely implications – the benefits and costs – of one course of action over another?

This is leadership *in* complexity and change. What we were experiencing brings the highly dynamic picture of continuous change, connectivity, and intricate interdependencies into sharp relief. It offers a vivid portrayal of huge uncertainty and unintended consequences on a global scale, as new patterns of behaviour emerged from the accumulation of small decisions made by many millions of people. It exposed how government and business policies were shaping people's behaviour at the same time as that behaviour, and that of the virus, was shaping government and business policies.

Leadership in complexity and change

This is a book about leadership that does not talk about leaders. The reason for that, as you will see later, is that leadership emerges between people, rather than existing in individuals. I tend to refer to managers as a useful shorthand, however you do not need a position in a hierarchy to benefit from the insights in this book. It will be useful to anyone who is feeling curious or perplexed about how organisational life really works and why the working world does not simply work as many of the management books suggest it should.

The extraordinary events of 2020 put leadership in the spotlight and brought the dynamics of complexity and continuous change into clear focus as they played out intensively, and very publicly, on a global stage. Suddenly, the inherent uncertainties and ambiguities of leadership were starkly revealed for all to see.

While 2020 was exceptional, leadership in complexity and change is not. It has become an ordinary state of affairs for managers at all levels and in all sectors. Managers everywhere have been grappling with the practical challenges of leadership in complexity and continuous change for years.

Yet complexity denial, in various forms, is still fairly common. As you can see from the examples below, this often results from mistaken assumptions about complexity:

- Sometimes we hear those in charge denouncing complexity and calling for it to be managed or simplified. The mistaken assumption is that complexity is an excess of bureaucracy that should be removed or reduced. But what they fail to recognise is that internal complexity enables organisational *adaptation* in challenging and changing conditions.

- At other times, people turn to technology such as artificial intelligence (AI) and machine learning to deal with complexity. The mistaken assumption is that complexity is just extremely complicated. Yet they do not realise that computers lack the common sense to deal with the very ordinary complexity that humans effectively navigate every day.[5]
- Another common response to complexity is to assume that, if we cannot control complexity, then anything goes. The mistaken assumption here is that complexity is something special that is unrelated to what we each say and do every day. However, what we say and do matters in all kinds of expected and unexpected ways.

So, let me be clear about a few things. First, complexity is not an anomaly. It arises whenever you have lots of people working together, so it is inherent in organisational life whatever type of enterprise you work in. Second, complexity is not bad or bureaucratic. Indeed, without it we would lack the capacity to adapt in changing conditions. Third, complexity is not extra complicated. It is qualitatively different to complicated machines, which is why trying to manage or control it is the wrong response.

Complexity is not going away, and nor would we want it to as it enables organisational adaptation in a changing world. So, if we want to make leadership count, then we need to better understand why things work as they do. Once we have built that conceptual foundation, we can explore how to practically engage with complexity and work through it.

Complexity science, the science of uncertainty

The view from complexity science

I bumped into complexity science accidently through Gareth Morgan's image of organisations as flux and transformation (Morgan, 1997). It was a revelation. That is how the world *really* works, I thought. Finally, I had found something that explained my experience of organisational life, and beyond. It explained why even the best planned change was often so messy, surprising, and unexpected in practice. Suddenly, I understood why a big initiative may have little or no effect, whilst an impromptu comment from a senior executive might reverberate wildly through the business. It made sense of my experience where I had previously thought there was no sense to be made. I was fascinated.

Complexity is the science of uncertainty (Stacey, 2010). It is a multidisciplinary science that argues that the reality of the living world is complex, uncertain, and

---

5 For an excellent discussion on the inability of machines to navigate common sense, see Melanie Mitchell's *Artificial Intelligence: A guide for thinking humans* (Mitchell, 2019).

changing (Boulton et al., 2015: 28). So, what does complexity science tell us about how the world, and the social world, in particular, really works? Let us start with a few principles:

- **Change is the norm.** Counterintuitively, complexity science reveals that, far from being stable and certain, the familiar patterns of everyday life are dynamically re-created. We create a sense of stability – what we might call normal life – through a multitude of small adjustments that we each make to one another, and to the physical world, every minute of every day. (In complexity terms, this is known as **local interaction.**) Note: brief explanations of the complexity science terms in **bold** can be found in the glossary.
- **Things are entangled.** Over time, complex social systems tend to become more entangled, which means that effects can spread rapidly across a system. Increasing globalisation, fuelled by the ease of travel and the power of technology, has created an intricate network of interconnections between countries. Supply chains are global. Financial markets are global. Technology and communications platforms are global, enabling information and misinformation to spread rapidly. (This is **interdependence.**)
- **Effects may escalate.** In a complex system, small changes in behaviour can escalate into larger patterns. A run on a bank is an extreme example, while culture change is a more ordinary one. They both emerge from small changes in people's behaviour, amplified by communication and interaction. (In complexity terms, this amplifying effect is known as **positive feedback.**)
- **Radical change may happen accidently.**[6] In more extreme conditions (in complexity terms, this is known as **far from equilibrium**), we are more likely to experience irreversible system-wide change without anyone intending it. An extreme example is climate change, and a less extreme one is reliance on digital technology. Importantly, the system *itself* creates the new normal, or not. (In complexity terms, system adaptation to a 'new normal' is called **self-organisation.**)
- **Large changes may have little effect.** Lots of small adaptations by lots of people may neutralise large change efforts. (This dampening effect is known as **negative feedback.**)
- **The future is unknowable.** Our future is being co-created in the here and now by what everyone is saying and doing. But cause and effect get entangled in iterative interaction (**non-linearity**), so we cannot know ahead of time how those words or actions might change the whole system. (In complexity terms, this is known as **emergence.**)

---

6 This is a reference to Plowman et al. (2007).

This short preview of complexity science's explanatory potential is designed to convince you of its usefulness in understanding the changeability of the world. We will unpack it further in Part I.

Conceptually alluring, potentially confusing

Although many people refer to complexity theory (e.g. Morrison, 2010, Chiles et al., 2010), there is no single theory of complexity (Cohen, 1999). Complexity theories emanate from biology, chemistry, physics, maths, evolution, and computer science (Mitleton-Kelly, 2003). Insight from these "numerous theoretical strands" (Chiles et al., 2010: 11), such as **chaos theory, dissipative structures,** and **complex adaptive systems,** have combined to form a valuable body of knowledge. So, rather than talking about complexity theory, I prefer to talk about complexity science.

Complexity science is conceptually alluring. Its multidisciplinary roots imported new and intriguing terms into the worlds of social and organisational science. Before we go further, I want to inject a note of caution. While complexity science is incredibility useful in informing leadership in complexity and change, it needs careful translation.

When ideas from complexity science first made their way into the business and management domain, business leaders were variously encouraged to loosen control, to adopt simple rules, and to develop new and exciting organisational forms, so that organisations could self-organise to greater levels of fitness. Unfortunately, all that misses the point that organisational systems self-organise anyway, whether those in charge intentionally 'let go', or not. Complexity science does not tell us how the world *should* work, rather, it provides a fuller explanation of how the world works now.[7]

Unfortunately, it is all too easy for conceptual confusion to arise unless there is careful translation from the natural to the social worlds. For example, self-organisation in complexity science is quite different from self-management in organisation science.[8] Understanding those differences matters if we are to realise the promise of complexity science in informing leadership practice. When the application of ideas becomes untethered from the underlying science, the potential for that science to inform practice, and for practice to inform the evolution of the science is severely reduced.

---

7 The view I am taking throughout this book is that complexity science offers a fuller explanation of organising and changing because it bridges perspectives (Boisot and McKelvey, 2010).
8 For more on this, see Stacey (2010).

From hype to firm foundation

The early hype around complexity has had some unfortunate unintended consequences:

- Misunderstandings about processes of emergence only working in special circumstances allowed complexity science to be divorced from the mainstream in management and organisation studies. Complexity was conveniently put in a box (the irony!), only to be pulled out in special circumstances.
- Heralding a "new science" for leadership (Wheatley, 1999) is great for catching attention and bringing powerful ideas to a new audience. Unfortunately, it is also divisive. Pitching new against old polarises people into two opposing camps, with little common ground for fruitful dialogue. Complexity became an either/or choice (again, the irony!), you either accepted it, or you rejected it.
- Another problem with a faddish use of complexity science concepts (Maguire and McKelvey, 1999) is that fashion is fickle, always searching for the next big thing. Some of the quiet progress in complexity research has therefore been overlooked.

Over the past 20 years, however, scholars and practitioners have been working together to make solid progress in understanding the implications of complexity science in the business and management domain. Much of this has taken place beyond the confines of the mainstream management journals. For example, the dedicated complexity journal *Emergence: Complexity and Organization* actively encouraged inter-disciplinary and international conversations connecting different perspectives.[9] Many complexity scholars have chosen to share some of their best work in books because they allow a fuller discussion of key ideas.

We now have much firmer foundations to inform leadership practice. There are no simple answers, but we know a lot more to help people make informed leadership choices amidst uncertainty. Now is the time to take complexity science insights seriously in leadership practice. If not now, when?

---

9 The *Emergence: Complexity and Organization* journal published between 1999 and 2018 deliberately sought to bridge three gaps: (1) the distance between academic theory and professional practice; (2) the space between the mathematics and the metaphors of complexity thinking; and (3) the disparity between formal idealizations and actual human organizations. You can see more at: https://journal.emergentpublications.com/aims-and-scope/ (accessed 10/07/2020).

Engaging with complexity

Ambitions of this book

Drawing on complexity science, particularly complex adaptive systems, this book paints a picture of an interconnected world that is in constant motion, where leadership is enacted *in the midst* of complexity and change. The view taken here is that the working world really *is* complex and in constant motion. This is an important statement because it sets out a clear worldview[10] in which we are to understand what follows in this book.

An important implication of this worldview is that theory about complex systems can aid our understanding of how the working world really works. By understanding that world better, executives, managers, and professionals, like you, will be better placed to engage with its challenges and opportunities. This book will help you to:
- recognise where some of the challenges you are facing come from
- understand why those challenges persist
- engage with the ***dynamic patterning*** of organisational life
- appreciate the scope you have for leadership
- recognise the choices you can make
- choose how to manage yourself.

Complexity cannot be simplified. However, the language of complexity can be made more accessible. My aim here is to introduce some key ideas from complexity science in a straightforward manner, to make it easier for a range of managers and professionals to begin to grasp the implications of the science of uncertainty.

Structure of this book

There are three parts to this book. Part I invites you to see the world and your position in it differently. Part II introduces principles and practices of learning informed leadership to help you engage with that world. Part III explores being in that world and the personal aspects of leadership in complexity and change.

Part I brings complexity science to life. It explains *how* the working world is qualitatively different than many people assume and *why* that matters for leadership and change.

---

10 In academic parlance, this is an ontological statement. Boulton et al. (2015) make a similar statement. If you read this book and then find you want to take a deeper dive into embracing complexity, their book would make a good next step.

Chapter 1 paints a picture of a world in constant motion and introduces the idea of the dynamic patterning of organisational life. The key message of Chapter 1 is that organisational stability only arises through continuous changing. Yes, it does feel counterintuitive, but it is really important to understand. The familiar patterns that we experience in our working lives are dynamically created, through lots of small and large adjustments. When an organisation appears not to change, it is not due to a lack of change. Far from it.

Chapter 2 offers a straightforward view of key complexity science concepts by relating them to real-world organisational challenges facing managers. It introduces the **Complexity Conundrum** and explores entanglement, uncertainty, patterning, and emergence, then considers the leadership implications. A key message of Chapter 2 is that, as soon as humans get involved, complexity enters the room.

Chapter 3 positions leadership in the midst of complexity and change. It explains why it matters what we say and do when we interact with other people, how to make differences count, and it explores the advantages and challenges of being insiders. The key message of Chapter 3 is that leadership emerges through *active participation* in the dynamic patterning of organisational life. It ends by introducing the **complexity learning cycle**, a valuable tool for learning informed leadership.

Having built the essential conceptual foundation in Part I, Part II invites you to break some ingrained habits and to develop some new habits that are better suited for a world in constant motion. It begins by considering how we can invigorate existing tools and techniques with a new mindset. The subsequent chapters then explore some essential tools and techniques for **learning informed leadership**.

Chapter 4 explains why how we think about what we do matters a lot. It introduces the idea of opening our **mental aperture** to engage with more real-world complexity. It argues that the uncritical use of leadership models and tools is an unhelpful habit that inhibits thinking and invites you to adopt a new habit of critically employing multiple models to help you in thinking and learning for yourself.

Chapter 5 invites you to break the habit of assuming that small changes will not make much difference and instead to pay close attention to noticing what is changing. It proposes that **small data** in the here and now, which is freely available but often overlooked, provides valuable clues about emerging issues and opportunities. It encourages busy managers to slow down their thinking by bracketing time to enhance their noticing.

Chapter 6 introduces the four **vital signs of change.** It invites you to take your noticing to the next level by broadening and deepening your attention to help you in spotting the vital signs of change sooner. Then it considers how you might pull it all together to become a better noticer.

Chapter 7 encourages managers to break the habit of jumping to conclusions. It invites you to explore connections, contradictions, potential patterns, and possibilities in your noticing data, and to develop multiple interpretations without becoming too attached to the sense you make.

Chapter 8 recommends breaking the habit of leaping into action because what we say and do matters in what emerges. It invites you to explore your space for action and to choose your next response into the dynamic patterning of organisational life wisely. It encourages a more exploratory approach to adapting as you learn and to cultivating enabling conditions.

Part III explores the more personal aspects of leadership in complexity and change.

Chapter 9 considers an orientation to leadership practice where we consciously use ourself as the main instrument. It encourages you to think about leadership development in terms of a lifelong journey of deepening and broadening your use of self, your complexity of mind, and your practical judgement.

Each chapter concludes with a summary of key insights, followed by a section called 'noticing and noting', which invites you to relate some of the material covered to your own working context. You might want to start a reflective journal to note down what you are noticing about engaging with complexity and change in your leadership practice.

Back to you – noticing and noting

We are moving into new territory here. So, if you feel uncomfortable with anything you read in this book – such as you are in charge, but not in control – I encourage you to notice your discomfort. Perhaps pause to note it down, so that you can come back to it later. Just note it, without trying to analyse it. Your feeling of discomfort might signify that you have come across something that confronts your 'obvious'; the way you habitually view the world.

Perversely, our own ways of viewing the world can be so ingrained that they fail to be obvious to us.[11] To make them even harder to detect, our own ways of seeing the world are likely to be similar to those of the people around us because they are developed through shared life experiences. In sociology, this social patterning of ingrained habits, skills, and dispositions is known as habitus (Bourdieu, 1998). To use a sporting metaphor, habitus is a bit like having a feel for the game. Since we develop a feel for the game by playing the game, it is likely to be shared by those playing the same kind of game, for example, by people working in the same organisation, by those working in the same function in different organisations, or those working in various enterprises within the same sector.

---

[11] This blog from Dr Rob Warwick considers why and how our own 'obvious' is so obvious that we do not even notice it: https://metisexploration.wordpress.com/2020/05/18/obvious-its-obvious-really/ (accessed 28/05/2020).

Maybe what you will notice in yourself as you read on is a palpable sense of relief, or some excitement. Again, notice it, note it, but do not analyse it. Your positive feelings may signify that you have been feeling less than comfortable with taken for granted assumptions about leadership and change. Perhaps you have been on the receiving end of more and more data that does not fit the existing narrative. If so, what I am talking about may feel more natural to you.

I would encourage you to note any feelings of relief or discomfort as you go through this book and to wait until the end to make sense of them for yourself. It may be that new things become obvious to you as you go through this book and relate the ideas to your own experience. Perhaps you will notice yourself pattern switching.

Stating my obvious

I will be upfront with you. Complexity science has irrevocably influenced the way I understand the world. I can no longer imagine the universe as stable and unchanging. Instead, I notice the dynamic patterning (my term, more about that later) of the world. I find myself noticing what is new, different, surprising, puzzling, and unexpected. I try to pause before making that new data fit my existing mental models, to question what might be happening, to look for alternative explanations, to ask whether something new might be emerging.

Since I am being very honest here, I will admit that I find it easier to do that critical thinking in my work life. In my personal life, I am more likely to act out of habit, but I am working on it!

I am also really curious about the connections and interdependencies that create systems. Thinking in terms of relationships, networks, and systems has caused me to care more deeply about my place within those systems. I think and care more about ethics, power, influence, diversity, and inclusion/exclusion. For me, leadership comes with responsibility.

Part I: **A dynamic landscape for leadership and change**

Have you ever felt as if you are in the midst of complexity and change? Have you ever wondered; is it just me? Well, you *are* in the midst of complexity and change. It is not just you.

Part I portrays a dynamic landscape for leadership and change. Chapters 1 and 2 each draw on complexity science to explain what is going on. They invite you to reexamine your mental models, which you might find an easy leap, or a more challenging one. Chapter 3 then paints you into the picture and conceptualises leadership in the midst of complexity and continuous changing.

Chapter 1
In constant motion

Our dynamic world

Change is the natural state of the universe. We live and work in a world that is in constant motion. As philosopher William James puts it, reality is "in the making" (James, 2012: 138). In the flux of life, change is not an achievement. Stability is the achievement. This is important, so I am going to repeat it. In the flux of life, change is not an achievement. *Stability is the achievement.*

Have you ever tried to keep your mind or your body completely still? If so, you will probably have discovered that stillness does not come as naturally as you might have thought. It takes practice. So, why does conventional wisdom about leadership and management suggest just the opposite? Managers at all levels are expected to be 'on top of things', which assumes stability. They are also expected to 'shake things up', which assumes things are not changing. They are then expected to demonstrate their leadership of change, which assumes that things are unmoving unless there is deliberate leadership action.

This chapter unpicks a lot of conventional wisdom about the context for leadership. That conventional wisdom largely assumes that organisations are stable, and change is an accomplishment. Even in a VUCA environment,[1] one that is volatile, uncertain, complex, and ambiguous, organisations are largely thought of as stable and needing clear leadership to change, and thus to stay relevant in that highly dynamic environment. Not so, say Tsoukas and Chia (2002), who explain that organisational life is a process of "becoming" and that, counterintuitively, change comes *before* the more orderly state of organisation.

As we will see in this chapter, assumptions about stability have been hardwired into our thinking and practices over the past 100 years. They provide the foundations for many of our taken for granted ways of working, even influencing the language we use to describe how we do things, and how we think about what we do. It is extremely difficult to challenge this thinking because it has become so ingrained in our mental models of leadership and change that we do not even notice it.

Unfortunately those mental models of organisational stability create unhelpful traps (Argyris, 2010, Garvey Berger, 2019) that keep people stuck in prevailing patterns of thinking, talking, and behaving. Getting out of those traps can be difficult. Most managers have been trained and conditioned to talk and behave *as if* organisations are relatively stable, certain, and thus controllable. Such beliefs often run deep; they get entangled with our own sense of our professional identity and in social norms of what we should say and do and how we should be in our working lives. Changing our minds can, therefore, feel uncomfortable in our bodies as we challenge the certainties of ourselves and others.

https://doi.org/10.1515/9783110713343-001

In this chapter we will consider the trap of assuming that organisations are naturally unchanging when they are actually in constant motion. I call this dynamic patterning. We will then challenge the implications for how we think about and talk about leadership and change. In order to do this, we will need to surface our own obvious, challenge it, and perhaps replace it with a new obvious. I will call on complexity science here to provide us with a coherent conceptual foundation to underpin this important work. Complexity science is ideal for the job as it is "the science of evolutionary change, adaptation and self-transformation" (Merali and Allen, 2011: 43).

Is it just me? A world in constant motion

Everything is changing

Many managers tell a familiar story of working ever harder and longer in a continuous struggle to keep up with things, to get on top of things, and to stay on top of things, without ever getting there. When I introduce managers and professionals to complexity science ideas, their sense of relief is often palpable. Oh, I thought it was just me, they say. Let me be clear, it is not just you. The world really is in constant motion.

We have known this for a long time. Some 2,000 years ago, Greek philosopher Heraclitus, known for his doctrine that things are constantly changing and flowing (the idea of universal flux), argued that it is not possible to step into the same river twice.[2] In the early 20th century, French philosopher, Henri Bergson, prioritised movement over the things that move by arguing that existence is change. To paraphrase: "To exist is to change, to change is to mature, to mature is to go on creating oneself endlessly".[3] Around the same time, William James, the American pragmatist, advised; "philosophy should seek this kind of living understanding of the movement of reality, not follow [Newtonian] science in vainly patching together fragments of its dead results" (James, 2012: 138).

But is this just poetic fancy? We can turn to complexity science to explain what is going on (more in Chapter 2). Key terms, first instance in **bold**, can be found in the glossary.

Complexity science explains how **complex systems** are naturally dynamic, due to "continuous internal processes of exploration, experimentation and innovation at their underlying levels" (Allen, 2014: 265). In the working world, this encompasses all the different ways in which different people continually adapt and respond to one another as they say and do things in the normal course of working together. Ralph Stacey refers to this everyday interaction as **complex responsive processes** of relating (Stacey, 2001; 2012).

These everyday ways in which we adapt and respond to one another are so ordinary that we rarely think of them as change. But the amazing thing is that these micro dynamics are the source of large-scale patterns of change. A helpful analogy to bring this idea to life is to think of a large flock of starlings (known as a murmuration) and the amazing patterns the birds create in the sky as they fly over their roosting site in early evening. These fascinating patterns are complex and continuously changing. The constant motion and the fact that the larger patterns never repeat makes it mesmerising to watch. If you have not had the chance to see this stunning phenomenon for yourself, you can find plenty of murmuration videos on the internet.

The dynamic patterning here is co-created by the flocking behaviour of tens of thousands of starlings, sometimes millions, as each bird adapts to the other birds immediately around it and to the prevailing conditions. Complexity science explains that small differences between the individual starlings and in how they respond and adapt in the moment create novel patterns across the flock. Like a river, those dynamic patterns are never the same twice, even when they look similar. The beauty of this example is that it shows coherent patterns of change arising rapidly across the flock *without anyone being in control of making that change happen.* Change emerges from interaction without management or deliberate leadership. (In complexity science this is known as **self-organisation.**)

The dynamic patterning of organisational life

Now, let us take this analogy into organisational life. Here we have many people adapting and responding to other people, as they communicate with one another in the normal course of their everyday working lives. If you receive a meeting invitation, you might accept, decline, send a counteroffer, forget it, or ignore it. Your response might depend on what else is going on at that moment, who sent it, and how important it is to you. When people are gathered in a meeting, they may build on others' contributions, challenge them, overlook, or ignore them. (In complexity science this adaptation is known as **local interaction.**)

Rather than being physically connected like birds in a flock, individuals in an organisational system are often spread out across different places – different rooms, buildings, cities, countries, and so on. Yet, people can easily adapt and respond to other people who are in different places through the wide range of communication methods at their disposal. Interaction might involve real time conversations (synchronous communication), or there may be time lags like there are in email exchanges (asynchronous communication). As well as adapting and responding to other individuals, people are also adapting and responding to changing organisational conditions, such as different policies, strategies, technologies, workplaces, and so on.

Through the multitude of communications that happen every day – our "communicative interactions" (Stacey, 2012) – organisations are also in constant motion. Like the patterns of the flocking starlings, organisational patterns ebb and flow, they are never the same twice. (In complexity science this is called **emergence.** More in Chapter 2.) Importantly, we can see now that there is a whole lot of change going on in the normal course of working life. Indeed, on a very ordinary day, there is so much change going on that it would be absurd to think anyone could be on top of it.

Dynamic patterning is my term to convey the constant motion of organisational life. Importantly, it connects complexity (patterning) and continuous change (dynamics) to illustrate their interdependence (illustrated in Figure 1.1). In **complex adaptive systems**, complexity and change come as a package. Thinking about organisational life as a process of dynamic patterning draws attention to vitality – changing and enduring – in a way that we can engage with both. It invites us to notice what is changing in familiar patterns so that we can make our leadership count by choosing our responses into that patterning. (We will explore this in depth in Part II.)

Figure 1.1: Dynamic patterning.

Hidden depths of change

Change at multiple levels simultaneously is a key principle of complex adaptive systems. In a murmuration it is easy to see the constant motion at two levels of analysis. At one level, the individual starlings are in constant motion (**micro-level**). At the other, the flock is also in constant motion (**macro-level**). From our vantage point as outside observers, we can watch the interaction of micro and macro-change – the birds and the flock – physically play out across the sky.

A murmuration is a good example to begin with because the idea that micro-level change somehow co-creates macro-level change does not really challenge our mental models. Indeed, it is common to think about organisational change as some kind of accumulation of individual changes; if individuals change, then the organisation changes. However, complexity science shows it is *not* a simple sum of the parts since change is **non-linear**.

What makes the notion of multilevel change so intriguing is that constant motion at a micro-level may also re-create *familiar* patterns at a macro-level. When this happens, it can look a lot like nothing is changing when a great deal is changing. For example, organisational culture is often referred to as sticky.[4] Yet, it would be a mistake to think that persistent cultural patterns are unmoving or unchanging. Familiar cultural patterns ebb and flow as they are dynamically re-created by "the way we do thing around here" (Deal and Kennedy, 1982: 4), that is, through all the things we say and do every day as we adapt and respond to one another. Change is a multilevel phenomenon, but whether we notice change or stability depends on the level we are looking at.

Stability is dynamic

It may take some mental gymnastics to get your head around this idea of change enabling stability, so let me illustrate what I mean with a non-human example.

I used to work in the offshore oil and gas industry. The company I worked for laid a 1,166 km (725 mile) gas pipeline along the seabed between Norway and the UK. Doing this kind of work involves continuously welding twelve metre lengths of steel pipe on board a pipelay barge which, crucially, moves at the speed of the work to ensure that the pipe is carefully laid on the seabed without breaking. 'Dropping' the pipe is ruinously expensive. One such incident on another project cost $90 million. The pipelay vessels use a dynamic positioning system – a series of propellers and thrusters mounted all around the ship – that continuously adjust to weather and sea conditions to help keep the vessel on course so it can lay a continuous run of pipe. As you might imagine, in the North Sea this is essential. So, keeping the vessel on course (stability) in changing environmental conditions relies on numerous small adjustments (continuous changing), which we do not immediately notice.

Stability and change co-exist. The curious thing about stability is that things only remain stable in dynamic conditions because they are constantly changing. If we think about human beings now, we maintain physical stability (i.e., balance) by making lots of micro-postural adjustments in response to sensory data. It normally feels automatic, so we rarely notice it. But try standing on one leg and then closing your eyes, and you will notice your body adjusting to try and maintain your balance. Maintaining our balance whilst moving (e.g., walking) is quite a bodily achievement.

These hidden levels of change make it easy to convince ourselves that the working world is more stable than it is. Surprisingly, patterns of business as usual also arise from constant motion. In the working world, many people making a multitude of small changes may help to keep an organisational system metaphorically 'on course' in a changing business environment. The financial services case (Box 1.1) clearly illustrates how a multitude of micro changes enabled a financial services company to stay on course in the context of huge disruption.

Box 1.1 Rapidly changing to stay the same

A challenging environment: Early in the Covid-19 pandemic many of us experienced significant change in how we lived and worked. In late March 2020, the UK followed other countries and entered a period of lockdown. Schools were closed. Households were physically isolated from one another. Everyone was asked to stay home and to work from home if they possibly could.

Yet, with global financial markets apparently in freefall, many people were concerned about their personal finances. Suddenly, the volume of calls to pension and investment companies shot up. Financial services businesses were deemed 'essential' by the UK government and were expected to continue operating, while also adhering to government advice and protecting staff. These companies were expected to deliver business as usual in a highly challenging and rapidly changing environment.

A risky business: No wonder then, that operations risk professionals in a large financial services company were on high alert. Under pressure, they anticipated an increase in operational risk events, so they wanted to keep a close eye on what was going on. They began identifying high risk operational processes by considering business criticality and the degree of pressure on the process created by the extraordinary environment of Covid-19.

Business-critical processes under pressure: Unsurprisingly, they found some business-critical processes (e.g., dealing with customer calls in a timely and effective manner) were under significant additional pressure from multiple factors. Higher levels of sickness absence, along with reduced opportunities to recruit and on-board new staff, left fewer staff to deal with higher volumes of customer calls. The remaining call centre staff were thrown into working remotely from their homes and facing multiple challenges.

People under pressure: In the office, call centre staff were provided with ergonomically designed chairs and desks equipped with multiple computer screens and state-of-the-art headsets. Colleagues and supervisors were around to assist when needed. At home, many call centre staff found themselves ill-equipped with space and equipment, learning how to work remotely, whilst dealing with multiple demands and domestic pressures. Some had little more than a smartphone in the corner of their bedroom. Parents of young children found themselves juggling childcare, home schooling and work, while variously trying to keep the domestic ship afloat.

Yet risk incidents did not increase: With this sudden and significant increase in pressure, the operational risk team expected to find an increase in risk incidents with business controls failing to operate effectively. Surprisingly, their analysis found that the number of risk incidents over March/April 2020 *did not increase*.

Lots of tiny adjustments: Through qualitative interviews, they found lots of people making lots of tiny adjustments to keep things going in challenging and changing conditions. For example, some people with young families varied their working hours to accommodate both work and family life. Staff outside the call centres who had their own laptops returned their work-issued machines to support those in greater need. IT technicians worked 16–20 hours a day to rebuild and reissue laptops. Various people revised manual processes, such as signing documents, on the fly. Everyone modified their communication patterns and methods to accommodate remote working.

Huge change to ensure no change: The risk team found that people in the operational and support teams had managed to rapidly adapt to a radically different working environment (huge change). However, the review showed that controls were operating effectively (no change).

Emerging issues: Interviews revealed that people were under increased pressure from dealing with unprecedented changes in their work and home lives, with some just about holding it together. The risk team identified the emerging risk as sustainability. Concerned that increased pressure and long hours might increase the likelihood of errors being made, they adapted their questions to reflect the new conditions and asked; what new risks are emerging here?

Continuously adapting

The financial services case (Box 1.1) illustrates how the people doing the work rapidly changed how they were working during the early stages of the Covid-19 pandemic to keep business critical activities going. It shows that lots of people making lots of small adjustments were able to maintain stability in the face of massive disruption. This is a huge achievement. But this amazing achievement was not a one off. It happened over and over, in many different places and contexts.

The extraordinary circumstances of the pandemic – where environmental disruption was both rapid and extensive – suddenly revealed the workings of organisational life. Incredibly, many people in many places matched the speed and extent of the environmental disruption by coordinating with one another to make numerous small adjustments. Collectively those numerous small adjustments matched the large changes (e.g., everyone working from home) to enable many organisations to continue operating in turbulent conditions. In complexity science, this is known as **requisite complexity** (Boisot and McKelvey, 2011a).

These adaptive responses were so fast and so widespread that they could not be convincingly explained away with the usual stories of 'heroic' individual leaders stepping in and rescuing the situation. Any heroics were created collectively through lots of small, everyday actions. So, what can we learn? The learning here is not about re-creating the extreme circumstances of the pandemic. As Box 1.1 illustrates, that intense pressure has human costs and is not sustainable. But there are two important points to take from this experience:

1. There was no central coordinator. These rapid adaptive responses emerged from people coordinating with one another. Those in charge were thrown into it, along with everyone else. Any central coordination came after the fact as a tidying up exercise.
2. Organisational life is in constant motion. The bigger patterns are continuously created from numerous small changes that we may not even notice under normal circumstances.

Such creative and resourceful human behaviour is not restricted to pandemics or extreme events. Yet these amazing capabilities that enable us to keep things in balance while the world is in constant motion normally go unnoticed. We fail to notice them because making small changes is so routine. This is what **adaptive agents** in complex adaptive systems do every day. We can see the same kinds of adaptive behaviour going on in ordinary circumstances, if we pay close attention, as Box 1.2 illustrates.

Box 1.2 Keeping things going

Managers at a Higher Education Institution had an unpopular cost-cutting programme to imple-ment. Richard, one of the senior managers, told me he had put in "a ridiculous amount [sic] of hours trying to keep things . . . going". He described how he was adapting processes "almost on a daily basis" to correspond with new institutional priorities. In a changing context, effec-tively he was changing his behaviour to ensure that the organisation was not changing. John, another senior manager, told me that he had become "more resourceful" and was also putting in more hours to counter the effects of behaviour that he was unhappy with. While Jan explained how she had come at a problem "from a couple of different ways" to pursue one of her change goals, which had not progressed at the rate she would like, owing to the changing environment.

The lesson here is that, in a dynamic working world, business as usual is under-pinned by a continuous process of changing at a micro-level. Ongoing adjustments by individual birds keeps the flock of starlings in motion over their roosting site. Ongoing adjustments by the various thrusters and boosters in the dynamic position-ing system keep the vessel on course in stormy seas. Ongoing adjustments by many people keep the organisation on course in a changing environment.

From change to changing. From organisations to organising

Talking about change

Drawing on complexity science, we have seen that the landscape for leadership and change is a working world in constant motion. So, let us now consider how we talk about change in the work environment.

We often talk about bringing in *a change* such as an office move, a new organisa-tion structure, a different way of working, a streamlined process, or a system upgrade. Or we talk about making a change to a process, to technology, or even a change to/of people. We might talk about organising activities in a change programme, and we might raise a change request, use a change process, or a change approach to formal-ise the procedures for this work.

It turns out that we use the word 'change' to refer to various things. But notice, they are all *things*. In the working world, change is often described in terms of static states ('as is' and 'to be') and the choices and activities used to move from one to another over time. Curiously, despite all this talk of change, nothing is moving.

Losing the dynamism

What is really striking is how there is nothing dynamic about change in the way we commonly talk about it at work. The movement itself has been lost and we no longer see a world in constant motion. Talk about change projects and processes conceptualises defined "episodes" (Weick and Quinn, 1999) of change, with start and end points, which serve to punctuate the equilibrium (Romanelli and Tushman, 1994) of organisational life. We have artificially separated 'change' from 'no change' and assumed that 'no change' is the norm.

Moreover, in talking about 'a change' or 'the change', we have treated change as an abstract concept (Tsoukas and Chia, 2002, Stacey, 2010), rather than an ongoing process. We have focused more on the static "accomplishments" of change (Tsoukas and Chia, 2002) i.e., the 'ends' in terms of what will be different, rather than thinking about how change is accomplished i.e., the 'means'. When we talk about change in the abstract like this, it becomes difficult to point to precisely when and *how* change is happening, or indeed to notice *who* is making it happen.

All this talk about change has distanced us from it. We have conceptualised 'change' as if it is separate from us and from leadership. When we talk in these ways, it is easy to lose sight of the people involved and to overlook the many, creative ways that people continuously adapt to one another, and to a changing environment, in the course of their everyday work.

Talking about changing

Another way to see change is as a process of chang*ing* where we focus on the movement, just as we did in the murmuration. Using the term 'changing', as I do in this book, brings the dynamism and the people back in.

Imagine, for example, that we make a structure change by creating a new position in a team and bringing someone in to fill that position. Inevitably, there will be some procedural actions required for that to happen. Yet nothing has actually changed. The dynamic process of changing begins as people make adjustments in anticipation of the new person joining the team. The new person and existing team members are then involved in the process of changing as they adapt and respond to one another in the course of their work.

Or consider the example of introducing new software. Changing is happening as people anticipate the arrival of the new technology and what it will mean for them in various ways. Changing is continuing as people engage with developing and using the software. Changing is still ongoing as people tell stories about their experience of using the technology and as they reflect on their experience of how it was introduced, and so on.

In these examples, changing begins from the moment the idea is articulated. There is an *anticipatory effect* in complex human systems. Changing often continues long after the person or the technology has been introduced. Indeed, changing can continue after the person has left or the system has been replaced through the stories that are handed down about what happened and how people feel about what happened.

Conceptually, changing is "continuous" (Weick and Quinn, 1999), an ongoing process of "flux" (Weick, 2011), with no particular start and finish. Changing is also active, interpersonal and context specific: it is "enacted" and "performed" by specific people, in specific situations (Tsoukas and Chia, 2002). Changing is personal: it is something we "experience" (Tsoukas and Chia, 2002) and are "immersed" within (Stacey, 2010). Changing is also interpersonal as we make "situated accommodations" (Orlikowski, 1996) to one another.

Importantly, we have to step into the ongoing process of changing to "perceive" and sense what is happening in the "flux" of our experience (Weick, 2011). We understand that changing by checking out our conceptual "hunches" (Weick, 2011) with the specific happenings in our lived experience. Our own subjectivity becomes an asset as we use our five senses to pick up what is going on and to enact leadership in the midst of changing. (Much more about that in Part II.)

These views of change and changing are quite different, so I have summarised them in Table 1.1.

Table 1.1: From change to changing.

From change	To changing
Change is episodic (with beginnings and ends)	Change is continuous (and ongoing)
Change is an accomplished event	Change is enacted (it is embedded *in* action)
Change is abstract (it is hard to point to)	Change is experienced (by people)
Change is generalised (in a plan)	Change is performed (in a specific context and by specific people)
Change is understood objectively through abstraction (i.e., by stepping out) and making conceptual hunches about what is going on	Change is understood subjectively through immersion (i.e., by stepping in) and perceiving what is happening within the flux of our own experience

Source: Adapted from Weick and Quinn (1999), Tsoukas and Chia (2002), Stacey (2010), Weick (2011).

Experiencing changing

Changing may be likened to playing a team sport. While we might anticipate the kinds of moves other players will choose to make, we cannot precisely predict them ahead of time. While we know the kinds of moves that we might make, and we might practice and prepare for them ahead of time, we can only make them *in the moment*. Then we notice what is going on in and around the field of play, so that we might adapt to what is unfolding, to make our next move.

When we and others are experienced at playing a particular sport, we normally become more skilful in making our own moves and in anticipating other people's likely moves. When new players come in there might be a period of adjustment. Bringing in new kit or equipment might take more time and effort to get used to. New rules of the game might disrupt play until everyone gets used to them. Learning a completely new sport whilst playing a familiar one might be more disruptive still. In changing, the challenge is that the game never stops. It is an infinite game (Carse, 2011).

The word 'change' has fallen out of fashion in some work environments. In some places, it has been replaced with terms that sound a bit grander (e.g., transformation), more fashionable (e.g., agility), or more acceptable (e.g., continuous improvement). Whatever synonym you choose (transformation, continuous improvement, upgrade, evolution, agility, etc.), the important thing is to remember to add the *-ing*. By talking about transform*ing*, continuously improv*ing*, upgrad*ing*, evolv*ing*, *becoming* agile, etc., you are emphasising the dynamics and reminding yourself that you are enacting leadership in continuous changing.

Talking about organisations

Thinking and speaking in terms of changing, rather than change, is a bigger leap than it sounds. It is entangled with the question of whether we primarily think about organisations (as entities), or whether we think about organising (as a process). These are two quite different views of reality.

It is common to speak of organisations as distinct things which exist separately to the people involved. For example, we might refer to 'an organisation' or 'the organisation'. Then we talk about *the* organisation doing things such as making decisions, setting strategies, or pursuing policies. For example:

The organisation had a 'robust partnership' with the US which it hoped to scale up.[5]

The organisation that rules the internet's body language is having to perform a cultural and political dance.[6]

Essentially what we are doing here is treating the organisation *as if* it is a special person with human powers to act. Implicit in the above examples, is that an organisation has some independent agency to do things such as managing a change process or even doing a dance! There is also an implicit assumption that an organisation can have an intention to create effects, such as developing robust partnerships, or navigating politics. By talking about 'organisations' *as if* they are social actors (King et al., 2010), we have reified (made real) and personified them.

Talking about 'the organisation' treats the organisational collective as if it is a single person when it is not. By aggregating behaviour in this way, and then attributing it to the organisation, we are more likely to miss the important differences and interactions between the many people involved in organisational life. Complexity has been airbrushed out, so we fail to see the dynamics at play.

Many of the words we commonly use to refer to businesses and social or governmental enterprises reinforce this mistaken idea that they are static and unmoving. 'Firms' sound so fixed; 'institutions' sound so ingrained; and 'organisations' sound so orderly and organised. Therefore, I tend to talk about organisational life, which brings the vitality back in.

Talking about organising

In contrast, when we speak about social processes of 'organising', it brings the actions and interactions of the many different people involved in organisational life back into focus. People do things. People have agency to create effects through their social interaction. Differences between individuals matter a lot in change (Stacey, 2010: 63, Boulton et al., 2015: 22). As people interact, these small differences (**micro-diversity**) may combine to create true novelty; a bit like the grit in the oyster that co-creates a pearl.

People create organisation (familiar patterns of behaviour) through their organising. In this view, 'organisation' is an impermanent pattern (Weick, 2012), or a transitory outcome (Livne-Tarandach and Bartunek, 2009) in an ongoing process of human organising. An organisation cannot organise. Only people can do that, and they do it by repeatedly interacting and coordinating with one another.

As soon as diverse human beings along with their diverse human 'doings' become part of the picture, the dynamics of organisational life become visible again. When we let this complexity back in, we can see what is changing.

Diving deeper

The differences between these two views are not trivial. They represent two contrasting world views that are bound up with fundamental questions about reality and existence (see Table 1.2). We are now in the philosophical realm that academics refer to as ontology.[7] A huge amount has been written in the academic literature about these kinds of questions. Some papers have focused on the differences between the two views, as I have done here. Others have considered the relationship between them, as I have done elsewhere (Varney, 2013).[8]

Table 1.2: From organisations to organising.

From organisations	To organising
Organisations are relatively stable structures	Organisation is a temporary, transient, impermanent pattern in a dynamic process of organising
Organisations are social actors in their own right	Organising is a social process of interaction between many people
Organisations perform organising (e.g., they set strategies, pursue policies, etc.)	Organising creates patterns of organisation

Source: Adapted from Livne-Tarandach and Bartunek (2009), Weick (2012), King (2010).

The practical problem of talking about 'organisations' is that this convenient short-hand masks the dynamic and very human aspects of organising that we experience in organisational life. From a leadership perspective this is vitally important because engaging with the micro-level changing in human organising is how we make our leadership count. (We will explore this in Part II.)

From change management to managing in change

Managing in change

When we talk about organisational life as a continuous process of changing, it becomes clear that some assumptions about leadership and change have outlived their usefulness. As we watch the rapidly changing patterns in a murmuration, we do not ask which starlings are the leaders, which ones are in charge of making that change happen? It would be absurd. So, why do we think that organisational change can be managed?

The issue arises when we equate 'change' with 'a project'. Trying to squeeze change into a project is a bit like trying to stuff a cloud into a box. The aspects of change that can be managed and scheduled via a project approach are limited to a few tangible elements, for example, the written plans and schedules, allocation of resources or equipment, legal and contractual procedures, and the design of formal engagement, communication and training.

Yet, these tangible elements are just the tip of the change iceberg! Hidden from our gaze lie the countless intangible aspects of change that cannot be managed or scheduled through project management, but which are *vital to successful delivery of hoped-for benefits*. These are the kinds of things that might be conveniently labelled under the extremely broad banner of 'human behaviour'. This banner of human behaviour includes all the ways in which people choose to show up; how they follow prevailing social norms, or not; their sense of themselves and others; all the power dynamics and the political behaviours at play; all the informal conversations that happen every day, and so on.

When we think of change in terms of the informal, human dynamics, it seems inconceivable that we would think of change as a *thing* that can be managed. All we can manage are a few tangible aspects of the project. As these tangibles are often linked to costs, managing them is useful. However, if we want to realise the benefits in continuous changing, we need a different approach that prioritises learning. (We will explore learning informed leadership in Part II.)

Why we think change should be managed

The misunderstanding that change is a thing that can be managed is compounded by the common change management assumption that change *should be* managed. The short history lesson below briefly unpicks where these misleading ideas have come from and considers why they remain so pervasive more than a century later.

Organisations as machines

Frederick W. Taylor, a mechanical engineer by training, was one of the most influential organisational theorists of the last century (Morgan, 1997). His scientific management principles sought to standardise work processes through detailed analysis and control. As Morgan (1997) explains, those principles and the underpinning assumptions, principally that *organisations are like machines*, had a profound influence on work design during the 20th century and beyond.

Indeed, Taylor's ideas have become so embedded in work and organisational design that it is difficult to see them for what they are: a world view. His scientific management ideas have shaped our experience of the working world and therefore our understanding of that world and the role of leadership and management within it.

Taylor's ideas have also shaped the language we use. This is where 'change management' fits in. The embedded assumption is that change can be and should be planned and managed because organisations are unchanging, like machines.

Over time, continued use of mechanistic language (e.g., planning, designing, implementing, monitoring, controlling) has created what Stacey (2010) calls the "dominant discourse" in and about organisational life. Language plays a curious role. It imports a ready-made set of socially constructed norms that shape our understanding of reality. For example, using the term 'change management' imports deep-rooted Taylorist assumptions about organisations as unchanging machines.

Why 'change management' needs to go

The term change management has been enshrined in the IT Infrastructure Library (ITIL) standards since the 1980s as a way of controlling risk in IT projects. Indeed, it has been widely adopted in all kinds of management contexts. When terms like 'change management' are in common usage, we rarely notice the embedded assumptions imported through our everyday language. By using those terms, we pass on the embedded assumptions – for example, that change *can* and *should be* managed – without necessarily being aware of doing so.

Where people commonly talk about 'change management', they are more likely to act and interact with one another as if change can and should be managed. For example, they are more likely to talk about and to produce project plans for managing change. Those plans then reinforce the idea of 'change management'. You can see from this example how the language we use structures how we communicate and interact with other people "in the living present" (Stacey, 2010: 155). So, in addition to shaping our predominant *understanding* of reality, the language we use then shapes our ongoing *experience* of reality.

My invitation to retire the label and language of change management is not a call to abandon all planning or management. It is an encouragement to change how we talk about change. If we begin to talk about *managing in continuous changing*, we will think rather differently about what we do and what is possible.

Thinking about planned and emergent change

The notion of planned change has dominated both the change literature (Burnes, 2005) and change management practice (Burnes and Cooke, 2012) for many years. Planned change came from Kurt Lewin's work in the late 1940s. He reputedly coined the term "to distinguish change that was consciously embarked upon by an organisation" (Burnes, 2009a: 328). Planned change is understood as a formal procedure, that is actively managed, to move an organisation from one state to another through pre-planned steps (Livne-Tarandach and Bartunek, 2009). Does that sound familiar?

However, if we are busy noticing the planned aspects of change, we will be predisposed to overlook how much organisational change simply bubbles up autonomously, as Weick (2000) puts it, with no one managing it. Weick used the term emergent change to provide a contrast with planned change. 'Emergent change' has since been used as a headline banner for critics of planned change (Burnes, 2005).[9] The practical problem for managers is that, if we are predisposed to think in terms of planned change, we may be prone to overlook the more intangible aspects of change, such as emotional energy (Bruch and Vogel, 2011, Sanchez-Burks and Huy, 2009), and other human experiences.

Thinking in either/or terms is unhelpful in complexity. In practice, planned and emergent aspects of change are entangled (more about entanglement in Chapter 2). As Stacey (2010: 139) explains, organisational change will be emerging in the *interplay* of people's plans and intentions.

Missing the obvious

Whether we see more of the planned or more of the emergent aspects of change depends on what we are looking for. As we have seen, language creates perceptual distortions by emphasising a particular "way of seeing", which creates "a way of not seeing" (Morgan, 1997: 10).[10] We tend to perceive reality to fit our world view, so we see what we expect to see. More importantly, we may miss things that later seem so obvious.

Missing the obvious

The tendency to notice what we pay attention to and to overlook other perceptual cues is known as inattentional blindness (Mack and Rock, 1998). During dynamic events, for example, in the midst of changing, we may fail to notice even large changes to objects and scenes over a period of time (known as change blindness), and we may fail to perceive specific objects (known as inattentional blindness).

Simons and Chabris (1999) illustrated this in their well-known 'invisible gorilla experiment'.[11] They found that 50% of people who watched a short video of six people playing basketball, and who were asked to count the number of passes made by those in white shirts, failed to notice someone in a gorilla suit walking through the scene.

While we continue to talk in terms of 'change management', we are primed to notice those aspects of organisational change that lend themselves to being planned and managed. Importantly, however, we may miss valuable data that does not fit with that view. For example, we may overlook the countless examples where change happens without any one person or group deliberately managing it. We may discount people's natural adaptability and creativity. We may fail to notice how organisational stability arises from a myriad of adjustments and adaptations that people make to one another and to the changing environment in the course of their everyday work together (as we saw in the financial services case in Box 1.1).

In Part II we will explore ways of mitigating these risks by adopting ways of thinking designed to enlarge your worldview. I will introduce you to multiple lenses – the vital signs of change – that will help you to notice more widely and deeply than you otherwise would.

Change in the flow of changing

Thrown into the flow

As we have seen in this chapter, organisational life is in constant motion. Even familiar patterns of behaviour are dynamically re-created as people adapt and respond to one another and to their perception of changing organisational conditions. Just like the murmuration, or the river, those familiar organisational patterns of behaviour are never exactly the same twice.

Therefore, any change project you work on is *thrown* into this flow. Change interventions take place in continuous changing and you cannot know ahead of time precisely what effect they will have. You know there may be ripple effects (to stick with the river metaphor a while longer), so the chances of any plan landing exactly as you intended it are extremely small.

Many managers approach change projects as if the world is going to stop while they do it. It is not! They also assume that change will stay on the straight and narrow, as if it travels along some kind of path. It does not! As soon as you say or do anything, it potentially ripples out into unknowable areas. Even talking about the possibility of change can create ripples; this is the anticipatory effect that we considered earlier. For example, anticipatory effects might arise from rumours of a reorganisation; or hopes, fear and expectations related to a new senior executive who has yet to join the team.

Plans are general statements that tell you what should be happening. But any plans you make will quickly be out of date in the flow of changing, unless you pay close attention to emerging changes and use them to adapt your approach in response to what is actually happening.

Understanding change projects as taking place in the flow of continuous changing means thinking differently about the effects of change interventions. Thinking in terms of 'outcomes' makes little sense when changing is continuous. It is more useful to think in terms of intended and unintended consequences in change.

Intended and unintended consequences

Let us now consider five common patterns of intended and unintended consequences. I will unpack typical assumptions about what is going on and consider how we might reframe what is happening.

1. Nothing much changes

When a new organisation structure, computer system or process does not realise its intended effects, conventional thinking suggests that not enough was done to overcome resistance to change. Typically this refers to individuals' resistance to change because the assumption is that organisational change is some straightforward accumulation of individual change. It is not.

But, what if lack of change has nothing to do with resistance to change at all? What if people's enormous capacity for innovative, adaptive behaviour means that changes to formal structures, systems and processes just have less effect than you might imagine? As we saw in Box 1.1, rapid adaptation at a micro-level is what helps an organisation to survive in a turbulent environment. Those micro-changes create organisational **resilience** – a vital capability in a dynamic environment – and not something organisations would want to lose. Resistance and resilience are two very different animals, and they require very different approaches.

Another common explanation for a lack of change is that the new organisational structure or system was the wrong one. So we go back to the drawing board and tinker with the solution to *redesign* something that is a better fit. Remember, an organisation is not a static thing, but a continuously changing pattern of behaviour. So, looking for the right 'fit' is rather missing the point.

An HR manager for a local authority told me how she was continually being asked to redesign the organisation structure. "Re-org-ing the re-orgs", she called it! There is a whole lot to unpack here. For now, I just want to point out how repeated change projects may create no real change at all. Even with the best of intentions, our change efforts may reinforce the status quo.

2. Nothing much changes in the here and now

Sometimes nothing much seems to change in the here and now. However, the seeds may have been planted which create effects that become noticeable further away from the time and place of the intervention.

At one level, the announcement of a merger between two UK government departments DfID (Department for International Development) and FCO (Foreign & Commonwealth Office) is a machinery of government change – note the mechanistic language.[12] Civil servants are used to structural changes, so I trust they will manage the technical aspects competently. If so, the short-term effects may look something like business as usual.

While DfID and FCO both have worldwide roles, they have very different goals. DfID leads the UK's work to end extreme poverty, while the FCO is responsible for protecting and promoting British interests worldwide. Mergers and acquisitions always have a political dimension, but this one is highly contentious, with entrenched party political divisions.[13] One view sees DfID reform as "long overdue", while another sees it as "political vandalism".[14]

When you bring significant cultural differences, entrenched party political differences and a highly volatile world stage together, you create a catalyst for unintended consequences. So, while no one can know what will happen, we do know that conditions are being created now whereby large effects may happen further down the line. These unknowable effects may be felt far away from Westminster, in other spheres of life, years from now. They may also affect people in the UK in ways that cannot be predicted.

3. Things change in expected ways

When a change project seems to change things in the ways we expected, or better, we pat ourselves on the back, enjoy the plaudits, take full credit and breathe a huge sigh of relief. Job done!

Unfortunately not. In a dynamic world, problems do not stay solved. The world is still changing, so a solution that lands at one point in time, does not necessarily stay landed over the longer term. We therefore need to pay attention to how the change and the changing context are **co-evolving**.

Conventional change management has an answer for this. It is 'embedding change'. Embedding means fixing an object firmly in a surrounding mass, a bit like hammering in a nail. Unfortunately, this has thingified both the change and the organisation again. Can you imagine nailing change into a river?

I prefer to talk about 'absorbing change'. This comes from the idea of absorptive capacity (Cohen and Levinthal, 1990), a useful concept from organisational learning. Thinking in terms of absorbing change into business as usual helps in a few different ways. First, absorbing something takes time, so it reminds us to keep an eye on how things are going. Second, absorbing change encourages us to zoom out from focusing on a single change to considering multiple changes; there is never just one change game in town. Third, it changes the nature of the work from a push (doing the embedding), to a pull strategy (creating conditions for absorption). Fourth, it recognises the importance of learning in altering deeply embedded knowledge and habit (McKenzie and Van Winkelen, 2004).

4. Things change in unexpected ways

I worked with a large charity where the director of fundraising announced in a Town Hall style meeting with his team; I want us to put our supporters at the heart of everything we do. It was an off-the-cuff comment, designed to fire people up and thus prepare the ground for some projects that were coming later that year.

Unexpectedly, some two hundred people took it as a mandate to do just that. They rushed off, full of enthusiasm and began adjusting their work to put the charity's supporters at the heart, as they saw it. This was not what the director had intended, but it shows how a comment from someone in a position of power can have ripple effects. We will pick this up in Chapter 3.

In this kind of situation, suddenly you are off plan and working live. A natural reaction is to think, where have I seen something like this before? Then you pull out something that was a bit like this and respond as if it was *exactly* like this. Acting out of habit tends to work well if nothing has changed. In changing conditions, however, it may have unexpected effects. So, in the midst of change, we need to slow down our thinking (Kahneman, 2012, Cilliers, 2006).

5. Unexpected things change

Unexpected things changing is very common. As we will explore in Chapter 2, everything is entangled. For example, while organisational downsizing and redundancy programmes often focus support on those who are leaving, we know that survivors may also feel anxiety, stress and guilt (e.g. Mayton, 2011). Yet, it is easy to neglect this survivor effect until it happens. Unfortunately, once it has happened, suddenly we can see all the warning signs. It is a reminder that everything is obvious, once you know the answer (Watts, 2012).

One reason that we miss what later seems obvious is the tendency to equate change with projects. While we are busy focusing on what is *in scope*, we are prone to miss anything that is outside of scope. (Did anyone see that gorilla?) Frankly, there is normally so much activity in scope in a large change project, that it is often difficult to pay attention to anything beyond.

In complexity and continuous changing, however, we need to broaden our gaze to take in more of what is changing in the dynamic patterning.

Influencing dynamic patterning

Designated change leaders often worry about projects not delivering intended changes. They tend to be concerned that it will not look good for them because they are expected to *deliver* change. Failing to deliver can make them feel bad about themselves as well as feeling anxious about looking bad in other people's eyes. I fully understand this concern, I have been there too.

However, if nothing much changes at least you know roughly where you are. The bigger risk is of change interventions having effects that cannot be predicted in advance. This is the risk of unintended consequences. In a complex and changing world, the likelihood of unintended consequences is high. People often assume that unintended consequences are bad. Sometimes they are. But they may also take the form of unexpected benefits and opportunities that you would not want to miss.

Reframing our mental models of change can help more than you might imagine. Once we reframe change projects as being part of a wider experience of changing, we attune ourselves to expect the unexpected. Paying attention to unintended consequences may help us to spot weak signals about emerging opportunities and issues sooner so that we can choose to fan the sparks of emerging opportunities and dampen the ground around emerging issues.

In the dynamic patterning of organisational life, leadership is not about getting change to happen, it is about influencing the change that is already happening. We will explore some useful tools and techniques to help us do that in Part II.

What does this mean for leadership?

Involved in the dynamic patterning

Striving to be 'on top of things' when our working world is in constant motion is a never-ending journey to nowhere. As we will see in the Complexity Conundrum in Chapter 2, we can never know enough detail to be on top of everything that matters. As Cilliers (2002) explains; we cannot know complex things completely.[15] Even if it was possible, in a changing world it would be momentary. So, let me be clear, not being on top of things is not a personal or leadership failure. It is impossible.

Striving to be top of things is a bad idea anyway. With so much going on, it forces us to narrow our field of vision to the manageable. The job of leadership in complexity and change is to broaden our perspective to take in more of the dynamics.

Our aim is to "catch reality in flight", as Pettigrew (1992: 10) puts it, by spotting the vital signs of change in the dynamic patterning of the here and now. That means paying attention to our involvement in the flow of dynamic patterning and, as Schein (1997) puts it, treating everything that happens as new data. Being involved enables us to pick up valuable data for learning informed leadership.

Leadership is in the relationship

Interestingly, the things that matter in complex systems are not 'things' at all, they are relationships. Bradbury and Lichtenstein (2000) refer to these invisible connections as "the space between".

If we return to the murmuration, the individual starlings are in no sense coordinating the pattern. The incredible dynamic patterning arises in the space between the individual birds. It emerges from in-the-moment relationships between specific starlings, as they adapt and respond to one another and to changing air currents, weather patterns, predators, and the particularities of the landscape. Human relational dynamics are considerably more multi-faceted than a starling murmuration, but it serves to make the point.

From a complexity science perspective, leadership does not sit within individuals, it is activated through relationships as people adapt and respond to one another in specific situations. There are two main implications. First, 'effective' leadership is highly context specific. It is different in different times and places and with different people. Second, who is 'a leader' at any particular moment is fluid and may shift around a group (Stacey, 2010). Therefore different people will emerge as adaptive leaders (Schreiber and Carley, 2006), and the ability to effect leadership may run counter to the authority structure (Schneider and Somers, 2006: 356).

Questioning our certainties

Throughout this chapter, we have seen how assumptions about stability are embedded in our language and in the mental maps that influence how we act in everyday situations. Argyris and Schön (1974) call these mental maps our theories-in-use and they guide our leadership action.

People are often unaware of their own theories-in-use, such as 'change' needs 'management'. When we fail to explore our theories-in-use, we may inadvertently create mind traps that prevent us from thriving in complexity (Garvey Berger, 2019). We may also co-create organisational traps through collective, taken for granted ways of thinking (Argyris, 2010).

We create mental traps when problems are upsetting and threatening (Argyris, 2010). So, dismantling those traps – including assumptions about stability – can feel unsettling and disorienting. As I said at the outset of this chapter, most managers have been trained and conditioned to talk and behave *as if* the working world is relatively stable, certain, and controllable.

Unravelling ingrained mental models may include confronting deep-seated beliefs about what it means to be a good leader or change manager. Questioning our certainties is challenging, especially if they are bound up with our personal and professional identity.

Noticing how it is landing for you

Throughout this chapter, I have been introducing ideas from complexity science to help you to notice your own language and assumptions (your theories-in-use). I have invited you to redraw your mental map of leadership to reflect the dynamic patterning of organisational life by seeing the working world as being in constant motion, even when – and this is the tricky bit – you feel stuck in rather familiar organisational patterns. I have introduced you to the terminology of changing and dynamic patterning to help you think and talk about a world that is in constant motion.

Right now you might be thinking; of course that is how the world really works. Thank goodness I have found something that explains my experience! You might be feeling energised and liberated from habitual ways of thinking. Alternatively, you may be feeling distinctly uncomfortable. You might be thinking; these are fine words, but that is not how things work here; or I have got a big change project to land and there is a lot riding on it. You might be feeling unsure, threatened, or even angry. Those, too, are common reactions, and they are perfectly understandable.

Over the past 15 years working with executives, managers, and professionals from a wide range of sectors, I have found that complexity science often polarises people into these two broad camps. Of course, this is a sweeping generalisation, and your reaction may be somewhat different. Whatever your reaction, it is perfectly okay. Just notice it and explore how it feels without passing judgement. Then spend a few minutes noting what it is like for you in words and pictures. The prompts at the end of this chapter will help you.

As I mentioned in the Introduction, noticing and noting is an important practice for leadership in complexity and change. It sounds easy, but it takes some skill to do it well, so I have offered you some prompts for noticing and noting at the end of every chapter.

Key insights
- Organisational life is in constant motion, a process of dynamic patterning
- In a dynamic world, business as usual is created by many people making many small changes
- Organisational patterns are never exactly the same, never completely different
- How we talk about the world affects what we see in the world
- Talking about 'changing' helps us to reframe our mental models and see more of the dynamism
- In practice, planned and emergent aspects of change are entangled
- Change projects are thrown into the flow of continuous changing
- Leadership in change means influencing the change that is already happening
- Leadership is activated through our involvement and relationships between people
- Developing leadership for a world in constant motion means questioning our certainties

thrown into the flow
many small adaptations
dynamism question our certainties
involvement
in constant motion
continuous changing
dynamic patterning
reframe our mental models
relationships

Noticing and noting

I would encourage you to take a few minutes, right now, to notice how you are feeling about what you have just read in this chapter. Then spend a few minutes noting it down.

Try to be factual (e.g., I think . . . or I feel . . .) rather than judgemental (e.g., I am . . . or I am not . . .). The following prompt questions may be helpful:

- What is going on in your head? What do you *think* about what you have read?
- What is going on in your body? What do you *feel* about what you have read? What physical and emotional affects is it having on you?

Notes

1 The US army developed the term VUCA (volatile, uncertain, complex, ambiguous) to describe the changing and challenging nature of military engagement in the theatre of war.

2 See *Stanford Encyclopedia of Philosophy* https://plato.stanford.edu/entries/heraclitus/ (accessed 11/06/2020).

3 See *Stanford Encyclopedia of Philosophy* https://plato.stanford.edu/entries/bergson/ (accessed 11/06/2020).

4 Stickiness is a general economics term that applies to any variable that is resistant to change.

5 See *Financial Times* February 2020 https://www.ft.com/content/cef96328-475a-11ea-aeb3 -955839e06441 (accessed 11/06/2020).

6 See *Financial Times* November 2019 https://www.ft.com/content/2c8f959a-045b-11ea-9afa- d9e2401fa7ca (accessed 11/06/2020).

7 Ontology is the philosophical study of being that is concerned with the nature of reality and existence.

8 Complexity science, particularly the branch of complexity science known as Complex Adaptive Systems (CAS) has done an important job in explaining why we need to pay attention to micro-aspects of organising and changing. However, it is not purely a bottom-up science. Understanding the co-evolutionary macro/micro and the micro/macro relationships is central to complexity science. We will consider both in this book. My position on this matter is that organisation and organising are co-constituting (Juarrero, 2011).

9 'Emergent change' is a broad banner used to describe unplanned aspects of change, whereas 'emergence' in complexity has a specific meaning that we will look at in Chapter 2.

10 *Images of Organization* (Morgan, 1997) has become a management classic, inviting readers to see how our language creates powerful images of organisation and management that offer both insights and distortions.

11 More at http://www.theinvisiblegorilla.com/gorilla_experiment.html (accessed 26/05/2020).

12 As reported in the *Financial Times* 10/12/2019 https://www.ft.com/content/efaf9090-1aa7-11ea- 97df-cc63de1d73f4 (accessed 17/06/2020).

13 As reported in the *Financial Times* 17/06/2020 https://www.ft.com/content/3839fdef-cb51-4386- aa0a-f373b9652f9a (accessed 17/06/2020).

14 As reported in the *Daily Telegraph* https://www.telegraph.co.uk/opinion/2020/06/17/dfid-reform- long-overdue/ and the Guardian https://www.theguardian.com/global-development/2020/jun/16/polit ical-vandalism-dfid-and-foreign-office-merger-met-with-anger-by-uk-charities (accessed 17/06/2020).

15 Complex systems are 'irreducible', meaning they cannot be more simply described or understood.

Chapter 2
Complexity, straightforwardly

Our complex world

As soon as humans get involved complexity enters the room, therefore we need to understand something more about the science of complexity.[1] In this chapter, I offer some straightforward explanations of the theory[2] by relating them to real-world organisational challenges facing executives, managers, and professionals.

Complexity, however, is anything but straightforward. As Chris Rodgers so aptly puts it, complexity is 'wiggly' and leaders need to get to grips with that real-world wiggliness (Rodgers, 2021). It is a useful metaphor because it reminds us that complexity is not about straight lines, but loops (more about that later). Wiggly things tend to get tangled. Just think of the wires on your earphones before the move to wireless ear pods.

When we come across 'wiggliness' in organisational life, it is a clue that we may be in "the zone of complexity" (Stacey, 1996). Here the patterns of working life are *both* familiar *and* unfamiliar, predictable *and* unpredictable, at the same time. This entangled and paradoxical nature of complexity (that wiggliness again) is important to understand and tricky to navigate.

Chapter 1 considered dynamism in some detail. In Chapter 2, we will explore four more core characteristics of complexity – entanglement, uncertainty, patterning, and emergence – and consider the challenges they present for leadership:

- **Entanglement means that we can never be fully in control.** The entangled nature of organisational life means that we cannot simply pull things apart and deal with them one bit at a time. If you change one element, you potentially change everything. Entanglement, and the unpredictability that comes with it, is what makes complexity so difficult to engage with at a practical level.
- **Uncertainty means that we can never know how actions will play out.** Inherent uncertainty comes along with entanglement, and with the dynamism we considered earlier. When you are in charge, and everyone is looking to you for certainty, it can feel extremely uncomfortable to realise that you cannot provide it. Uncertainty, and the anxiety that comes with it, is what makes complexity feel personally demanding.
- **Patterning means that we can pretend the world is more stable and certain than it is.** The characteristic patterning in complexity is incredibly helpful in many ways (more about that in Part II), but it can easily lull us into a false sense of familiarity. If we assume the world is stable and unchanging, when the opposite is true, we may cling onto old habits of action.

https://doi.org/10.1515/9783110713343-002

- **Emergence means that surprises are common.** Remaining stuck in old patterns of leadership can blind us to what is changing (the dynamic patterning from Chapter 1). This can leave us woefully unprepared for shocks and surprises arising from processes of emergence where interactions generate something new and unpredictable.

Understanding the science behind these challenges helps us to appreciate why they are so persistent. If we develop a fuller understanding of how the working world really works, then we are much better positioned to engage with complexity and continuous changing.

Complexity is complex. Can we just simplify things? (Entanglement)

The challenge of entanglement

What managers generally want is to get a good grasp of what is going on. However, as the name suggests, complexity is complex. It is difficult to get a good grasp on complexity, so our very natural response is to want to break complexity down and simplify it. Big management consultancies often advise leaders to *crack* complexity, to *manage* it, or *put it in its place*.

For anyone who is feeling overwhelmed by complexity, that desire to simplify is very appealing. But can we? The short answer is no. The challenge here is one of entanglement. Let me explain.

Complexity (from the Latin *plectere*) means braided or entwined. Once the basic ingredients have been entwined to form a complex system, something new has been formed which cannot meaningfully be untangled into its constituent parts (this is emergence). Take mayonnaise, for example. Once you have combined eggs, oil, and lemon juice to form mayonnaise, you cannot simply take it apart again. Even if you could chemically separate the elements, how would you get the lemon juice back into the lemon, or separate the beaten eggs and get them back into their shells?

In everyday life, the words 'complicated' and 'complex' are often used interchangeably. As I highlighted in Chapter 1, people often mistakenly think that complex means extra complicated. If something is complicated, it can potentially be simplified. If it is complex, it cannot. Like mayonnaise, complex systems are **irreducible**. It is vital to understand these differences so we can decide how best to act in each context (Snowden and Boone, 2007).

Complicated or complex?

One way to illustrate the difference between a complicated and a complex system is to contrast a clock and a cat. A clock is a complicated system, whereas a cat is a complex system. As Gamble and Blackwell (2001) explain; with the right expertise, you can disassemble a mechanical clock, oil the cogs and levers, replace the worn parts, and then reassemble it to make it work better. However, if you were to disassemble a cat into its constituent parts, your chances of ending up with a working cat once you have reassembled it are pretty slim![3] Furthermore, the day-to-day behaviour of a fully working cat is far less predictable than that of a clock.

Snowden and Boone (2007) contrast a Ferrari and a rainforest to explain the difference between complicated and complex systems, respectively. With the car, the whole is the sum of the parts. Regular, expert maintenance serves to keep the car working predictably. In contrast, a rainforest is more than the simple sum of its parts. The various species of plants and animals interact with one another, with the natural features of the landscape, and with the changing weather in a complex ecosystem. A 'working' rainforest does not stay the same, it is in constant flux. Complicated systems do not change until they are changed. Yet complex systems do not stand still.

Let us now think about human systems. Norman (2011) contrasts rocket science with education science. He argues that the former is (very) complicated, whereas the latter is complex. Rocket science is **deterministic**. What that means is that the many parts in a space rocket combine in predictable ways, a bit like the Ferrari, or the clock. The effects of one part on another can be known and isolated. Overall, therefore, the effect of any specific part – when constructed to precise tolerances – on the behaviour of the overall **system** (the space rocket) is, ultimately, knowable.[4]

In education science, however, precise learning outcomes for any individual are unknowable. The reason for that is, unlike in rocket science, the relationship between inputs and outputs is non-linear. In other words, educational outcomes are not proportional to and cannot be precisely predicted from the inputs. Theories of learning tell us what happens in general (i.e., what tends to work for a population of particular kinds of people, in controlled conditions), but they cannot tell us what will happen for a specific individual in real life.

Take a formal leadership development programme, for example. The specific learning outcomes for a specific individual cannot be predicted from educational inputs because those learning outcomes are affected *by that individual* and by the detailed nuances of their particular context.

Feedback loops

What we have in leadership development are **feedback loops** between individual learners and other variables in the learning context, which affects learning outcomes. For instance, a manager who feels inspired may find it easier to get into the "flow" of learning and to experience a deeper level of attention (Csikszentmihalyi, 2014). Learning with others who are 'getting it' may provide scaffolding to help people develop and learn (Vygotsky, 1978), and such a cohort of learners may spur one another on to higher performance, by reinforcing collective belief in their abilities to learn (Bandura, 2000). There may also be a feedback loop between the learner and their emerging learning outcomes. Feeling that they are doing well may reinforce someone's belief in their ability to learn, which encourages them to put more effort into their learning (Bandura, 1977). These are all examples of positive feedback, which *amplifies* the change (i.e., the learning in this example) by *reinforcing* the effect of inputs.

Conversely, negative feedback *dampens* the effect of inputs and thus serves to maintain the *balance* of the status quo more closely. In the educational example, we might imagine how finding the subject or the teacher uninspiring, combined with unwelcome distractions, previous and current struggles to learn, and the lack of a supportive cohort, could reduce the attention and energy that an individual gives to their learning, thus reducing the degree of learning.

An important point about feedback loops

Somewhat confusingly, positive and negative feedback loops in complexity science do not relate to either the positivity of the message or the outcomes:

- Positive feedback fuelled *both* the boom and the bust cycles of the dot-com bubble in the early 2000s. Expectations of rapid share price growth fuelled actual share price growth way beyond the value of the underlying knowledge assets, until the bubble burst and expectations of a share price crash exacerbated the share price crash.
- Positive feedback, in the form of large financial returns, also fuelled rapid growth in increasingly riskier sub-prime mortgage lending in the United States and the plethora of increasingly complex financial products that enabled it to continue over many years. More and more institutions jumped on the bandwagon that seemed to keep on giving, until its spectacular collapse in the global credit crunch of 2007–2008.

To avoid confusion, sometimes people refer to 'reinforcing feedback' to denote positive feedback that *amplifies* the direction of system change, and 'balancing feedback' to denote negative feedback that *dampens* or opposes the direction of change to maintain the status quo (e.g. Meadows, 2008).

Cause and effect are entangled

The presence of feedback loops means that outcomes cannot be predicted. Emergent effects arise from the interaction of the various elements, including back onto themselves (known as emergence). Therefore, in complex systems cause and effect cannot be separated because they are intertwined.

Snowden (2002: 105) brings this strange concept of **mutual causation** (Juarrero, 2011) to life by contrasting a complicated aircraft system and a complex human organisation:

> Consider what happens in an organisation when a rumour of reorganisation surfaces – the complex human system starts to mutate and change in unknowable ways and new patterns form in anticipation of the event. On the other hand, if you walk up to an aircraft with a box of tools in your hand, nothing changes.

We often assume that organisational change is a simple sum of individual behaviour changes, but it is not. Feedback loops between individuals (local interaction) and between the organisational system and individuals within it (**co-evolution**) mean that it is not additive, it is multiplicative! Therefore, causes and effects are entangled in organisational change. For example, if you and I both work collaboratively, we might draw forth *more* collaborative behaviour from one another as we interact and we might also create a micro-culture for collaboration that enables *even more* of that behaviour from ourselves and others. (This is an example of positive feedback which amplifies change).

Table 2.1 summarises the differences between complex and complicated systems. While they share the characteristic of having many elements, the similarities between complex and complicated systems end there. (Note: A simple system has the same characteristics as a complicated system, but with fewer elements.)

Table 2.1: Complicated or complex?

Complicated	Complex
Many elements (variables)	Many elements (variables)
that combine in predictable ways (linear)	that combine in unpredictable ways through positive and negative feedback (non-linear)
so that the effects of the parts can be isolated (reducible)	so that the effect on the whole cannot be extrapolated from the parts (irreducible)
and their overall impact on the system is ultimately knowable (deterministic)	and their overall impact on the system is ultimately unknowable in advance (emergence)

'Complicatedness' – why it's not so simple in practice

Now that we have neatly differentiated between complicated and complex systems in theory, I would like to introduce the notion of **complicatedness** to expose how difficult it is to separate the two in practice. In organisational life, complicated and complex systems become entangled.

Price (2004) uses the term complicatedness to describe the burden of organisational bureaucracy, and what he calls 'non-simplicity' that many people will find familiar. He claims that complicatedness tends to increase, over time, as organisational complexity naturally increases. (I will explain why organisational complexity increases, and why that is useful, later in this chapter.)

As organisational complexity increases, it is often accompanied by a proliferation of management tools that are introduced to control that complexity. Commonly used management tools include organisational structures, systems, policies, processes, and procedures. They are designed to regulate people's behaviour to keep it within clear bounds, thereby reducing variability. Management tools tend to become more complicated, over time, as they are tweaked and redesigned to take account of new people and new circumstances.[5]

The good news is that these complicated management tools can be redesigned and simplified. In practice, however, that may not be as straightforward as it sounds, as Boxes 2.1 and 2.2 clearly illustrate.

Box 2.1 Simplifying a global travel policy

A global energy company had a lengthy travel policy that attempted to cover all eventualities, for all people, in all circumstances. But it became hugely time consuming to read, understand, maintain, and update this enormous document.

Some years ago, managers decided to simplify the complicated travel policy and reduce it to a few principles that were far easier to understand and apply. They allocated travel budgets to each department and replaced the lengthy document with a short set of principles to guide teams in making local decisions about what was reasonable within that framework.

It worked well in simplifying an over-engineered process. Everyone was happy. I spoke to another manager at the organisation more recently and he confirmed that devolved travel budgets were still in place more than 15 years later. However, over that time, the policy behind it had been centralised. Once again, it ran to numerous pages as it sought to standardise action across the globe. The complicatedness had crept back in.

Box 2.2 Introducing a single parking policy

Over the years, a variety of formal and informal rules and exceptions had developed across an NHS Trust to regulate who could park on site and in what circumstances. The result was a complicated and unwieldy bureaucracy. It was full of idiosyncrasies and many people felt it was unfair. Managers therefore developed a single parking policy which they felt simplified and standardised the rules to make them clearer and ensure they were fairly applied across the Trust.

The issue of where you park your car might seem trivial in the grand scheme of issues that face people working in a busy acute hospital. Yet it was anything but trivial for those concerned. As one nursing leader in the Trust explained, people felt aggrieved at being expected to change their embedded behaviour and establish a new routine. She went on to say; "this change affected the whole hospital and every member of staff, having a negative impact on staff morale". She described a big backlash from angry staff which had a huge knock-on effect across the hospital.

The introduction of a single parking policy served as a powerful catalyst for staff to vent their dissatisfaction and distrust of their management, which went way beyond issues of parking.

In both the practical examples, complicated written policies were simplified. Yet, as computer simulations have shown, complex and unpredictable behaviour still arises when **simple rules** govern the interaction of adaptive agents in a complex system.[6] So, while it is theoretically possible to simplify complicated aspects of organisational life, 'complicatedness' means it is virtually impossible to untangle the complicated from the complexity it is enmeshed in.

As I explained at the very beginning of this chapter, as soon as humans get involved, complexity enters the room. It is an important implication because it means that organisational systems cannot be 'designed', 'reorganised', or 'transformed', without tripping over complexity.

Can we see what's coming? Why prediction doesn't work (Uncertainty)

The challenge of uncertainty

As well as gaining a good grasp of what is going on in the entangled present, managers generally want certainty about what will happen in the future. For example, business leaders want to be able to predict economic conditions to help them plan for those future conditions and make appropriate strategic and tactical decisions to successfully ride upswings and downswings. It enables them to create plans and roadmaps for action.

Managers and professionals, at all levels in the hierarchy, and in all kinds of organisations, also want certainty to help them make robust decisions. They want certainty about the implications of their actions in advance and they want to avoid surprises, particularly nasty surprises. But is that realistic? Unfortunately not. With complexity comes the kind of uncertainty that is here to stay (Boulton et al., 2015: 214).

Working in a VUCA world

I mentioned VUCA in Chapter 1, but I want to unpack it more here. VUCA refers to an uncontrollable environment and the term has rapidly gained currency in the business world. It is often used as shorthand for saying "hey, it's crazy out there!" (Bennett and Lemoine, 2014: 217). But is VUCA just a buzzword, or does it have important implications for leadership?

VUCA unpacked

Volatility signposts the highly dynamic nature of the environment, featuring instability, wild fluctuations, rapid and unexpected change. As volatility increases, more things change, more quickly.

Uncertainty draws attention to a lack of predictability and a capacity for surprises, signalling that information is incomplete and imprecise. As uncertainty increases, predictability fails and the future truly becomes unknowable (Stacey, 1992).

Complexity highlights that a multiplicity of factors may already be, or may become, salient. Those factors often have hidden interdependencies and feedback loops, with no straightforward cause and effect. As complexity increases, it becomes impossible to know the outcomes of our interventions in advance.

Ambiguity reminds us that we must act in the here and now, perhaps with only a hazy view of what is going on. Events become open to more than one interpretation. As ambiguity increases, the harder it is to reach clarity and agreement about the meaning of events (Stacey, 1995).

The real challenge of VUCA arises from the fact that it comes as a package. Our working world is becoming more volatile *and* more uncertain *and* more complex *and* more ambiguous than ever before. VUCA is descriptive – and the hundreds of managers I have introduced it to have readily recognised these factors in their own contexts – but it does not tell us how the factors interrelate.

Complexity science offers a way of understanding the leadership implications of VUCA as a package. It explains that complex systems are, well, complex. We cannot know complex things completely (Cilliers, 2002) and anything we leave out may turn out to be hugely important in terms of how that system behaves (Cilliers, 2005), but we cannot know that ahead of time, even when it seems obvious after the fact (Watts, 2012). When complexity is combined with the volatility of continuous changing, we end up in the Complexity Conundrum (see Figure 2.1).

In short, when we have *volatility*, there is too much happening, too quickly, to ever take it all in; yet there are so many interdependencies (*complexity*), that it is never safe to leave anything, however small, out of the picture when making a decision. The context for leadership, therefore, is perpetual *uncertainty* and *ambiguity*.

As a package, VUCA signifies a fundamental shift to a qualitatively different working world, a world where many of our tried and tested management strategies and tools no longer work reliably. Complexity means that they only provide partial answers and volatility means they only provide temporary answers. If we are going to work in the ambiguity of perpetual uncertainty, it is important to understand it a little better. Broadly speaking, uncertainty takes two forms: 'known unknowns' and 'unknown unknowns'. We will consider both.

• **Volatility** –
there's too much happening, too fast,
to *ever* take it all in when making a decision

\+

• **Complexity** –
things are so connected that it's *never* safe to
leave anything out when making a decision

} creates perpetual
Uncertainty
\+
Ambiguity

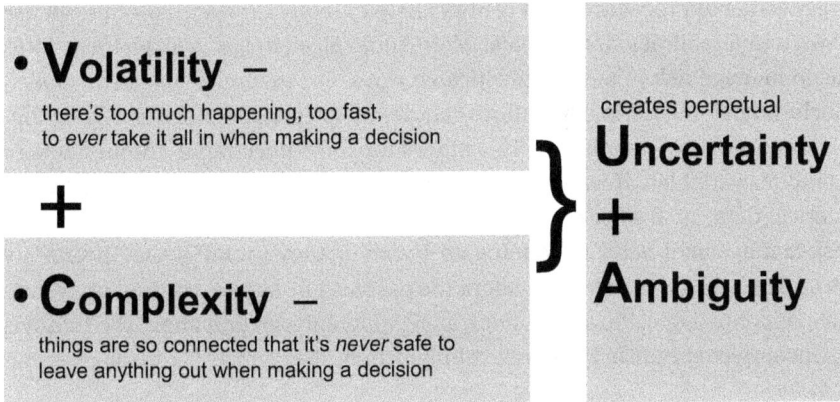

Figure 2.1: The Complexity Conundrum.

Managing known unknowns

The common way of thinking about uncertainty is in terms of known unknowns. We mitigate known unknowns with risk management as we do when we make travel plans.

Arriving on time

We know that traffic jams, train delays and flight cancellations are likely to happen from time to time. The unknown is whether those hold-ups will affect a specific future journey.

Imagine you have a business meeting with an important client. Knowing that delays might happen, you could look for data on when and where they are more likely, for example, busy times and junctions on motorways; on particular train routes or airlines; or at particular airports. If arrival by a certain time is especially important, you might decide to leave extra time for a car journey, or to catch an earlier train or flight to allow for 'normal' delays.

This is risk management. We weigh up the impact and likelihood of a risk – formally or informally – and gather information to help us to make a more informed decision about whether to and how to mitigate that risk.

In large and mature organisations, risk management is typically more sophisticated, wide ranging and formalised. It includes a variety of controls designed to regulate activities and prevent losses. These controls might include security passes to manage access to buildings and car parks; passwords and encryption to limit access to information systems and their contents; agreed levels of authority to regulate spending; and strategies and plans to direct how people should spend their time. On projects, risk management activities often focus on ensuring delivery on time, on budget and to pre-agreed quality standards. In other words, risk management is designed to increase certainty that the project will deliver what it is expected to deliver.

Organisational procedures and controls help to reduce known risks in response to known vulnerabilities and threats. More sophisticated risk management tools help us to manage risk in more sophisticated ways. For example, stochastic modelling (including Monte Carlo simulations) allows us to estimate probability distributions under a range of conditions. This allows for some uncertainty through one or more random variables. However, those random variables are usually constrained by historical data, such as past market returns.

Risk management helps us to mitigate *known* unknowns. But some uncertainty always creeps back in. Information about the past may be sparse, contradictory, ambiguous, or context-specific so it is not transferable. Information about the future is always incomplete because it has not yet happened. We cannot risk manage uncertainty away.

Airbrushing uncertainty

Management and uncertainty sit uneasily together. Unfortunately, many of the statistical tools and even the mindset of management, remove uncertainty from picture. Let me explain.

Assumptions about management are generally based on historic data and past experience, which presupposes that natural and social structures remain broadly stable and that any instabilities are normally distributed around the mean in the manner of a traditional bell curve (see Figure 2.2). For example, organisational performance management systems often assume that individual performance is normally distributed. Some people will perform better or worse than the average level of performance, and few will perform much better or much worse.

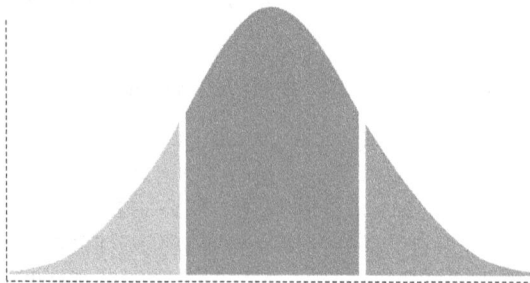

Figure 2.2: Normal distribution.

As the name suggests, a normal distribution focuses on the norm. Large deviations are treated as outliers and are statistically normalised through processes of data standardisation.[7] These neat bell curves (**Gaussian distributions**) simply airbrush uncertainty from view.

However, the mindset of normal distributions ignores two critically important aspects of uncertainty: extreme events and systemic events. These are relatively rare, but in the social world, they are not all that unusual. They are also unpredictable, even if they seem obvious after the fact (Watts, 2012).

Extreme events may be one-offs, for example, the invention of the World Wide Web, the storming of the Bastille in Paris, and the 2001 attack on the World Trade Center (i.e. 'black swan' events, Taleb, 2010). These rare and unpredictable events each had an extreme impact which has triggered wider transformation in the underlying social structure (Watts, 2012). Yet outlier events at or beyond the extremes of a normal distribution are more common than you might think. Blockbuster films with huge box office takings are relatively rare, but they are not one-offs (Andriani and McKelvey, 2007). Similarly, relatively few social media posts go viral, but those that do can have a large impact.

Normal distributions assume that the world is constituted by a collection of separate objects, where "social events are independent of each other" (Boisot and McKelvey, 2010: 416). However, the entanglement we explored earlier means that events are *not* independent at all. Under tension, tiny events can trigger "a causal chain reaction" which may generate an extreme outcome (Boisot and McKelvey, 2010: 416). This has become known as the 'butterfly effect' (Lorenz, 1972/2000).[8]

Wherever there are interdependencies, for example in supply chains, there will be chain reactions from time to time. Many will be dynamically stabilised by lots of small adaptations (as we saw in Chapter 1), which introduce negative feedback into the system to keep things in balance. Sometimes there will be a more extreme outcome. For example, in January 2021, wine merchants and others struggled to obtain delivery boxes due to a 'perfect storm' created by Christmas demand; stockpiling related to the UK's exit from the European Union; plus, extra demand on home deliveries and recycling problems due to the Covid-19 pandemic.[9]

Extreme and systemic events are impossible to predict, even with the most sophisticated statistical tools.[10] However, they have a considerable impact when they occur. The big problem here is that normalising outliers makes us overly confident in the certainty of the world. This "Great Intellectual Fraud" (Taleb, 2010), whereby outliers are airbrushed from our view makes us feel assured that we have tamed uncertainty when we have not.

While large events are less common than small events, their impact can be much greater. Large events have the potential to tip us into uncertainty where familiar patterns break down. We cannot simply absorb these events. They change the dynamic patterning of everyday life. A series of small, connected events can have the same effect. They shift the ground we walk on.

Paying attention to outliers

In contrast to the bell curve, **Pareto distributions** characteristically have long tails to the right, as illustrated in Figure 2.3. You might have come across Pareto's 80/20 principle, where 80% of the effects come from 20% of the causes, for example, 80% of revenues come from 20% of customers. These long tail distributions bring potentially interesting outliers back into the picture.

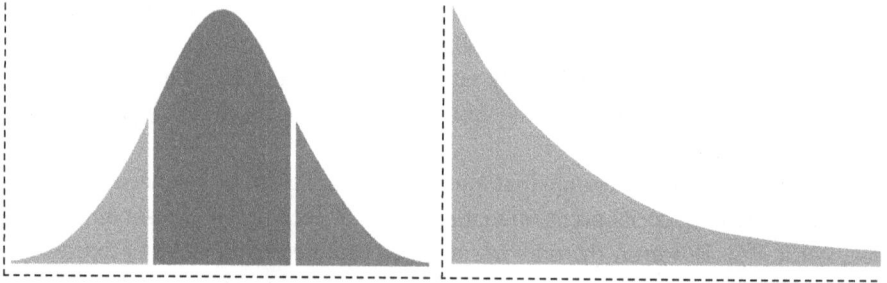

Figure 2.3: Normal and Pareto distributions.

In complex natural and social systems, Pareto distributions (known in complexity science as **power laws**) are everywhere (Boisot and McKelvey, 2010). Andriani and McKelvey (2007) highlight 40 natural world and 40 social world examples where power laws apply, from avalanche sizes to film and book revenues, firm sizes and salary distributions. Indeed power laws have been discovered in such volume and diversity that some scientists have dubbed them "more normal than 'normal' [distributions]" (Boisot and McKelvey, 2011b: 121).

While normal distributions treat everything as separate, power laws allow for the connectivity, interaction, and interdependencies that we find in complex human systems. If we return to the example of organisational performance management systems, 'normalising' performance scores to a normal distribution curve assumes that an individual's performance is unrelated to anyone else's performance, or to anything else. This would make a nonsense of the idea of high performing teams, where people spur each other on, or exceptional managers who enable exceptional performance.

With power laws, outliers, such as exceptionally high performing teams, are treated as "meriting attention" (Boisot and McKelvey, 2010: 417) rather than being disregarded as statistical anomalies. While statistics treats exceptions as outliers, management time and attention are often taken up by responding to anomalies and one-offs and adapting to the threats and opportunities arising from extreme events. So, we want to ensure we adopt ways of looking at things that bring them into view.

In a dynamic and entangled world, outliers are interesting because they may offer clues about newly emerging patterns. Rather than ignoring them, we should actively look out for them. We should be curious and ask searching questions about what might be going on. In Part II, we will pay particular attention to noticing, interpreting, and responding to outliers.

Engaging with unknown unknowns

Uncertainty also takes the form of *unknown* unknowns. This is a bit trickier to understand, as US Secretary of Defence Donald Rumsfeld famously discovered.[11] An unknown unknown is something that *cannot* be known ahead of time (Knight, 1921, in Boulton et al., 2015: 214). One reason for this deeper uncertainty is change. "Change of some kind is prerequisite to the existence of uncertainty; in an absolutely unchanging world the future would be accurately foreknown, since it would be exactly like the past" (Knight, 1921).

Continuous changing means that gathering additional data about the past will not reduce inherent uncertainty about the future. In a dynamic world (as we explored in Chapter 1) certainties only hold true over short time scales. For example, pre-industrial assumptions, such as work being small scale, handmade, and produced for the purpose of consumption, seemed quaint in the large scale, machine made, industrial era of production for profit. While industrial era assumptions, like the focus on centralised work 'places', no longer hold true in our post-industrial era where knowledge workers are technologically equipped to work from pretty much anywhere.

As we explored in Chapter 1, in spring 2020, millions of knowledge workers around the world rapidly flipped from physical workplaces to virtual workspaces pretty much overnight. A gradual trend towards virtual working took a completely different trajectory. We are not talking about normally distributed variability around a mean here. We are talking about fundamental changes in the structure, fabric, and underlying relationships in society. The effects of this change are unknowable.

Complexity science reveals the "fundamental uncertainty of the universe" (Stacey, 2012: 21) whereby the effects of entangled causes cannot be known in advance. But we do know that unknown unknowns are likely to emerge – there is some certainty in that. What we do not know is when, or where, or what form they will take. By actively bringing outliers into our view, we are aiming to *engage* with unknown unknowns as they emerge and become more knowable.

As we will see in Part II, widening our mental aperture may help us to appreciate more of the real-world complexity that lies beyond the bounds of a normal distribution and which may reveal more interesting possibilities for action:

> The "normal" world that we believe ourselves to be inhabiting is but a small and stable corner of a much broader and more complex one in which we are actually immersed. Indeed, the most "interesting" possibilities for action ... often reside in the tails of a PL [power law] distribution.
> (Boisot and McKelvey, 2011b: 120)

Haven't we been here before? The illusion of stability (Patterning)

Patterns and patterning

Entanglement and uncertainty force us to let go of the idea of predictability in complex systems. However, we are not living and working in a world of complete randomness. Complex human and organisational systems are patterned. Patterns are important. Patterns of social structure, for example, help us learn how to act and interact in the world.

The starling murmuration in Chapter 1 helped us to understand the world as being in constant motion. It is also a particularly useful analogy to help in understanding the concept and importance of patterns in complex organisational systems. Photos of this flocking behaviour sometimes capture a recognisable pattern such as a large bird, a whale, a tornado, or a heart. (Try an image search on 'murmuration' and you will see many examples.) This label is the human brain giving some intelligible form to what it sees – people are "pattern seekers" (Kahneman, 2012: 114) – rather than an orchestrated attempt by the starlings to create a particular form.

There is some regularity in a murmuration. This regularity means that we can know general things such as when and where a murmuration is most likely to happen, and the kinds of numbers likely to be involved. But the irregularity means that we cannot know precisely when and how any particular flock will form, or what exact shapes the murmuration will create. In the organisational world, we can know general things about how people are likely to interact in a meeting, but we cannot know exactly what will happen ahead of a particular meeting. While we are in familiar territory, the detail of the patterning of interactions in a meeting is never the same twice.

Such pattern is also fleeting, gone moments later. I therefore prefer to talk about pattern*ing* (rather like the idea of chang*ing* that we considered in Chapter 1). Any particular moment of pattern is abstracted from the ongoing process of dynamic patterning. As we saw in Chapter 1, these patterns are *never exactly the same* twice. Importantly, however, they are *never completely different*.

The science of patterning

Complexity science offers valuable insights into how such patterns are created, established and changed (Boulton et al., 2015). What we have in complex systems are "relatively stable mutually sustaining interactions", that is, behaviours, "leading to relatively stable aggregate forms" (Boulton et al., 2015: 244), that is, patterns.

The science of patterning

Let us return to the familiar murmuration example and unpick what is going on using complexity science principles.

Before they roost for the night, thousands of starlings (**adaptive agents**) come together as a flock (**complex adaptive system**) for warmth and protection (**interdependence**). The rapidly twisting and turning flocking behaviour over the roosting site (relatively stable mutually sustaining interactions) is known as a murmuration (a relatively stable aggregate form).

Small differences between the individual birds (**micro-diversity**) and in how they respond and adapt in the moment to the starlings immediately around them (**local interaction**) create novel and changing patterns (**emergence**) across the flock (**macro-level**). A gust of wind, or the appearance of a hawk (**perturbations**) also affect the shape of the patterns.

Note: **bold** terms are in the glossary.

So, what does 'relatively stable aggregate form' really mean? Essentially, it is a recognisable pattern. For example, flocking starlings create organic shapes which rapidly twist and turn. However, a migratory flock of geese fly in a v-formation, with minimal changes in direction. So, while the detailed patterning of flocking starlings and geese will be different every time, you would never confuse the two kinds of pattern.

'Thingifying' again

As we saw in Chapter 1, the dynamic patterning process creates relatively stable patterns in the working world too. These patterns are stable enough that we give them neat labels like 'organisational culture', 'agility', 'risk aversion', 'corporate responsibility', 'the organisation', etc.

Yet, as we saw earlier, familiar patterns are dynamically re-created by what everyone is saying and doing every day. For example, a 'team-oriented culture' might persist where people repeatedly talk and act in ways that enable collaboration and co-production, and where mistakes are used as a source of learning. Whereas an 'aggressive culture' might persist when people work in ways that continually pit individuals against one another, where the language is laden with threats, and where mistakes are punished.

These labels thingify the patterns in a convenient shorthand that glosses over the adaptive behaviour in the patterning process and makes the working world seem much neater, more controllable, and less human than it really is. Rather than describing a messy, dynamic process of human interaction and sensemaking involved in forming, re-creating, and changing patterns, we simply refer to the relatively stable pattern it creates as *a* culture, or *an* organisation.

We then treat 'the culture' or 'the organisation' *as if* it is a static thing that can be changed from the outside by things done to it. This contrasts with the complexity science view where 'organisation' or 'culture' is a temporary pattern in a dynamic process of patterning, which is changing itself (or not) from the totality of interactions within it. (We will explore outsider and insider views in more depth in Chapter 3.)

Similar, but not the same

The challenge of patterning is that macro-level patterns, such as organisational culture, are often familiar enough that we dismiss the differences – not a good idea in complex systems. Entanglement in complexity means that it is never safe to leave anything, *however small*, out of the picture when making a decision (see Figure 2.1 The Complexity Conundrum.)

Whether we get similar patterns (we might label this 'continuity'), or different patterns (that we might label as 'change') emerging in the dynamic patterning of organisational life depends on the balance of positive and negative feedback in the organisational system. As we saw earlier, positive feedback in micro-level interactions produces more of a particular type of behaviour which creates *patterns of change* at a macro-level, while negative feedback reduces variability to re-create *patterns of continuity*.

The challenge of patterning is making sure we are not beguiled by familiarity into thinking that things are more stable than they are. We need to look more deeply at familiar patterns and to ask ourselves, in what ways are these patterns not the same? What are the small ways in which this pattern is changing? What is new, different, surprising, puzzling, or unexpected in this pattern? For example, in an 'aggressive culture', we might look out for small ways in which people are being less aggressive or more collaborative. Or in a 'high performing team', we might look out for ways in which team members are not performing optimally.

In what has become known as 'The Stacey diagram', Ralph Stacey (1996) depicted "the zone of complexity" as a state where there is both order and disorder; both regularity and irregularity; both predictability and unpredictability.[12] This illustrates the paradoxical nature of complexity, where one phenomenon and its opposite "exist simultaneously and persist over time" (Smith and Lewis, 2011: 382) and challenges us to see *both* 'same' *and* 'different' in the dynamic patterning of organisational life.

If we continue to focus on similarities (the regularities), and make the conceptual leap that things are the same in all important ways, we may miss small, but important clues (the irregularities, including outliers) about where and how they are changing. In Part II, we will explore some straightforward ways in which leaders can refocus their attention to notice small irregularities, potentially valuable weak signals about how relatively stable patterns are changing.

Can we turn back the clock? Why complexity is a one-way street (Emergence)

Entangled wholes

The mayonnaise example earlier in this chapter illustrated the one-way nature of complexity. Once the ingredients have become entangled into mayonnaise, something new has emerged that was not there before. It cannot simply be reversed or undone. This is one of three ways in which complexity is a one-way street.

Earlier we made a distinction between complicated and complex organisational systems and acknowledged a tendency for them to become entangled. For example, formal organisation structures and hierarchies get entangled with informal relationships and power dynamics to form 'the way we do things around here'. The ingredients have combined to create something new.

'The way we do things around here' comes as a package. If we want to redesign the organisation to work differently, for example, then we need to engage with the whole package. We cannot just re-engineer the complicated bits (e.g., by redrawing the structure chart, changing the formal reward system, and so on), we must work with the entangled whole.

The implication is that organisational designers must do much more than simply design. Redesigning parts is missing the point when the whole is not a simple sum of its parts. Changing how the organisation works means engaging with the dynamic patterning of the entangled whole and the uncertainty that comes along with it.

Lichtenstein (2014: 1) explains that "organisation is an emergent entity: it arises as a whole-system out of the combined interactions and relationships of elements, but does not exist 'in' any one of those elements". If we refer to the business Amazon, for example, we are not referring to a collection of parts, but to a whole, like an ecosystem. Amazon is not in the people, or in the places, the website, the transactions, the branding, or the governance. Amazon is Amazon.

When we think in terms of engaging with whole systems and influencing the dynamic patterning, we start bumping into the concept of emergence. Emergence is at the heart of complexity science (Lichtenstein, 2014), but it is tricky to grasp, both conceptually and practically.

Understanding emergence

Goldstein (2000: 5) describes emergence as "a construct amid a thicket of conceptual snares" and explains that "the more one tries to get a clear grasp on the concept, the more it can prove to be elusive and murky".[13] Simply put, in emergence, something that was not there before comes into existence. In organisational life, that invariably means a new pattern.

Practically, it is hard to pinpoint emergence in the making, as it is an invisible patterning process that happens beneath the surface. We talked about these hidden depths of change in Chapter 1. Emergent structures do not exist . . . until they do. As Lichtenstein (2014: 1) explains; "when emergence happens, something new and unexpected arises, with aspects that can't be predicted even from knowing everything about the parts of the system".

Yet, in other ways, we all recognise emergence because it is a familiar part of organisational life, indeed it is part of life. As one manager aptly put it "emergence is the thing that comes along and pisses in your cornflakes!" You might sense the intense frustration in her choice of words.

Emergence is full of surprises because cause and effect are all tangled up (mutual causation). In the complex responsive processes of relating, my behaviour invites your behaviour, and your behaviour invites mine in an entangled gesture and response (Stacey, 2001). As we saw earlier, my collaborative behaviours enable yours as your collaborative behaviours enable mine. Even in this simple example of two people and one broad type of behaviour, cause and effect are entangled.

Human systems tend to be strongly emergent (Lichtenstein, 2014). One reason for this is that individuals are all different (**heterogeneity**). People are not standardised resources that are fully interchangeable (i.e., we are not homogeneous). Therefore, tiny differences may amplify as people interact, which may matter an awful lot in what emerges. It is another reason why emergence is full of surprises.

Lichtenstein (2014: 1) argues that "emergence is the creation of order, the formation of new properties and structures in complex systems". Yet the order that Lichtenstein refers to may not feel very orderly. That is why I prefer to use the term dynamic patterning to describe the ongoing ordering process that produces emergent patterns in complex human systems.

History matters

History matters in complex systems because it shapes the current context (this is known as **path dependence**). Comments cannot be unsaid. Events cannot unhappen. They shape the landscape of what is now possible (see Box 2.3). This time ordering of events is the only linear aspect in the wiggly world of complexity. It is the second way in which complexity is a one-way street.

Box 2.3 What is said cannot be unsaid
I vividly remember being in a town hall style management meeting where a would-be candidate for the Managing Director role set out his vision for the future, ending with the challenge; "you're either with me, or you're against me". Two hundred people immediately made up their minds which side they were on and it quickly became clear that most people had not sided with him.

Until that moment, I doubt whether many people in the room had given that idea any thought. Once said, however, it could not be unsaid. We all took a position and the damage had been done. Going forward, he could only try to mitigate the effects by softening his approach, with limited success.

The executive in this example (Box 2.3) could not unsay his ill-judged comment, the 200 people in the room could not unfeel their reaction. They could not move backwards and change that history. That event shifted the pattern of how that director was perceived, which co-created the new context for action whereby executives took a more inclusive approach to gaining buy-in, which was a shift to a new pattern.

But why was "you're either with me, or you're against me" so controversial? To understand why, we must go backwards and understand the history. We were working in a privately-owned company that started as a family business, which was part of the story that had been handed down. The company was mainly female, albeit the executive team was not, and the predominant culture was fun-loving. I imagine he had intended a rallying cry, but in that particular context his call to arms failed to have its intended effect. In other places, it might be seen positively as a sign of strength. Here, many people found it overly aggressive and confrontational.

Boulton et al. (2015: 29) explain that "the future is a dance between patterns and events". What this means is that what can happen in the future is affected by what has happened, that is, the order and sequencing of events in the past. However, what will happen next cannot be predicted from what has happened because it is affected by events in the here and now.

With processes of emergence, we end up with an uncertain connection between past, present, and future that can only be understood backwards. For example, Duncan Watts (2012) asks why the Mona Lisa is the most famous painting in the world. The answer, he explains, is because it is the Mona Lisa. The more famous it has become, the more fame it has attracted, the more famous it has become, and so on. Its history at the Louvre in Paris includes theft and, later, vandalism, which have both fed into its fame. (This is known as **increasing returns.**)

Complex systems will have more than one possible path in moving forwards. Yet, once they reach a **tipping point**, they cannot move backwards and change that history. As grains of sand are added to a sandpile, it reaches the point where another grain of sand creates an avalanche and thereby creates a new base for a new sandpile. (This phenomenon is known as self-organized criticality [Bak, 1996].) In human systems, a tipping point is better understood as a new pattern across a population of people. For example, train travellers are now more likely to read the news on their phone than to buy a newspaper.

Complexity supports survival

Organisational complexity is necessary for survival over the longer term in a complex and changing environment (Allen, 2014). As McKelvey (2013: 96) explains; "it takes internal complexity to develop strategies suitable for strategic success in a complex external environment". In complexity science, this is known as requisite complexity.

Requisite complexity means that complexity *inside* an organisational system must match (or exceed) the complexity outside the organisational system (Uhl-Bien et al., 2007). Firms that do not achieve requisite complexity may not survive in a complex and changing environment. Firms that do survive tend to become more internally complex as they adapt and respond to increasing complexity in their environment (see Box 2.4). This is the third way in which complexity is a one-way street.

Box 2.4 It takes complexity to deal with complexity
Somewhere around the turn of the century, the retail world shifted. Technological developments and adoption brought us online shopping from upstart tech companies like Amazon and eBay. At that time, it was a niche activity. Traditional retailers were divided.

Some retailers increased their internal complexity by experimenting with 'bricks and clicks' and developing an e-commerce website alongside their shops. This early speculation was costly and time consuming. No wonder then that many profitable retailers chose to stick to what they knew and continued to milk the cash cows in their prime locations. They made a strategic choice to *exploit* current certainties, rather than to *explore* new possibilities (March, 1991) such as e-commerce.

With the benefit of hindsight, that failure to develop an online offering looks strangely short sighted, and many retailers were left playing a costly game of catch up. At that time, however, diversification into bricks *and* clicks added complexity and cost to the business, and would have diverted resources, such as management attention, away from the main business. They could not have known then how ubiquitous online shopping would be now. It is just shopping.

Importantly it is the strategic choice to explore, experiment and innovate that allows requisite complexity to emerge. Yet we make that choice in full knowledge that many of those experiments will fail. This means tolerating a higher degree of redundancy, in the engineering sense. In engineering, redundancy means the inclusion of extra resources, which are not strictly necessary to immediate functioning, to support the main system. The reserve resources are redundant because they are not needed for normal operation, but they can be invaluable if the primary system fails. A familiar example is backing up your computer. You only need the back up if the main system fails.

Developing resilience

We only know whether any particular path will turn out to the be the right one with hindsight. Going back to the retail example, it is obvious *now* that retailers need an online presence because we know the answer (Watts, 2012).

We know that in spring 2020 many countries entered a period of lockdown to slow the spread of Covid-19. Physical shops were shut, so only online retailers could operate. But what if the virus circulating in spring 2020 had been a virulent computer virus? What if the computer systems that we rely on had been wiped out, or unavailable for an extended period? Then the investment in bricks and mortar retail would now seem like the *obvious* choice. In that scenario, online retailers who had experimented with physical stores would be the ones lauded in the press. This second scenario could also happen.[14]

Whether a specific experiment will help specific businesses to survive and thrive in the longer term is unknowable. We simply do not know what is coming down the road until it begins to emerge in the here and now. So, developing resilience in a changeable world is about increasing internal complexity through multiple experiments and by developing a culture that fosters experimentation and exploration to increase the chances of survival.

A pure exploitation strategy might deliver efficiencies and returns in the short term. But in reducing redundancy, and thereby complexity, it may compromise longer term survival. Relentless pursuit of efficiencies tends to shut down the kind of exploration, experimentation and innovation that together build adaptive capacity, and thus resilience in a complex and changing environment. We need both if we want to enable adaptability in increasingly dynamic and demanding environments (Uhl-Bien and Arena, 2018). Simple either/or answers lack the requisite complexity that enables adaptation. Therefore, for every complex problem, there is an answer that is clear, simple, and wrong.[15]

What does this mean for leadership?

Complexity is here to stay

Complexity is inevitable in organisational life. As soon as we have many people interacting to achieve particular ends, complexity becomes an intrinsic part of the picture.

Whether you are working in a nimble tech company, a financial institution, a government body, a healthcare provider, a retailer, a university, a big charity, a manufacturer, a logistics company, a large consulting firm, or any other sector for that matter, complexity affects us all. Complexity is there in bureaucracies and in flexible, adaptable organisational forms such as Uber and Airbnb. Complexity embraces us all, whatever sector or type of business we are working in.

If you replaced many of your human workers with machines, people would still be involved in making decisions, selling things, and so on. People would also be involved as customers and suppliers. Inevitably people will continue to interact, so you will still have complexity in the wider organisational system. There is no such thing as a little bit of complexity. Arguably, if you let some complexity in, then you get the whole lot.[16]

As have seen, complexity is a one-way street. There really is no going back, complexity is here to stay. Therefore, the first implication for leadership is that we must learn to engage with complexity.

Humans beat machines in complexity

Unlike machines, which are good at a narrow range of tasks, human beings are well adapted for complexity. We have been dealing with human complexity throughout our lives. Our experience in the world affords us the opportunity to develop rich contextual understanding. We have learned to adapt and respond to unexpected events in ways that machines just cannot do.

Easy things are hard

Even if you like the idea of a machine-driven world, there are significant downsides for a world in constant motion. Machines are incredibly good at doing some things, in some circumstances. Yet, as Marvin Minsky, co-founder of MIT's AI lab puts it, "easy things are hard". AI still struggles to interpret and describe the complexity of scenes and actions as humans do (Mitchell, 2019).

Highly optimised robotic systems work well in a narrow range of situations, but, if those conditions change, then your system will need to adapt. Machine learning does not enable your AI system to do something completely new. That is where you need humans.

Most of us have become surprisingly good at coping with the complexities of organisational life. We navigate a complex set of relationships with a variety of different people, and we use multiple channels to communicate. We work out how to conduct ourselves in a wide range of work situations and we successfully deal with an assortment of day-to-day challenges. In so doing, we are continually adapting and responding to other people, and to the events that happen, while re-creating the familiar patterns of working life. Incredibly, we manage to contend with the normal fluctuations of working life without really noticing the complexity of what we are doing. No machine could do this.

Furthermore, we are often doing this while accommodating a multitude of small adjustments to our working conditions. For example, we cope with new people joining and others leaving; we adapt to new priorities and demands; we learn new ways of working; and we find ways to absorb new technologies into the ways we work. All the while, we are incorporating new routines as we are re-creating the familiar patterns of working life. The complexity of what we are doing is astounding. Yet, we rarely stop to notice it.

Engaging with complexity

Generally, we each take the dynamic patterning of organisational life in our stride. We do not appreciate the complexity in which we are enmeshed. When our own complexity matches the external complexity, we can easily overlook it.

We only begin to notice complexity when the environment changes more profoundly, perhaps due to a large change event, or when the accumulation of small changes exceeds what we can readily accommodate. When it is revealed, however, that complexity can feel overwhelming and we may feel that we are in over our heads (Kegan, 1994).

There is some good news here. Theories of adult development suggest that humans can develop greater capacity to cope with complexity throughout their lives (Kegan, 1994). Garvey Berger (2011) calls this self-complexity. The idea is that adults can develop their internal complexity to make sense of an increasingly complex environment (requisite self-complexity). We will pick up on these ideas in Part III.

As we have seen, the challenges of complexity are vastly different to those of a machine-like world. Working harder or faster will not help us to engage with the challenges of entanglement. Putting more effort in will not help us to figure out how to act in uncertainty. Longer hours will not help us to notice small differences in familiar patterning which might provide important clues about some of the surprises in emergence.

If we want to learn how to engage with complexity, then we must understand more about how complexity arises and be prepared to review our understanding of the world. Leadership in complexity and change requires us to accept that organisational life is dynamic (as we saw in Chapter 1), and that it is entangled, uncertain, patterned, and emergent. What is more, we are *in the midst* of it all.

Key insights
- As soon as humans get involved, complexity enters the room
- Complexity means engaging with loops not lines
- Everything is entangled including causes and effects, changing one thing may change everything
- The conundrum of volatility + complexity = perpetual uncertainty and ambiguity
- Outliers are really interesting and more common than you might think
- Patterns are fleeting moments in an ongoing process of dynamic patterning
- Familiar patterns can lull us into a false sense of familiarity, so we fail to notice what is different
- The challenge of emergence means that surprises are common – expect the unexpected
- Developing internal complexity helps in adapting to external complexity
- Human beings beat machines in engaging with complexity

complexity outliers
dynamic patterning
VUCA surprises are common
complexity conundrum
entangled patterns
emergence loops not lines
engaging with complexity
uncertainty **human beings**

Noticing and noting
- How do each of the four characteristics of complexity that we considered in this chapter show up in your working world?
  Entanglement
  Uncertainty
  Patterning
  Emergence
- Which one(s) feel more challenging for you?

Notes

1 Thanks to Paul Zonneveld from Mobius Executive Leadership for introducing me to that phrase.

2 Students of complexity science will want me to be more specific here. My research has taken a complex adaptive systems (CAS) perspective, so when I refer to complexity science, this is my theoretical home territory. I have spent over 15 years researching complex adaptive organisational systems, so it is not a simple lift and shift from the natural sciences as was common, and somewhat problematic, in the early applications of complexity science to organisational science.

3 I would like to reassure cat lovers that no cats were harmed in the production of this metaphor.

4 This does not mean that everything is fully known. Norman (2011) references the NASA space shuttle Challenger disaster of 1986 where behaviour of the O-rings at low temperatures, which led to a fatal malfunction, was not fully known at that time by those making the launch decision. However, it was knowable.

5 David Stephenson brings this idea to life in his story of 'The Palace' (Garrow and Varney, 2013).

6 Reynolds (1987) developed a programme called BOIDS which simulated the flocking behaviour of birds using simple rules.

7 Typically, data sets are cleaned to normalise data that is more than 3 or 4 standard deviations from the mean.

8 'The Butterfly Effect' (Lorenz, 1972/2000) is an analogy to illustrate sensitivity to initial conditions in nonlinear systems whereby a small change in initial conditions can create a significantly different outcome.

9 See https://www.bbc.co.uk/news/business-55878062 (accessed 11/02/2021).

10 To explore the unpredictability of complex systems and the social world in more depth, see Watts (2012).

11 US Secretary of Defence Donald Rumsfeld is famously remembered for his use of this term in a 2002 NATO speech https://www.nato.int/docu/speech/2002/s020606g.htm (accessed 23.04.2020).

12 Professor Ralph Stacey is one of the leading thinkers on complexity science in the business and social world and his work has been highly influential for practice. He has now distanced himself from his idea of different zones with different tools (Stacey, 2012). I tend to agree. It oversimplifies complexity and makes it seem more certain and bounded than it is. Yet, I have found that 'the Stacey diagram', as it has become known, can be a useful learning tool to help people as they begin to conceptually engage with complexity. Stacey has developed his confidence and competence to discard those stabilisers, and I have too. Maybe by the end of this book, you too will understand complexity well enough to join us.

13 Jeffrey Goldstein (2013) and Benyamin Lichtenstein (2014) have both offered greater conceptual clarity around the term emergence.

14 The University of Cambridge's Centre for the study of Existential Risk considers both technological and biological risks: https://www.cser.ac.uk/ (accessed 17/07/2020).

15 This aphorism is normally attributed to American journalist and satirist H L Mencken.

16 Nonlinearity means that small actions or events can have large consequences, so it makes no sense to talk about degrees of complexity. A system is either complex, or it is not. Once you let people in, you get complexity.

Chapter 3
Leadership in the midst

Being in the midst

Having painted the picture of a working world that is inherently complex and continuously changing, I now want to put you back in that picture. The good news (and the bad) is that you are right in the midst of it all.

We are all insiders in the social world, entangled in a web of relationships. We are involved in the flow of events and the patterning of behaviour and we are affected by them. A key message from complexity science is that we cannot step out from this continuous flow of events and dynamics of patterning, of which we are part, to *be* a leader, or to *do* leadership. Therefore, *leadership is enacted in the midst of complexity and change by involved insiders, not by detached outsiders.*

Being inside and an integral part of what is emerging puts us in a privileged position. Firstly, it provides us with first-hand understanding of the patterning of the world we inhabit through our everyday experience. Being in the midst offers us direct access to rich contextual data about the particularities of what is going on through our five senses. Secondly, our capacity for language enables us to engage in communication about our world with others. Thirdly, being entangled within organisational systems puts us at the heart of the action. This is what makes the things we say and do count in processes of emergence.

As we will explore in this chapter, what we say and do matters when we are connected with others in a web of relationships. Leaders (i.e., those with formal authority and/or informal influence) are not in control of what happens, but nor are they passive recipients. Like everyone else, leaders are *active participants in the dynamic patterning of organisational life.*

Yet being in the midst can sometimes feel like being in the mist; it is hard to get a clear view.[1] At best we will have a glimpse of what is going on, we can never see the whole picture. Making sense is challenging when we only have fragments of a changing scene, so we must act in perpetual uncertainty and ambiguity (the Complexity Conundrum). Moreover, we are by no means in control of how events and even our own actions play out across an organisational system – even if we are in charge and accountable for what happens.

Being in the midst of the dynamic patterning of organisational life is inherently paradoxical. We are simultaneously initiators and on the receiving end of what is happening. Being in the midst of complexity and change can feel extremely demanding. Yet, being an insider and in the thick of action is the *only* place to enact leadership.

In this chapter, we will explore more deeply what it means to be in the midst of complexity and continuous changing. We will consider how the world is relational; what it means to be insiders; why differences are so important; and the implications

https://doi.org/10.1515/9783110713343-003

for leadership. In doing this, we will highlight two more important characteristics of complexity, namely relationality and paradox.

Yes, it does matter what you say and do

Thinking in terms of relationships

Chapter 1 briefly introduced the idea that leadership is in the relationship and indeed in the "space between" (Bradbury and Lichtenstein, 2000). We considered the notion that leadership arises between people as they interact and that who is a leader at any time is therefore fluid and rather context dependent.

All this is rather different to conventional ways of thinking and talking about leadership which focus on the leadership *of* individual organisations, leadership *of* complexity, and leadership *of* change. The unspoken assumptions are that individuals are separate from one another, separable from organisations, detached from phenomena like complexity and change, which are somehow distinct from one another. Leadership is treated as if it is something special that can be differentiated from other ways of being and doing.

That kind of thinking views the world as a collection of independent objects. Boisot and McKelvey (2010: 416) call this an "atomistic ontology" (i.e., a worldview) because the focus is on individual parts. In this view, events, actions, individuals, and organisations are distinct from one another. In contrast, complexity science takes a "connectionist ontology" which brings higher levels of interaction and interdependence among actors and phenomena into the picture (Boisot and McKelvey, 2010: 420).

Moving from an atomistic to a connectionist view means thinking in terms of relationships, rather than individual entities. We already know that relationships are important in leadership, after all, power and influence are both relational concepts. Yet, we probably think primarily in terms of individuals forming relationships with other individuals (an entity perspective). Complexity science takes a more overtly relational view. It concentrates on the connections, interactions, and interdependencies themselves. It is interaction, rather than independent action, that creates change and continuity in a dynamic world.

The space between

So, let us think about 'the space between' in its own right and bring the idea to life, starting with physical space. In the now familiar murmuration, change the space between the starlings in the flock and you change the patterns that are co-created. This works in the human world too.

Changing the space between

Many countries and states brought in policies of social distancing in the early months of the Covid-19 pandemic in 2020. By changing the physical relationships between people, literally changing the space the between them, political leaders sought to change the macro-level patterning of coronavirus infection rates (known as the R value)[2] across the population. The space between people really mattered. This is a stark reminder of our interdependence; that what we do affects others with whom we are connected.

Human relationships are multi-faceted, so the physical space between human bodies is just one dimension of the many ways in which we are connected and interdependent. In organisational life, the space between is crammed full of the really important stuff of the social world that gives meaning to our words and actions. We have named some of them. For example, trust, respect, communication, influence, and social capital are all properties of relationships rather than individuals. Leadership itself is a relational word, so is followership and friendship.

Many important organisational phenomena are created in the relationships between people. For example, organisational learning and organisational change both emerge in the many micro-interactions between people, rather than in people. Knowledge is also created in the space between people (Nonaka, 1994, Nonaka and Konno, 1998) because context is what gives knowledge meaning.

The power of social norms

Our involvement in society brings social norms into play. We relate to one another through culturally specific norms which serve to regulate individual action in terms of what is seen as socially acceptable behaviour in a particular context. For example, we have created different conventions in greeting one another in different countries and in different situations. Often these social norms get entangled with material artefacts and physical relationships in shaping individuals' behaviour. (This is sociomateriality, Orlikowski, 2007)

Knowledge workers' rapid flip to working from home in spring 2020 clearly illustrates how quickly social norms develop and become established, and how powerful they soon become in shaping people's behaviour (see Box 3.1).

Box 3.1 You're on mute

In spring 2020, millions of knowledge workers found themselves suddenly working remotely from their colleagues. Meetings moved from physical places to virtual spaces and many people found themselves using unfamiliar technology. "You're on mute" became a familiar refrain. It quickly went from being a helpful prompt, to being a bit of a joke, and then being a bit irritating as the familiar chime disrupted the flow of meetings long after we expected everyone to be adept at using the technology.

Social norms of having your video on/off in meetings as a default also became established very quickly. Where the norm was video on, not having your camera on without explanation might be seen as antisocial and not being fully present, for example, 'he/she is probably doing his emails'. Where it was video off, it was harder for an individual to go against the grain and have their camera on, for example, 'he/she clearly wants to be seen'.

Different social rules emerged for one-to-ones, small group and large group meetings, and non-work meetings. Differing team and organisational norms emerged around the default of having cameras on/off which rapidly became hard to shift. Therefore, social norms had to be renegotiated for meetings and events involving people from different organisational contexts.

In this simple example, we can see the power of social norms in influencing behaviour. Once a recognisable social pattern of behaviour has been created, it becomes harder to go against that norm. Each time individuals choose to go with the social norm, it reinforces the pattern (negative feedback). This social pressure can make us feel stuck in familiar patterns. This is what Lewin (1947/2009) is referring to when he talks about social patterns as being frozen in a quasi-stationary equilibrium and therefore requiring an unfreezing of social habits to change the pattern.

The entangled individual

We can see from the virtual meetings example how individual and social behaviour are entangled. As psychoanalyst Joan Hodgson Riviere explains, thinking about an individual in isolation "is a convenient fiction . . . . There is no such thing as a single human being, pure and simple, unmixed with other human beings" (in Mitchell and Aron, 2013: 116).

Box 3.1 illustrates a complex relationship between an individual and the various social groups that individual identifies with. Where there is some freedom of choice, a person's decision on when and whether to switch their video camera on/off for meetings affects the choices of other people with whom they are directly interacting. If I show up to a one-to-one meeting with my camera on and say, 'it would be great to see you', you might reciprocate by turning your camera on. If three of us show up with our cameras on, and you are on the only one who is incognito, you might feel some peer pressure to join in.

In complexity science, this process of mutual adjustment is known as local interaction. As we interact, our behaviours and choices (e.g., camera on/off) play a role in shaping the behaviours and choices of the people we are directly interacting with, while their behaviours and choices play a role in shaping ours. What we are doing here is enabling and constraining (Juarrero, 2011) one another's behaviour in a process of gesture and response (Stacey, 2001, 2012). The prevailing social patterning (i.e., the history of choices made in a particular context) also enable and constrain that behaviour by making some choices *more likely* and other choices *less likely* in a given situation.

Embedded in context

One knowledge manager who regularly joins the monthly Community Coffee sessions at The Henley Forum[3] told me it is the only time that he sees anyone's face because the meeting default is firmly 'camera off' in the government department where he works.

This illustrates that the specific context matters in socially priming the range of likely choices. The individuals involved in any specific meeting may choose to go against the socially primed default. Yet default bias (from behavioural economics) means they are more likely to stick with it, thus socially reinforcing the default position. It does not remove intentional behaviour from the picture, but the prevailing social patterning in a specific situation makes some behaviours more likely. This highlights the importance of understanding the nuances of local context, since what we say and do may land very differently in different places.

So, the patterning of our individual choices within specific settings creates the social context which influences the choices we then make in those communities. If that sounds circular, it is because it is. As we saw earlier, cause and effect relationships are entangled (known as mutual causation).

This social patterning is known as habitus (Bourdieu, 1998). Stacey (2012: 34) considers this amalgam of assumptions, attitudes, behaviours, feelings, and dispositions that we learn and inherit from one another to be a "second nature". As habits become second nature (habitus), they become so instinctive that we tend not to think about the choices we are making and the nature of the social patterns that our instinctive behaviours are reinforcing. We may therefore miss opportunities to respond in different ways.

Part II of this book introduces leadership practices, tools, and techniques to help you to notice and interpret the social patterning so you can break ingrained habits of action by choosing your responses into the dynamic patterning of organisational life.

The entangled nature of relationships

Managerial relationships are often set out in hierarchies of reporting relationships, which are enshrined in the familiar organisation chart. When individuals have a position of authority in a hierarchy, they have more 'say' (i.e., power) over other people's day to day working lives and over their longer-term careers. Managers have disciplinary power (Stacey, 2012).[4] People are therefore primed to take more notice of what managers say and do (and what they fail to say and do) and how they spend their time. It follows that what people in positions of authority say and do may have a disproportionate effect. Since managers at the top of the hierarchy may also get more sanctioned airtime, particularly with larger groups, what they say may have an even wider effect. However, it may not have the particular effect they would want or expect.

The formalised relationships in organisational life that confer positional power are just part of the picture. As you can see in Figure 3.1, the vast majority of relationships are informal ones, and they can be incredibly powerful in enacting leadership.

Figure 3.1: The entangled nature of relationships (Image reproduced with kind permission from Julian Burton at Delta7 Change Ltd.).

For example, in the oil and gas industry, wearing personal protective equipment (PPE) is mandated in many situations to protect people in the event of accidents and to save lives. Yet, in some social groups, wearing PPE is perceived as a sign of weakness. Such is the strength of peer-to-peer influence that some of those people routinely fail to wear mandated PPE, even in hazardous conditions. For them, the immediate influence felt through direct interaction with peers, and reinforced by being part of a particular social group, outweighs the formal influence of policies and more distant managers.

As Figure 3.1 illustrates, the formal and informal domains are intricately entangled in organisational life. In the formal domain, the patterning of relations is largely structured by power. In the informal domain, it is informal influence (personal and social power) that structures the patterning. Leadership is enacted through the entangled web of formal and informal relationships; that means actively participating in both the legitimate and the shadow systems in organisational life (Shaw, 1997, Houchin and MacLean, 2005).[5] It follows that you must be in it to change it.

You've got to be in it to change it

Outsider views of leadership and change

As we saw earlier, we are involved and entangled in what happens in organisational life. We cannot step out of ourselves to see the 'bigger picture' or to take a 'helicopter view'. Whatever our vantage point, we are all *in* the social world that we are trying to understand and thus affected by the patterns of social interaction (context) and deeper social patterns (habitus). Yet, taking an outsider view of leadership and change is common.

In the outsider view, leaders change organisations. They take a strategic stance, which enables them to stand back from the organisation so they can clearly see what needs to be changed. They convey the importance of the need for change, and they set out a clear vision for that change to get buy-in and make sure that everyone is aligned behind it. They ensure that the change is planned, managed, sponsored and supported appropriately. They empower action, sustain engagement, and celebrate successes until the change is firmly embedded in the organisation.[6]

The outsider view is the leadership partner to planned change, and the pervasive idea that change is something that *can* and *should be* managed, as discussed in Chapter 1. In this view, individual leaders are separate from the organisation and from the change (the atomistic ontology discussed earlier in this chapter). Individual leaders are "prime movers" in creating organisational changes (Weick and Quinn, 1999).

Surprisingly, another outsider view of leadership and change comes from the notion of emergent change, also discussed in Chapter 1. Emergent change is said to "bubble up" (Weick, 2000). It is variously seen as "accidental" (Plowman et al., 2007), "unintended" (Balogun and Johnson, 2005) and "unowned" (Mackay and Chia, 2013). In these organisational descriptions, individuals are largely left out of the explanation. If they are considered at all, individuals are portrayed as rather passive recipients of organisational change. The idea of leadership potency simply disappears.

An insider view of leadership and change

Complexity science takes an insider view of leadership and change. As I have illustrated in this chapter, far from being prime movers in creating organisational change, or merely passive recipients, individuals are *active participants* in the dynamic patterning of organisational life which is both changing and not changing. As Stacey (2010) points out, there is no "special force" in processes of emergence beyond what individuals are saying and doing as they relate to one another. In the social world, leadership potency is enacted from *inside* communities.

Being an insider positions us well to actively participate in the dynamic patterning of organisational life, which is where leadership happens. Firstly, we are already enmeshed in many formal and informal relationships that co-create familiar patterns of business as usual and unfamiliar patterns of change across the organisational system. Secondly, our direct experience offers valuable contextual knowledge about the specific situation and the particular people involved.

By contextual knowledge, I am referring to knowing something of the history and the patterning of events which have helped to shape the current context. This kind of knowledge, which can be codified in language and conveyed to others, is known as explicit knowledge (Polanyi, 1958). We could have this kind of knowledge as outsiders, although it would lack "thickness" (Geertz, 1973) in terms of the richness of contextual detail – and we know from the Complexity Conundrum that small details really matter.

However, explicit knowledge is just the tip of the iceberg. As insiders, we have privileged access to tacit knowledge (Polanyi, 1958) through our experience of participation in organisational life. Tacit knowledge is a form of social knowing that is not easily codified and shared because it must be experienced. We may not think of tacit knowledge as knowledge, and we may not even know that we know it, but this insider knowledge is invaluable because expertise (Nonaka, 1994) and practical judgement (Stacey, 2012) rely on it. To contrast the two, we could learn about a murmuration from the outside, but we would lack the rich tacit knowledge of being a starling and experiencing a murmuration from the inside.

Inside what? Systems, networks and communities

If we want to take this insider view seriously, then we need to ask; inside what? As we are taking a connectionist ontology, which views the world as constituted by relationships, it helps to think in terms of systems, networks, and communities. Each has slightly different nuances.

A system is a complex whole that is comprised of interdependent parts. It defines what we are talking about quite well, because an organisational system works as a whole, which is why people commonly default to referring to 'an organisation'. The people who comprise an organisational system are connected formally (e.g., through reporting lines) and informally (e.g., through conversations).

Organisational systems are open systems, which means they have permeable boundaries. For example, employees can join and leave the system, and non-human resources (e.g., budget, buildings) can be acquired and disposed of. Customers, suppliers, external consultants, and so on can become part of an organisational system temporarily through their interactions, so the system boundaries may be highly fluid. The problem with the word 'system' is that is sounds very impersonal and somewhat unhuman. Some people therefore prefer to talk about networks.

Thinking in terms of networks helps to focus attention on relationships. With the prevalence of social media, most people are familiar with the idea of influencing through connections in a social network. Networks draw attention to the structure of relationships, for example, who is connected to who else, the chains of influence, and who has informal influence in particular situations.[7] Networks also draw attention to the quality of relationships. For example, we might have a relatively small number of close connections with deep and trusting relationships (strong ties, Granovetter, 1973). These might be the people we work with regularly, for example, or those with whom we have shared interests, or a long history. We might also have a larger number of acquaintances, such as people we work with infrequently, or someone we bump into on a training course (weak ties, Granovetter, 1973). Weak ties are valuable, as we will see later, because they bring diversity into the network.

Social networks

In social networks, some people have large numbers of social ties ('friends' or 'followers'). What they say on social media can have large ripple effects across their networks, which is why they are often referred to as influencers. For example, a social media post might get a lot of responses in terms of likes, shares, or comments. Or people might respond by acting on the views or behaviours shared, such as buying particular products, wearing particular clothes, or sharing particular views.

However the fluidity of networks makes it hard to conceptualise system boundaries or to understand the purpose that holds the network together. I also find the structural approach can be rather impersonal. It drives us to think in terms of the paths to achieving goals (i.e., the ties between the nodes in a network). If we think of people in more transactional terms as nodes in a network, we may lose sight of all the important idiosyncrasies that make us all different as human beings. I therefore like to think in terms of communities.

Participating in communities

Thinking in terms of communities focuses attention on participation (Lave and Wenger, 1991). Communities focus attention on people and relationships, along with some kind of boundary. We may actively choose to participate in some communities such as organisational or professional communities; or informal communities of practice (Lave and Wenger, 1991) like women in tech groups. These communities offer some kind of purpose for interaction which creates a natural boundary, for example, working together, sharing knowledge, professional development, or making change.

We may also be part of other communities that we did not choose, based on our identity, for example, being a graduate, being a manager, being a female CEO, etc. (More about that in a moment.) We may even find ourselves in very temporary communities, when we just happen to be in the same place at the same time as other people, perhaps on a bus, in a coffee shop, or on a particular street. Just walking along a particular street makes us a temporary part of that community. As we and others adjust to obstacles and to one another to avoid collisions, we become an interdependent part of that local community through our participation in it.

Thinking in terms of communities makes it easier to recognise that we are involved in multiple communities, at work and out of work. Those communities often overlap in the manner of Venn diagrams. Any individual sits at the intersection of multiple communities as they interact at work and beyond. These overlaps serve to create interdependencies *between* as well as *within* communities.

From a complexity science perspective, we are insiders in communities through interaction. This is important because it means that boundaries are flexible and created from *within*; it is participation that dictates who is *inside* a particular community at any given moment, not personal identity. Membership of communities is therefore fluid, rather than being limited by who we are.

On boundaries and participation

Being in a particular community often means being 'in' the conversation. That matters because leadership is enacted through active participation in the dynamic patterning of organisational life, that is, through the things we say and do, and how we spend our time when we are connected with others.

So, let us come back to identity. Belonging to a particular 'club' may make it easier to access particular communities. For example, if you have a management position in a particular setting, membership of that club will open doors for you to participate in management conversations. Yet being seen as part of the management club may also make it more difficult to participate in conversations in communities of non-managers, and in many other informal communities.

This insider view of leadership and change invites us to think in terms of active participation in a range of communities. It encourages us to think about the communities and conversations we are part of; which ones we are not part of; and which ones we could be part of – either directly, or indirectly through intermediary relationships.

Making differences count

Valuing diversity

Complexity science shows us that micro-diversity within the system provides the necessary conditions for macro-level adaptation (Allen, 2001). So, if you are looking to create organisational change, diversity is like the grit in the oyster that co-creates a pearl.

If we go back to the simple video on/off example from earlier, diversity might involve going against the default option, or taking another path altogether such as a phone call or using avatars. If others do the same, or build on it (positive feedback), that may create a new pattern in the organisational system. Furthermore, *excess* diversity – that is, more than is currently required – helps to create internal resilience to changing future circumstances by introducing more potential pathways or options (Allen, 2001, Boulton et al., 2015).

From a complexity perspective, there is no point everyone looking different if we all think the same.[8] Yet, it is hard to maintain thought diversity from the inside. How many times do we bring people into the team for their great experience elsewhere and then expect them to fit in by speaking and acting just like us? Being different is tiring when you are expected to conform and fit in. This makes it hard for insiders to maintain their valuable differences over the long term.

Outsiders can bring diversity, but they lack the detailed web of relationships to make it count. For example, an HR director in a bank was telling me that the Board had commissioned a large consulting firm to develop a new operating model. This was their third round at developing a new operating model in as many years. She explained that the previous consulting firms had been fired as their models had failed to land. Neither of us felt confident of a different outcome this time around.

As we saw in Chapter 1, people do an amazing job at making small adjustments to keep an organisational system on course in a turbulent environment, but this also means that potentially valuable diversity can be lost through lots of small compensations (negative feedback). If you want diversity to land, you need to work closely with insiders (see Box 3.2).

Spanning boundaries

People who can bridge different communities are known as boundary spanners. Boundary spanners play a vital role in innovation (Tushman, 1977) and change (Cross et al., 2013) across complex systems because their boundary-spanning interactions mean that they are *insiders* in more than one community. In Box 3.2, Wendy Kelly brought diversity into the Aboriginal community, enabled by insiders like elder Daisy Ward.

> **Box 3.2 Making differences count**
> In Western Australia, Senior Constable Wendy Kelly transferred to the Aboriginal community of Warakurna and helped to bring huge change'.[9] She knew that she needed to work with insiders in that diverse community: "you have to have that community involvement . . . because they, at the end of the day, they will help you". By getting to know the elders, learning some of their

languages and getting to know them as people, she became accepted as an insider in various sub-communities. It broke down 'them and us' barriers between 'the police' and 'the community'.

Community elder, Daisy Ward, explained how Wendy Kelly brought valuable diversity: "there are things from what [the police] learned, what they did in uni [sic], bringing that in, and we from the bush side, giving what we have, and linking it together and working as one". This two-way relationship provided a platform for them to work together in addressing community issues such as break-ins. Community policing solutions were therefore created from the inside with the value of all the local knowledge.

What happened here was that Wendy Kelly acted as a bridge between the police and the elders. She therefore became an *insider* in those various communities. Elders, such as Daisy Ward, also acted as a bridge between the various social groups. Through the two-way relationships they developed – both teaching and learning – they actively made their diverse perspectives and specific knowledge count in creating change.

The extended case in Box 3.3 considers the value of boundary spanning in creating the conditions for change in social settings. I use it here because the boundaries between the various subcommunities are starkly drawn. Inside organisational communities, we often have many subcommunities with similarly entrenched boundaries.

Box 3.3 The value of boundary spanners

The problem: Residents on a large housing estate were regularly being disturbed by groups of teenagers. Many felt uneasy and threatened by open drinking and drug taking, noise, vandalism, and speeding cars late into the night. Things had got worse over several years. The police and council social services had been involved but had made little impact in resolving the problem. Dispersing groups and removing individuals had short-term effects, but anti-social behaviour persisted and became more entrenched over the long term.

Residents felt aggrieved that the authorities had not resolved the ongoing anti-social behaviour. The individuals involved from the police and social services – the authorities – each felt under pressure from their own service to resolve different aspects of the problem and there was little joined-up action. Yet they all felt under-resourced and frustrated that they were only scratching the surface of the issues. Relationships between the residents, police and social services were strained.

It is not clear what the groups of teenagers thought or felt, because their voices were not on record. They were an active part of the system, but they were not initially part of the conversation to change it.

What was going on: When complexity researchers mapped the social networks, they found lots of cliques. In social network terms, a clique is a group of people who have lots of interaction with one another, but few interactions with those outside their clique. As you can see from the lack of intersections in the simplified Venn diagram in Figure 3.2, effectively the people involved were in one community or another.

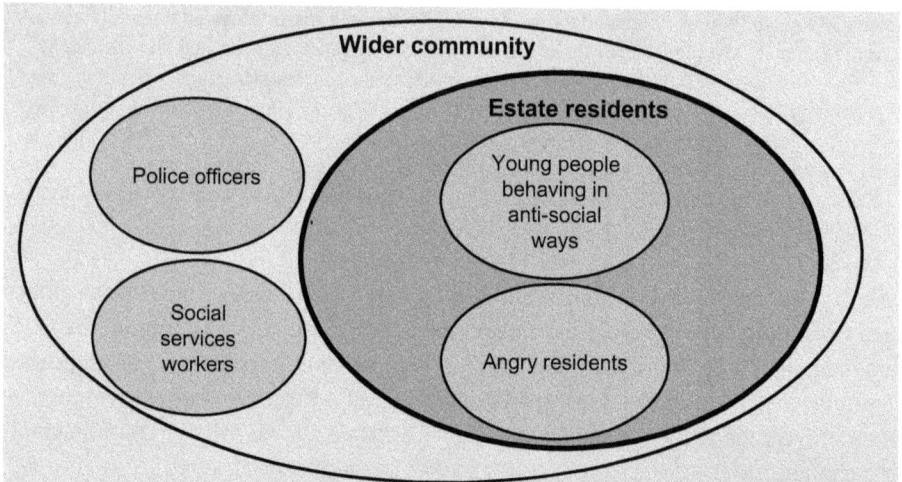

Figure 3.2: Communities and cliques.

What happened: Complex social problems are multi-faceted. So, this is not a story of overnight success, but of a turning point which helped to change the tone of the engagement between the various communities. The change came from enlisting the help of some volunteers among the wider estate residents to engage with the various groups. Being insiders, they could informally chat with other residents. By spanning the boundaries between the various communities, these volunteers managed to convene joint meetings with the various groups involved.

Getting people in the same room was a big achievement. It enabled differing perspectives to be heard and involved those embedded in the situation (the insiders) to participate in developing priorities for action. It paved the way for insiders to be part of the solution.

Boundary spanning is just as important in the corporate world. I remember attending a senior management meeting in a powerful region within a global business. People were talking openly and animatedly about their strained relationships with 'Group'. We *never* let them in here, one manager said, and everyone else agreed. Then he looked at me and added; oh, except you Sharon! My role was head of a group function and, like other group heads, I was expected to bring some coherence across the global group. Unlike other group heads, however, I had spent the previous year taking their views seriously, learning about their business and their challenges, and trying to develop solutions with them. I was therefore allowed in and was able to participate in both regional and corporate conversations.

Working in partnership

I remember joining a new organisation and being confronted with some tricky challenges around culturally integrating different businesses. I came across a dusty report that had been presented to the Executive Committee a couple of years earlier by some external consultants who had been commissioned to look into the same problem. It contained some really good work but had been ignored. Being an insider, I was able to re-engage the various communities and influence the conversations so that the new ideas could land.

Now, in my work as an external consultant, I work to bring valuable differences for my clients, including new ideas, different perspectives, and the legitimacy to ask different questions. When organisational communities are stuck in repeating patterns of behaviour, that diversity is a hugely valuable commodity. So, my start point is to discover, what do they need from me that they do not already have? It is important to keep that thought in mind. A consulting colleague of mine was reflecting recently; when we are no longer different enough, it is time to go.

Insiders make diversity count. My clients have valuable contextual knowledge and internal legitimacy to be part of a wide range of conversations. By working together in a joint endeavour, we can find ways to make our internal/external differences count.

The challenges of being insiders

We don't really know what is going on

While being an insider enables us to actively participate in the dynamic patterning of organisational life, it brings a few challenges. Like being in the mist, it is hard to get a clear view (Simpson, 2007). The challenge is that "emergence disguises cause and effect. We don't really know what is going on" (Sullivan, 2011: 89). We do not like to admit this, even to ourselves, so we get good at pretending that we do know what is going on.

Often we use hindsight to neatly explain away all the inconvenient ambiguity that disguises cause and effect in complex systems (Watts, 2012). Once we know what *actually* happened, we can conveniently ignore what else *might* have happened. This makes it easier to distinguish between the dots and the non-dots (Klein, 2013) in constructing plausible sounding narratives. Unfortunately, these convincing explanations only provide an illusion of control.

Our minds play tricks on us

Even though "the degree of complexity may lie beyond our cognitive limits" (Sargut and McGrath, 2011: 70) we are wired to make sense of things. The problem we all face is that the human mind is "a machine for jumping to conclusions" (Kahneman,

2012: 114). Our explanations tend to ignore complexity and explain it away when that is not fully justified. As Kahneman (2012: 118) puts it:

> We pay more attention to the content of messages than to information about their reliability, and as a result end up with a view of the world around us that is simpler and more coherent than the data justify.

Stories that we tell about reality therefore make "too much sense" (Kahneman, 2012: 114). We construct linear narratives about cause and effect to explain our complex, nonlinear world. Chance gets airbrushed out and the perpetual uncertainty and ambiguity of organisational life is explained away. What we hear about, then, are deliberate actions taken by individuals, which led to particular effects. This makes it much easier to bury the inconvenient truth about emergence.

We can't know what will happen

Armed with our linear explanations of cause and effect to explain what has already happened, we use them to inform actions and decisions in the present, assuming that such interventions will lead to similar effects in the future. We place too much faith (and faith is often what it is) in our causal explanations and overlook the inherent uncertainty in complex and changing organisational systems: "we have a tendency to think that certain causes will lead to particular effects . . . and we just don't know" (Sullivan, 2011: 90).

Since there is not a linear relationship between cause and effect, what will happen is unpredictable. Furthermore, the local context really matters, which is why 'best practice' so often fails to work. Conversely, sometimes solutions that should not work, do work (see Box 3.4).

There's no such thing as best practice

'Best' practice assumes a direct, linear relationship between cause (what we do) and effect (what happens at a system level). This thinking assumes that the answer is somehow *in* the solution – that the answer is in the strategy, the organisation design, the senior leaders, the technology, etc.

A 'best practice' mindset expects that what works in one setting will be transferable to another setting, or to a future point in time. The assumption is that all the important details will be the same from one context to another, and that nothing important will have changed.

Box 3.4 The surprising value of organisational values
Some years ago, I joined a rather fractured global business that was in serious financial trouble. One morning, the new senior executive team disappeared for an off-site and came back later that day with a set of organisational values.

They were not particularly well written; I am not convinced they were really values statements; and more importantly, no one else had been involved. The new values should not have worked, yet they did.

Over time, those statements played a part in enabling some coherence across a deeply divided business. The new values statements, albeit imperfect, worked at that particular point because people involved across the whole business made them work.

The important thing to understand is that solutions only work in complex social systems because people *make them work* in specific situations (Pawson and Tilley, 1997). What happens emerges from complex interactions between specific people doing specific things, in specific ways, in specific conditions.[10]

We're on the receiving end

It is easy to think of those who have more senior positions in an organisational hierarchy as initiators of change and to think of everyone else as recipients, but that is not the case. Feedback loops in processes of emergence means that individuals are both initiators and recipients of change *at the same time*. Even senior executives are on the receiving end (Balogun et al., 2015a). The illustration in Box 3.5 brings that challenge to life.

Box 3.5 On the receiving end
A facilities manager in a cash-strapped college was tasked by his senior management colleagues to make significant budgetary savings. He reset the central heating controls to reduce the active hours for heating college buildings and to lower the target temperature by a degree or two. He did not expect staff and students to really notice the difference. Unfortunately for him, they did.

He found himself on the receiving end of strong negative reactions from staff and students. Many saw it as tangible proof of their growing belief that; 'the senior management in this place don't care about us'. Senior management colleagues distanced themselves from his actions.

Over a matter of months, the facilities manager went from being on his way up in the organisational hierarchy, to being on his way out.

Being both initiators and recipients in the dynamic patterning of change holds true whatever your position in the organisational hierarchy. In this example, senior managers were initiators of cost-cutting measures, yet they were recipients of 'the backlash' against uncaring senior managers. Staff and students were on the receiving end of the cooler temperatures, yet they were initiators of the backlash towards senior managers.

Facing paradoxical tensions

Being *both* initiator *and* recipient in the dynamic patterning of change is an example of a paradox. In a paradox "contradictory yet interrelated elements . . . exist simultaneously and persist over time" (Smith and Lewis, 2011: 382). The persistence of contradictory elements creates tension for individuals that we cannot resolve, we can only work through them.

Complexity is inherently paradoxical. This is good for the system because it spurs adaptation.

Tension spurs adaptation

In complex systems "opposite modes are present at the same time in continuous tension with each other out of which some new form emerges" (Stacey, 2010: 101). Continuous tension between opposing forces acts as a catalyst for emergent system adaptation (Lichtenstein, 2009). In that way, tension is good for the survival of the system.

Tension between opposites generates novelty (generative emergence, Lichtenstein, 2014). No wonder this tension has been welcomed in the field of entrepreneurship and variously labelled in positive terms as "opportunity tension", "creative tension" (Lichtenstein, 2014), and "adaptive tension" (Uhl-Bien and Arena, 2018, Uhl-Bien et al., 2020).

Talking in terms of adaptive tension, for example, makes it sound desirable. While it may be good for the system, paradoxical tensions are rarely easy to cope with for the individuals involved. Normally we deal with tensions by separating them in time or space (Poole and Van De Ven, 1989). However, tensions between contradictory elements in a paradox cannot be resolved through separation because the elements are entangled. For example, we used to be able to disentangle work life from home life by separating them in time and space. We would leave our homes for several hours each day to go to a designated workplace. Mobile technology has made it much harder to separate work hours and workplaces from every other aspect of life. With mobile devices always on, work can reach out into all aspects of life and all hours of the day. We must work through the tensions that creates.

Pulled between competing demands

In 2020, 'stay at home' messages meant that many people found their homes also became their workplaces, schools, gyms, and everything else. The need to balance competing demands was ever present and there were no easy answers. Gradually people settled into a new dynamic pattern of responding to the co-presence of these tensions. The tensions were not resolved, yet many people found a new dynamic equilibrium (Smith and Lewis, 2011) through *actively* seeking both/and solutions to balance opposing forces.

Participating in organisational life is inherently paradoxical (Knight and Parou-tis, 2017), so we find ourselves pulled between competing demands in various ways. We often look for structural solutions to reduce the tensions between competing de-mands. For example, we might separate operations and innovation into separate de-partments. Yet, in practice, those departments are competing for resources such as budget and managerial attention. Furthermore, both exploitation and exploration are essential to survival (March, 1991). Operational performance ensures success in the present, while learning through research and development builds capabilities for the future (the learning-performance paradox, Smith and Lewis, 2011).

Paradox makes separation impossible, so any resolution is only temporary. Here, tensions between operations and innovation may become "salient" (Smith and Lewis, 2011) as they resurface in the interface between the departments. Working through this particular paradox requires enabling leadership to hold the tensions in an adap-tive space (Arena and Uhl-Bien, 2016, Uhl-Bien and Arena, 2018). We will explore the idea of adaptive space in Part II.

Sometimes the contradictory elements are separated in time. It is not unusual to see businesses flip-flopping between structural arrangements that favour central co-ordination (centralisation) and those that privilege local autonomy (decentralisa-tion). The new structure often appears to work *in the short-term* as it addresses the blind spots of the previous arrangements. However, longer-term it fails because it addresses one set of needs over the other. Failing to recognise the importance of attending to competing demands simultaneously, here the need for coordination and autonomy, is extremely expensive for businesses and hugely disruptive for those involved.

Coping with anxiety

Dealing with the various challenges we have explored in this section can create ongo-ing anxiety through a perpetual sense of something being amiss (Streatfield, 2001). Individuals who are nominally 'in charge', are expected to manage such tensions for themselves and for others, so the anxiety can be particularly acute for them.

As anxiety increases, people often look upwards in the hierarchy for resolution. Non-managers look to their managers, managers look to more senior managers, se-nior managers look to the Chief Executives, business leaders may look to policy makers. When there is a lack of clarity and certainty from those in charge, we find them wanting.

Yet, as we now know, being in charge does not give anyone control of the dy-namic patterning. We are all insiders in complexity and continuous changing. Fur-thermore, having high dependency on managers, and those nominally 'in charge', slows down people's responses to ambiguity and uncertainty (Stacey, 2012: 114).

While these challenges will persist, what we say and do matters in what emerges. For example, how we react to the opportunity tension can be generative, or it can be a dampening force (Lichtenstein, 2014). Leadership in the midst of complexity and continuous changing requires us to carry on *actively participating* with others, whilst holding the anxiety of not being in control.

What does this mean for leadership?

Getting in the conversations

As we have seen in this chapter, leadership is not something that an individual leader has or does; it is relational. Leadership emerges in the social influencing process (e.g. Kan and Parry, 2004, Yukl, 2008) and is enacted through a multitude of interactions between people.

Leadership is embedded in the ordinary words and actions that comprise our everyday interactions. As Stacey (2010) reminds us, there is no special force in emergence. Therefore, leadership is not something distinct that is different to other work, or that is only done by exceptional people, or via extraordinary acts.

When we are connected with others in communities through a web of formal and informal relationships, then what we say and do and how we spend our time matters. As they play into the dynamic patterning of organisational life, our words and actions become an integral part of what is emerging. They may reinforce familiar patterns of continuity, which gives us a sense of stability, or a feeling of 'stuckness'. Or they may amplify differences that accumulate to create unfamiliar patterns of change, or more radical transformation.

Our position in the organisational system will afford us entrance to some communities, but it will exclude us from others. Our social and demographic characteristics may do the same. Being in the elite club of management, or the even more exclusive club of top management may bring power and privilege. Yet the effects of that power are easily dampened down by the many actions of many people. So, influencing the conversation (i.e., leadership), or intentionally co-creating a new pattern (i.e., change) means getting involved in many conversations, directly and indirectly, through a network of relationships.

Diversity makes the difference

Broadening the scope of our interactions to encompass more conversations is necessary, but it is not sufficient. More of the same does not give you different. By spanning boundaries and bridging between communities, we are increasing variety by creating new relational flows that connect differences. It is diversity that makes weak ties so powerful (Granovetter, 1973). To borrow Bateson's (1972/2000: 462) phrase, the "difference that makes a difference" is diversity.

Connecting diverse communities tends to surface small differences, and that micro-diversity potentially enables new patterns to emerge. As we have seen, however, it might also make latent tensions in paradox salient. Since social habits tend to negate differences (negative feedback), we may want to choose our words and actions in order to hold the paradox open in a dynamic equilibrium (Smith and Lewis, 2011) and encourage the exploration of adaptive both/and solutions (positive feedback). For example, we might say and do things to hold open the ideas of autonomy *and* co-ordination across large businesses. We might work to enable understanding of potentially valuable differences at the interfaces between teams (Bromley, 2011). We might engage in behaviours that broker relationships between operational and entrepreneurial work to enable an adaptive space (Arena and Uhl-Bien, 2016, Uhl-Bien and Arena, 2018).

Actively participating

Paradoxically, we are simultaneously *both* initiators *and* recipients of change within the dynamic patterning of organisational life. What we say and do affects what is emerging, whilst what is emerging affects what we say and do. As we can see in Figure 3.3, there is a two-way generative relationship between the individual and the collective. Negotiating a paradox requires us to continuously balance the tensions between competing demands – here between being an initiator of change and a recipient.

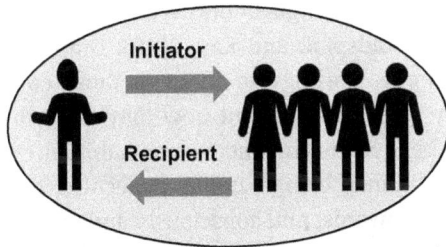

Figure 3.3: The initiator-recipient paradox.

However, conventional leadership thinking tends to ignore the tensions in this initiator-recipient paradox by separating them out. As you can see in Figure 3.4, the leader is positioned as an outsider and attention is focused on taking leadership action to influence the patterns of change. If the position of recipient is considered at all, it is normally framed in neat linear terms, whereby emergent patterns are treated as preexisting environment.

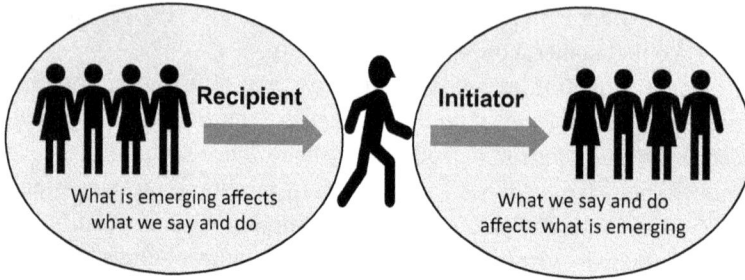

Figure 3.4: Conventional leadership thinking.

So, rather than thinking in either/or terms as an initiator or a recipient of change, I invite you to think of the initiator-recipient paradox in Figure 3.3 as maintaining *active participation* in the dynamic patterning of organisational life. Leadership as active participation requires us to attend to the entangled aspects of our initiator-recipient position at the same time. Rather than looking to the right in Figure 3.4, we must metaphorically look both ways, giving attention to both the emerging patterning and how we are playing into and influencing that patterning as it is emerging. Maintaining that dynamic equilibrium (Smith and Lewis, 2011) demands cognitive complexity to differentiate between and connect the two perspectives, and behavioural complexity to put it into practice (Lewis and Smith, 2014).

Making sense of what is going on

What makes complex human systems unique in complexity science is that humans have developed the capacity and the language to distinguish our 'self' from others and from the immediacy of our experience (Goldspink and Kay, 2010). Grains of sand have no sense of themselves in a sand pile. Starlings do not deliberately consider whether there are other choices they might make about how they flock together before they roost for the night. Their behaviour is instinctive and habitual.

Boulton et al. (2015: 108) explain that; "human beings, unlike molecules, can reflect on, analyse, imagine, create intentions towards, and consciously and unconsciously affect the social and natural systems of which they are a part" (Boulton et al., 2015: 108). Goldspink and Kay (2010) call this distinctly human form of emergence 'reflexive emergence' and Lichtenstein (2014) calls it 'generative emergence'.

As human beings, we can reflect on human doings and make choices based on that reflection. For example, we might look back and reflect on our experience of action in the past, and we might look around and reflect in action in the present (Schön, 1983). This ability to examine one's own beliefs, judgements and actions is known as reflexivity. We can use our capacity for reflexivity to develop insight into what is emerging and to choose our responses into those emerging patterns:

[Human] agents notice patterns that arise as they interact with others and distinguish those patterns in language…. Once distinguished and reified within a domain, agents can decide (on the basis of rational as well as values based or emotional criteria) how to respond.

(Goldspink and Kay, 2010: 56)

As we have seen in Part I, traditional thinking separates intentional behaviour from emergence, that is, it assumes we act *on* things that are separate to us and that there is a clear cause-effect relationship in what emerges. A complexity science view of leadership brings intentionality into the explanation of emergence in human systems. The assumption is that we act *in* a continuous process of dynamic patterning. Intentional behaviour therefore gets entangled in processes of emergence, so there is no direct cause-effect relationship. We must therefore stay alert to surprises by paying attention to learning in leadership.

Learning informed leadership

My adaptation of Goldspink and Kay's (2010) work on reflexive emergence is the complexity learning cycle in Figure 3.5, a continuous loop of noticing, interpreting and responding. In Part II, we will explore the mindset and skillset needed to apply this cognitive tool in much more depth.

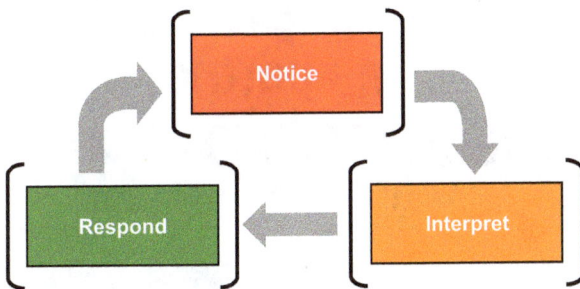

Figure 3.5: Complexity learning cycle.

As we have seen, leadership in the midst of complexity and changing has its challenges. We must cope with uncertainty, ambiguity, and paradox. We must accept that the dynamic and entangled nature of our working world means that we cannot fully know what will happen until it actually happens. We must also recognise that as what we say and do gets entwined with what everyone else is saying and doing, it may not matter in ways that we expect – even if we are in charge.

The good news is that being in the midst is a great place to be. Being insiders in the dynamic patterning of organisational life offers valuable data about the emerging patterns. Rather than acting out of habit, you can use this valuable data to choose your words and actions wisely, adapting as you learn. I call this learning informed leadership, and we will explore it in depth in Part II.

Key insights
- Leadership is in the relationship – think interaction, not independent action
- Social patterns enable and constrain our choices. Our choices create, reinforce and change social patterns
- Change is co-created by involved insiders, participating in diverse communities, spanning boundaries, and working in partnership to make differences count
- As insiders we have valuable first-hand experience, but we cannot see the whole picture
- Solutions 'work' because people make them work in specific situations
- Individuals are paradoxically both initiators and 'on the receiving end' of change
- The tensions involved in paradox cannot be resolved because conflicting demands are entangled
- Leadership emerges through active participation in the dynamic patterning of organisational life
- Reflexivity brings intentionality into processes of emergence
- We can choose our words and actions into the dynamic patterning of organisational life

first-hand experience interaction
leadership in the midst
social patterns make differences count
active participation
diverse communities **partnership**
tension relationship in the
reflexivity mist
intentionality **boundary spanners**
paradox

Noticing and noting
- Which communities are you part of in your working world? (Think about your organisation, business unit, level in the hierarchy; your functional, professional, and industry sector communities; and social communities)
- What communities are you part of beyond your working world? (Think about social, political, religious, ethnic communities, and so on)
- How does it feel to be *in the midst* of complexity and continuous changing?
- What are the benefits, to you, of being in the midst of complexity and continuous changing?

Notes

1 The idea of organising in the mist comes from Simpson (2007).

2 The R value is a way of rating the spread of a disease such as Covid-19. R is the number of people that one infected person will pass the virus onto, on average.

3 The Henley Forum is an applied research centre at Henley Business School, part of the University of Reading. The programme of research and events is designed to help the Forum's organisational partners advance their practice in developing more dynamically capable organisations https://henley.ac.uk/henleyforum (accessed 25/08/2020).

4 The notion of disciplinary power comes from Michel Foucault's work. Stacey (2012) offers a detailed explanation of how disciplinary power has emerged as the main form of managerial governance over people in modern workplaces.

5 The shadow side comes from Jungian psychology, reflecting unconscious aspects of our personality that we may not want to admit to having.

6 I have paraphrased John Kotter's (1995) popular 8-step change model here.

7 Organisational network analysis (ONA) may reveal some of the hidden influencers in transformation efforts.

8 Social diversity is important in its own right. Furthermore, social diversity can be a good source of thought diversity, provided the conditions are created for those differences to count.

9 See BBC News "Warakurna: How an all-Aboriginal police station brought 'huge' change" https://www.bbc.co.uk/news/av/world-australia-53830919 (accessed 21.08.2020).

10 This thinking comes from critical realism. Rather than direct cause and effect models, causality is thought of in terms of Context-Mechanism-Outcome (CMO) configurations.

Part II: **Tools and techniques for leadership**

So, here we are, in the midst of complexity and continuous changing. I suspect you already knew that from experience. However, as Part I has explained, this is not an extreme set of circumstances that can be managed away. It is how the world really works.

Faced with the perpetual uncertainty and ambiguity of the Complexity Conundrum, there are two main options. Option one is to ignore it and hope it will go away (it won't, this is how the world works). Option two is to accept it and adapt your stance to engage with the dynamic patterning of organisational life. I call this *learning informed leadership*.

Part II introduces five essential practices for learning informed leadership:
- Chapter 4 – Applying complexity thinking
- Chapter 5 – Noticing what is changing
- Chapter 6 – Spotting the vital signs of change
- Chapter 7 – Interpreting reality in flight
- Chapter 8 – Adapting leadership responses

Throughout Part II, I will be encouraging you to break some common habits that are unhelpful in complexity and continuous changing. Then I will invite you to replace them with new habits that integrate learning into leadership to better equip you for a complex world that is in constant motion.

Chapter 4
Applying complexity thinking

Rethinking how we think

Now that you have recognised the innate complexity and changeability of the world, you face the very practical problem of how to use that insight in leadership and management practice. As you can see in Table 4.1, the logics of complexity science and traditional management science are completely different, so you cannot engage with real-world complexity using traditional management logic. What we need here is a new way of thinking that takes complexity seriously.

Table 4.1: Contrasting complexity and management science logics.

Complexity science	Traditional management science
Dynamic	Stable
Entangled (interdependent)	Independent
Uncertain	Certain
Patterned	Controllable
Emergent	Predictable
Relational (between)	Individual (within)
Paradoxical	Either/or

Complexity thinking is a way of thinking, which embraces complexity (Boulton et al., 2015). It requires pluralism, open-mindedness, and humility (Richardson, 2008); a willingness to slow down thinking (Cilliers, 2006); and to approach complex problems indirectly (Chia, 2011).

How we think about what we do matters a lot. Opening your mind helps you to engage with more real-world complexity. It might help you to think of this as widening your mental aperture,[1] see Figure 4.1. The position on the left of this visual metaphor sees very little of the complexity of the world through its narrow aperture. As you

Figure 4.1: Complexity thinking as mental aperture.

https://doi.org/10.1515/9783110713343-004

move to the right, you have a larger view of the world which shows more of its complexity. You potentially enlighten your thinking as you admit more light.

This chapter introduces the principles of complexity thinking – thinking more 'complexly', as Richardson (2008) puts it. It begins by inviting you to break the habit of using leadership models and tools uncritically, as that closes thinking down. Then it considers why all models are wrong, and why some are useful . . . with the right mindset. It invites you to develop a new habit of employing multiple models and perspectives to open up your thinking in a complex world where we can only ever be roughly right. It encourages you to maintain a learning orientation to knowing in a dynamic world by taking a questioning and exploratory approach. That means adopting an open mindset, not a set mind.

Complexity thinking is a meta-level orientation that supports learning informed leadership. It provides an essential foundation for using the new complexity leadership tools that follow in this book. Applying complexity thinking will even help you to repurpose some of the old tools and techniques of management and leadership for a complex world.

Better to be roughly right than precisely wrong

All models are wrong

The aptly named George Box (1976) famously said that all models are wrong, and he is right. Unfortunately, complexity science shows us that *all* the tools and models of leadership and management, indeed of the business world, are wrong. All models of change are wrong. All models of strategy are wrong. All models of leadership are wrong. Every single one of them is wrong. Without exception.

Perhaps you were not a fan of tools and models anyway. Maybe you prefer to use your intuition. Unfortunately, all your conceptual models of how the world works are also wrong. Yes, every single one of them. Without exception. It is a sobering thought.

The reason all models are wrong is that models are simplifications of our complex reality. As we discovered in Chapter 2, complex systems cannot be simplified; they are irreducible.

But some are useful . . .

On a more positive note, George Box (1976) went on to say that some models are useful. The patterning that we explored in Chapter 2 means there is some merit to this idea. Let me explain.

John Kotter's eight step process for change leadership was based on his doctoral research studying the patterning of organisational change failure in more than 100 organisations (Kotter, 1995). The kinds of failures he highlights are all too common in organisational change programmes today. For example, he describes how many executives take a "let's get on with it" attitude and fail to convince people of the need or the urgency for the particular change that they are looking to make (Kotter, 1995: 60). Or they fail to "walk the talk" of the change they are advocating, leaving people confused and cynical (Kotter, 1995: 64). Others give up too soon, so that new ways of working fail to become part of the company culture (Kotter, 1995: 66). Does this sound familiar?

I have seen all these mistakes first-hand and I have read hundreds of MBA assignments where managers have used Kotter's model to evaluate change approaches in their own environment and found them wanting. Time and time again, those in charge of planned change fall into familiar traps. I have seen it in many different companies, contexts, sectors, and countries.

Using trial and error in planned change programmes is costly both in economic terms and in human terms. We know that change can be a hugely emotional process akin to loss and grief (Kübler-Ross, 1997) and that individuals may struggle to make a psychological transition and let go of the familiar (Bridges, 2003). Therefore, models that help us consider how to avoid common and painful pitfalls must surely have some utility.

. . . with the right mindset

We need to add a proviso to George Box's comment. Some models are useful *if* we apply a complexity thinking mindset. Adopting a complexity thinking mindset means understanding more about the limitations of what we *do* know and the limitations to what we *can* know (Richardson, 2008, Allen, 2010, Allen and Boulton, 2011).

Economist John Maynard Keynes reputedly said; "it is better to be roughly right than precisely wrong".[2] In a complex and continuously changing world, it is a useful maxim. Precision is misleading because it makes us feel as if we have mastered volatility and complexity when we cannot (that is the Complexity Conundrum). We are probably just looking through the left-hand lens in Figure 4.1.

Given everything we know about planned change, for example, we know that it would be roughly right to put time and effort into the human aspects of planned change programmes. It would be roughly right to allocate more time and effort to supporting emotional (Kübler-Ross, 1997) and psychological transition (Bridges, 2003) than senior executives might initially want to do. Yet, it would be precisely wrong to expect every individual to experience transition in the exact ways that Elisabeth Kübler-Ross and William Bridges set out.

Given everything we know about strategic change, it would be roughly right to consider key contextual factors such as the scope for change, time available, people's readiness, capability and capacity for change, and so on (Balogun et al., 2015b). Yet it would be precisely wrong to assume that the eight aspects in Julia Balogun and Veronica Hope Hailey's change kaleidoscope model are all that matters. It would be precisely wrong to think that Kotter's eight steps will lead to change success. Yet it would be roughly right to consider how to respond to the eight problems that Kotter identifies in your own context.

Expanding our mental aperture

Opening up thinking

Some models are useful, *if* you use them as a starting point to open up your own thinking. When you are an insider, they can prompt you to consider taken for granted aspects of the complexity in your specific situation, which you might otherwise overlook. The problem with models is that they can close down our thinking without us realising.

The shadow side of preferred change models

Some businesses identify preferred change models that they encourage everyone to use in planned change. They do this with good intent. There is some value in having a shared language and understanding around change, as it facilitates communication across community boundaries.

One change manager I was working with recently told me that her organisation 'officially' uses Kotter's eight steps and Kübler-Ross' change curve. While this might facilitate conversation and provoke some useful thinking, there is a shadow side.[3] The risk is that encouraging everyone to look at the same kinds of things in the same kinds of ways loses valuable thought diversity.

Some businesses subscribe to preferred change methodologies for change projects. Again, they often do this with good intent. The problem with detailed methodologies – such as agile development, lean principles, or any other methodology you can think of – is that they prescribe a way of thinking. Valuable thought diversity is therefore lost.

As it takes considerable time and effort to institutionalise these kinds of approaches, challenging them becomes socially unacceptable. Over time, therefore, methodologies turn into sedimented ideologies. They become "undiscussable" (Argyris, 1980) and valuable thought diversity is suppressed.

The issue here, as Kahneman (2012) explains, is assuming that What You See Is All There Is (WYSIATI). Assuming WYSIATI gets us into trouble because we can see very little of what matters in complex systems. If we go back to John Kotter's model as an example, turning the problems he found in change failure into eight steps for change leadership assumes that those things are *all* that really matter, which simplifies things too much. Even potentially useful models may prevent us from seeing anything else, simply because we are looking through too narrow an aperture.[4]

We know that, of course. If we stop to think about it, we know that all models are simplifications of a more complex reality. Therein lies the problem. In the midst of complexity and change, when we are caught up in the flow of events, we do not necessarily pause and think. Instead, we act out of habit. We might use a trusted model to focus our thinking. Or we do what worked in the past, that is, we replay a familiar conceptual model.

I am inviting you to break that habit by applying complexity thinking. A key principle of complexity thinking is to approach complex systems "from many directions" by taking a pluralistic stance (Richardson, 2008: 17). Using multiple perspectives helps us to mentally engage with more facets of the embedded complexity in the situations and challenges we face.

Taking multiple perspectives

Different models and theories take different perspectives. So, a practical way of applying multiple perspectives is to utilise multiple models. To illustrate this, we will return to the topic of planned change:

- **Social forces for/against change.** Kurt Lewin's (1951) field theory considers planned change in a social forcefield. In this perspective, some forces serve to drive the particular change that we are focusing on and others serve to restrain it. For example, changes in consumer behaviour might act as drivers in a move to a greater proportion of online grocery shopping, whilst lack of capital might restrain the pace at which a particular store is able to respond.
- **Management actions.** While Lewin's work encourages us to analyse the social field for change in terms of depersonalised forces, Kotter's eight steps focus on individual actions. Kotter (2001, 2012) invites executives and managers to take specific kinds of actions in leading and accelerating planned change projects. For example, he highlights the importance of communication and empowerment throughout the project, from conception until change is embedded.
- **Experiencing change.** Kotter takes the perspective of initiating change, while others consider what it is like to be on the receiving end. Kübler-Ross's change curve (Kübler-Ross, 1997), and its many variants, and Bridges's transition model (Bridges, 2003), both take a recipient's perspective in understanding common human responses to change. Together, these models draw attention to the emotional and psychological aspects of change.
- **Change agent perspectives.** Rather than focusing on initiators or recipients, the change paradigms (de Caluwé and Vermaak, 2004) offer insights into the perspective of change agents. This framework highlights the different mental models that change agents hold (often unconsciously), which influence their contrasting approaches to change.
- **Context for change.** The change kaleidoscope (Balogun et al., 2015b) zooms back out from the individual to focus attention on the context for change, as a precursor to making contextual design decisions. For example, it considers issues around power, capacity, and readiness for the change project.

- **Change domains.** The McKinsey 7-S framework (Peters and Waterman, 1988) focuses attention on the target for change and its relation to other interrelated human and technical domains. The message is that, if you change something in one domain, such as the strategy, you must consider how it will affect all the related domains. Galbraith's (1977) five-point star; Tichy's (1983) technical, political and cultural domains; and Burke-Litwin's (1992) 12-box model also highlight interrelated domains in planned change.

These various perspectives each shine a light on different aspects of our complex organisational reality. All are oversimplifications, even the more complicated models. Models, like metaphors, are paradoxical. They offer *both* ways of seeing *and* ways of not seeing at the same time (Morgan, 1997: 6). Applying multiple models invites multiple perspectives in relation to complex issues. It therefore helps us to mitigate the ways of not seeing that are embedded in each model.

Thinking for ourselves

In a complex world, we cannot rely on theories and models to do the thinking for us. "Blindly applying, and indeed uncritically accepting, models and theories" or expecting them "to deliver one unequivocal 'truth'" (Boulton et al., 2015: 79) is a very bad idea, even when we are using multiple models to broaden our perspective.

The true value in models and theories comes from using them to help us learn things for ourselves through real-life explorations of the unique idiosyncrasies of specific situations. Models and theories can be extremely helpful if we apply them to open up our thinking. They can help us to overcome individual and collective blind spots in taken for granted ways of looking at things.

Think of conceptual models and theories as a start point for learning. Models can open our minds to *noticing* other aspects of organisational life. (More on noticing in chapters 5 and 6.) Models provide a language to help us *interpret* what is emerging as we reflect on the "grittiness and granularity" of our experiences in the real world (Boulton et al., 2015). (More on interpreting in Chapter 7.) Models may also furnish us with more choices for action as we *respond* into the dynamic patterning of organisational life. (More on responding in Chapter 8.)

The planned change models and theories I talked about earlier can be valuable in helping us to have different conversations with ourselves about the specifics of what we are experiencing. We can also use them in opening up learning conversations in groups. For example, a retail manager who was leading a project relating to her company's online offering used a forcefield analysis with her stakeholders to consider the "social field" in which that project was taking place (Lewin, 1947a: 14). On reflection, she commented that this collaborative analysis "enabled a wider team understanding and healthy debate ultimately identifying where we were able to influence but not control".

What we are doing here is deliberately applying models and theories as heuristic devices. When we adopt a complexity thinking mindset, we use them to help us in thinking and learning for ourselves by reflecting on our experience in the midst of complexity and continuous changing.

Moreover, in recognising the imperfect match of *any* model, we open our minds to the 'not quite-ness' of things and all the difficult to name 'stuff' that does not fit. This is the space where we can really think and learn for ourselves.

Thinking about knowing in a dynamic world

Provisionality – the perpetual construction of knowledge

So far, we have considered the limitations of *narrow* ways of seeing in a complex world. We explored how to overcome those limitations by using multiple models and theories to open our minds to engaging with more real-world complexity.

Now we need to consider the limitations of *fixed* ways of thinking in a world that is in constant motion. That means going a bit deeper by thinking about the thinking and knowing process itself.

How facts change

Let us consider the facts. At one end of the fact scale, we have natural laws, such as Isaac Newton's law of gravity. Natural laws aim to have universal applicability; they are *always* true. This is the world of 'hard facts' where we assume that knowledge is definitely true and does not need to be questioned. Yet scientific thinking is underpinned by the notion of falsifiability. Facts and theories may be contradicted by evidence. For example, we can falsify the fact that all swans are white by observing a black swan. Facts change because an old truth is revised and replaced with a new truth.

Replacing old truths with new truths is a common way to think. We used to assume that asbestos was a good construction material due to its strength, insulating properties and heat resistance. We used to think that diesel cars were an environmentally friendly choice due to their more economic consumption of fossil fuels. Yet we now have evidence that the decomposition of asbestos and diesel emissions are hazardous to human health. Armed with this new knowledge, one set of accepted facts (the benefits of asbestos and diesel vehicles) has been replaced by another set of accepted facts (the dangers to human health).

'Hard facts', in terms of immutable universal laws, do not exist in social science. Even relatively stable facts are difficult to find. In a complex world, generalised facts are, at best, only ever roughly right in specific situations. Furthermore, in a dynamic world, 'the facts of the matter' are difficult to grasp because they are changing all the time. We saw that in the Complexity Conundrum (Figure 2.1).

Complexity thinking invites us to go even further by considering knowledge as provisional, or temporary. In complexity and change, "knowledge is under perpetual construction" (Stacey, 2001: 8). That is a strong statement because it means that knowledge is never fixed. We must therefore hold what we *know* lightly. We must be provisional and tentative about knowledge, and humble enough to admit we cannot be certain. As Richardson (2008: 21) aptly puts it; "complexity 'thinking' is the art of maintaining the tension between pretending we know something, and knowing we know nothing for sure".

Plausibility – determining fact from rhetoric

Knowing we know nothing for sure is not the same as saying there is nothing to know about. There is an enormous difference between taking a complexity thinking view that highlights our inability to know complex things completely (Cilliers, 2002), and taking a position that deliberately de-couples rhetoric from any factual basis. The latter is a political stance which is referred to as post-truth.[5]

Post-truth disregards the notion of there being shared, objective standards for making claims that something is factual or truthful. Little effort is made to ground assertions *in* fact. Instead, rhetorical appeals are often made to emotion and personal beliefs. Sometimes those appeals include a smattering of statistics. Such facts are selectively chosen for their ability to lend credibility to the argument that the person wants to make. Plausibility here is a rhetorical skill used to produce persuasive arguments that have an *appearance* of truth to achieve political ends.

In contrast, complexity thinking is concerned with making truthful knowledge claims, albeit held tentatively. Plausibility here is the skill of constructing explanations, based on all the available evidence, which are then held up to scrutiny. As I explained earlier, I have deliberately chosen to talk about complexity *science* in this book because it connects my assertions about leadership to an underpinning body of knowledge that has followed rigorous procedures in its development.

Three hallmarks of scientific knowledge
1. Rigorous application of explicit procedures to research. This helps us to verify whether the knowledge produced is trustworthy.
2. Pursuit of clarity about the boundaries of that knowledge. We explicitly consider the limits of knowledge transferability to other situations, so that we do not over claim.
3. Positioning truth claims in the wider context of the philosophy of science, that is, by explaining the world view taken (ontology) and what theory of knowledge is being applied to make those truth claims (epistemology). We are explicit about these academic '-ologies' to contextualise the kind of factual claims that we are making and the criteria against which they should be judged.

Holding knowledge claims and methods up to scrutiny help us to determine fact from rhetoric. As Cilliers (2002: 77) explains; "there is no reason not to believe that there is much to be learned. The argument is just that, as far as complex systems are concerned, our knowledge will always be contextually and historically framed".

There is a vast difference between understanding the ignorance in our knowing, and the ignorance that comes from thinking we know everything. Socrates had the former, developed through a lifetime of thinking deeply (Chia, 2011). I am sure we all know people who might fall into the latter category. It is the wise kind of 'not knowing' that we are aiming for in complexity thinking – and thus in learning informed leadership – not a blind kind of ignorance.

Plurality – listening to diverse voices

People are insiders in social and organisational systems. So, there are limits to what we can know in this sense too, because any understanding of our social or organisational world will always be made from within.

Being insiders means that we each have part of the puzzle in complexity. We experience some things up close and personally, but we cannot see the whole picture. What we know is partly shaped by our position within communities and by our local experience. For example, a senior executive might know what is really going on in the boardroom and in strategic decision making, while a front-line worker might know what is really going on with customers or service users and the nature of any operational workarounds in use. Listening to diverse voices widens our potential focus.

Our personal history and background also frame our understanding and thus further limit what we can know. The bottom line is that we can only ever have a subjective view of our objectivity. For example, someone new to the business and someone who has only worked in that business are likely to bring different mindsets to frame their understanding, even if they work in close proximity. Each perspective brings its own way of understanding and not understanding.

If we want to engage with complexity, then we must open the narrow confines of our limited experience by exposing ourselves to diverse points of view. Richardson (2010) calls this critical pluralism. While we will never have a complete picture, complexifying our thinking in this way helps us to appreciate more of the complexity involved in specific situations and aids us in mitigating our personal blind spots.

Practically, this means actively seeking out multiple perspectives, listening to other views, and particularly valuing those perspectives that are different to our own. Developing a mindset to deal with complexity takes time and effort. Investment strategist Michael J Mauboussin has been applying complexity thinking into his daily practices. He advises allocating a percentage of your time to exposing yourself to diverse points of view, for example, through reading, speaking to interesting people and engaging with unfamiliar ideas (Sullivan, 2011).

Earlier we considered the value of using multiple models in opening up thinking. Listening to diverse viewpoints and being curious about other perspectives, particularly when they differ from your own, is a practical way of opening your mental aperture to admit more complexity (Figure 4.1). Chia (2011: 194) proposes approaching complexity more obliquely by attending to the hidden, the inconspicuous, the marginalised and other outliers that reside at the periphery of attention.

While diversity is invaluable, it can be in short supply in organisational life. Typically, the higher up the organisational hierarchy you travel, the rarer it is to find true thought diversity. Senior management teams, in particular, are frequently plagued by a lack of thought diversity. The journey to the top often squeezes out people with genuinely different perspectives. Those that reach the top have often learned to hide potentially valuable differences under layers of normalised behaviour.

Recruitment practices typically search for people who will 'fit', so it is common to find whole businesses and industries populated with similar kinds of people. This is problematic because having the requisite internal complexity to engage with environmental complexity is vital in dealing with the changes and variations that will inevitably occur (Sargut and McGrath, 2011: 76). Rather than looking for people who will fit the existing culture, it is better to embrace the 'not quite'-ness of complexity by looking for people who do not quite fit. We should then aim to co-create a culture whereby the differences they bring are not squeezed out.

Thinking critically

Valuing diverse viewpoints is not the same as uncritically accepting every view expressed. 'Anything goes' is not the case if what we say and do matters in what is emerging now and in the future. Therefore every perspective is not equally valid in any given context (Richardson, 2008: 21).

Critical thinking is a deliberate process that invites us to reflect on our own thinking. It is akin to the 'slow' System 2 thinking which requires conscious mental exertion to overcome our natural tendency to jump to conclusions (Kahneman, 2012). Thinking critically involves asking questions about our thinking. It helps us in thinking and learning for ourselves. It can also help to reduce the effects of unconscious biases because we think more deeply about our assumptions.

As we have already seen, being insiders in complex systems means that perfect objectivity is not possible. Questions 1 and 2 in Table 4.2 invite you to be more objective in your subjectivity – to take an outsider view of your own thinking. Questions 3 and 4 then invite you to be more subjective about the imperfect nature of your objectivity – to take an insider view of your objectivity.

Table 4.2: Questions to encourage critical thinking.

Question	Why ask it?	Follow-up questions
1. What do I currently know or think?	It helps you to notice what you think – a vital first step in critical thinking	
2. How do I know this?	It helps you to analyse the process you used in getting to thinking what you think, or in getting to know what you know	– What evidence do I have? Where are the evidence gaps? – What sources am I using? How trustworthy are they? What sources am I neglecting? – How trustworthy are the processes I used to reach my conclusions?
3. Why do I think this?	It helps you to consider how your views of the world have helped to shape and affect your thinking	– What assumptions am I making about this issue, and about the wider world? – Why might my perspective be different from others?
4. How else could I look at this?	It helps to bring other perspectives into your thinking	– What am I seeing? What am I not seeing? – What other interpretations might there be? – What can I learn from opposing views? – What can I learn from bringing contradictory views together?

Questions, not answers

Developing an open mind

Questions offer a great way to open up thinking. Answers close it down. Answers are fine in a stable world where inputs have clear outputs, problems have knowable solutions, and interventions have predictable effects. We are not working in that world.

The problem with having an answer is that we frequently confuse it with having *the* answer. Our brains assume that WYSIATI (What You See Is All There Is) and we consider the problem solved. Answers work best when problems are separate and separable. Whenever they are entangled, which is most of the time when people are involved, then answers in one domain may cause or exacerbate problems in another domain.

Answers raise new questions

During 2020, national and local lockdowns reduced the spread of the novel Coronavirus. Yet those answers to reducing transmission rates saw economic repercussions and significant social hardship. Early data suggested that disadvantaged groups were disproportionately adversely affected by the virus and by measures put in to reduce its spread, thus reinforcing structural inequalities. Measures to ease lockdown and mitigate some of the socioeconomic issues were often accompanied by notable upturns in cases of Covid-19. We can see how answers in one domain have effects in entangled domains.

Looking backwards to evaluate lessons learned may suggest better answers. Yet retrospective learning is of limited value because we cannot rerun history. Although it sounds like a cliché, history never repeats itself in the same way, so answers based on retrospective learning are only ever roughly right. Asking questions can help us in developing more nuanced responses which better address the evolving situation and overlapping complexities.

We cannot stockpile answers and bring them out later, expecting them to work perfectly. Things will have moved on. Answers are highly context specific, so they do not simply 'work' at all times and in all places. That is why problems do not stay solved in a dynamic world.

Learning in the here and now

The only way to find better answers is to keep on asking questions. Asking questions keeps our minds open to new data. It is an orientation to learning in the here and now. Complexity practitioner Glenda Eoyang routinely asks three questions: What? So what? Now what?

There are no magic answers to the 'what', 'so what' and 'now what' questions. But the value is not in the answers, the value of questions is in the questioning. Their power comes from raising new possibilities and seeing problems in new ways.[6] Learning is never done because the here and now is continuously changing.

Complex and intractable problems cannot simply be solved, done, or ticked off. They are 'wicked' problems that persist, and leadership is full of them (Grint, 2005). Looking for answers to unanswerable problems can leave us stuck in patterns of inaction and repetition (Eoyang and Holladay, 2013). For example, the HR director for a large financial services firm wearily told me that executives had just commissioned a large consulting firm to design their third Target Operating Model (TOM) in around two years. They were still intent on finding a better answer, whereas they probably should have refocused their efforts on asking better questions.

Learning about the emerging future

In a dynamic world, the future is emerging in the living present. Therefore, learning about the emerging future involves continuously scanning our environment and asking: what is going on?

The trouble is that 'what is going on?' is a massive question. Paying attention to every detail, in every domain, all the time, is simply unworkable. Practically, it adds an impossible burden for busy managers who are under pressure to do things and deliver things that they cannot fully control.

Dynamic patterning creates both familiar patterns of continuity and unfamiliar patterns of change. While familiar patterns may not be especially productive, we have some practical knowledge of what we are dealing with and we probably have some idea of the risks and opportunities – the 'known unknowns'. There is a caveat here. Since human beings are natural pattern seekers (Kahneman, 2012), we must take care not to assume that more is 'the same' than it really is.

Rather than expecting busy people to stay on top of everything that is going on, I invite them to pay particular attention to the seeds of unfamiliar patterns of change. The risks and opportunities associated with unknown unknowns may be magnified when patterns are changing, so our aim is to notice the vital signs of change, so we can respond to emerging issues and opportunities sooner.

The key question is: what is changing? I add five further sensitising questions that prime people to broaden their focus and notice more about what is changing:
- **What is changing?**
- What is new?
- What is different?
- What is puzzling?
- What is surprising?
- What is unexpected?

Preparing yourself to learn

There is an academic term known as theoretical sensitivity which is used in the kinds of research that intensely scrutinise people's lived experience to generate theory from practice.[7] What it means is that researchers deliberately develop a broad understanding of the existing theoretical territory to sensitise themselves to noticing potentially important concepts arising in large amounts of unstructured data. What researchers are doing here is mentally preparing to learn for themselves. By broadening their thinking, they are opening their minds to notice more in their data.

We are trying to do something similar. We are mentally preparing to engage with complexity by applying complexity thinking to deliberately broaden our perspective and open our mental aperture. Maintaining a questioning orientation by asking 'what is changing?' then primes us to learn for ourselves in continuous changing. Asking 'what is changing?' in various ways – for example, what is new, different, puzzling, surprising and unexpected? – sensitises us to noticing weak signals of change in the overwhelming amount of experiential data that we are exposed to in the here and now. (More about noticing in chapters 5 and 6.)

Adopting a learning orientation

Learning in action

Complexity thinking is not a purely cerebral activity that is divorced from action. Thought and action are entangled. As Schön (1983) explains in his seminal book 'The Reflective Practitioner', professionals think in action. Rather than using the term reflection, which is often understood as a post-hoc activity (it is not), I prefer to talk about learning (notice the '-ing' again). Learning is continuous:

- **Learning before action**. Since what we say and do matters in what emerges, then we must think about our words and actions ahead of time. This is an imaginative activity which activates complexity thinking by opening our minds to considering possible scenarios. The focal question here is: *what is my next most promising step?*
- **Learning during action**. Since the unpredictability of complex systems means that we cannot know how our words and actions will play out ahead of time, we must learn as we go. The focal question here is: *how is this playing out?*
- **Learning after action**. Since history matters in what emerges, we might reflect on what happened during action and use it to inform our learning before action next time, for example, by using an After Action Review.[8] In complex systems, we are also looking to learn from the ripple effects of everyone's words and actions. The focal question here is: *what is changing?*

In complexity, the start point for learning is action. In other words, we act to learn.

Acting to learn

We can act to learn in various ways. Dave Snowden talks about "probing" first in complex systems (Snowden and Boone, 2007). Chris Rodgers describes "muddling through" complexity with purpose, courage and skill (Rodgers, 2021). Ralph Stacey (2012) advises exercising "practical judgement". Glenda Eoyang proposes taking "adaptive action" (Eoyang and Holladay, 2013). Ron Heifetz advocates "adaptive leadership" (Heifetz et al., 2009a). Essentially, they are all ways of experimenting.

With experiments, we have a theory about how something will work, then we try it out to learn how it *actually* works in practice. We pay close attention to the conditions and in learning from what happens in that context. Experiments in the working world are vastly different to experiments in a lab, however. We cannot control conditions. We cannot rerun or erase history, so our experiments play into the ongoing dynamic patterning of organisational life. Furthermore, our real-life experiments may have ripple effects beyond what was expected, so our learning must be equally broad based.

Being experimental does not mean that we are hesitant, or half-hearted in what we say and do. It takes both courage and humility to admit that nothing is certain. However, the conviction of a complexity thinking mindset is that we try things out in order to learn how they play out, that is, we learn and adapt as we go.

Double-loop learning

Not all learning is equal. Argyris (1977) differentiates between single-loop and double-loop learning.

Double-loop learning

An example of single-loop learning is a thermostat that turns the heating system on or off at a particular temperature threshold. Double-loop learning offers more possibilities. If you feel cold, you might choose to put an extra layer on, or make yourself a hot drink. You might move around, or go for a walk to warm yourself up. You may even decide to invest in better insulation, or to move to a warmer climate. In this example, the single loop has one habitual response, but the double loop helps us to actively consider a wider range of responses.

The single loop of if/then learning is faster and more automatic (Kahneman, 2012), but this kind of fast thinking ultimately returns us to the same place (Cilliers, 2006). Single-loop learning only works if everything important essentially stays the same. In a dynamic world, single loops can trap us in repeating patterns of action.

Breaking out of repeating patterns requires a different mode of learning. Double-loop learning is more deliberate and reflective. It involves thinking about your thinking and questioning your assumptions and beliefs to generate more possibilities for action.

Learning informed leadership

The complexity learning cycle (Figure 3.5) unpacks learning in action into a continuous process of noticing, interpreting, and responding. It is a reminder that there are no start or end points in dynamic patterning; changing is continuous.

The double loop in this learning cycle is stimulated by noticing what is changing. Rather than responding automatically, learning informed leadership involves *noticing* weak signals of change, *interpreting* emerging patterns, choosing your best *response* into those emerging patterns, and *noticing* what is changing in order to continue learning. Chapters 5–8 will explore noticing, interpreting and responding in more depth.

Key insights
- Complexity thinking is a meta-level orientation to engaging with real-world complexity
- Enlarging our mental aperture opens our minds to complex nuances in specific situations
- Models, including our conceptual models of the world, are never more than roughly right
- Employing multiple models and diverse perspectives helps us in thinking critically for ourselves
- Knowing requires provisionality, plausibility, plurality, and humility
- Asking questions is not about answers, it is about learning what is changing in the here and now
- We activate learning in action, by experimenting with conviction and courageous humility

Noticing and noting
1. Think about a leadership or change model that you have used before. (You might want to remind yourself of the model.) Now look at that model with new eyes. Ask yourself:
   - in what ways is that model wrong?
   - in what ways is that model useful?
   - what am I not seeing?
   - what other models could help me to see things differently?
2. Reflect on your mental model of good leadership or good change. (You might want to write yourself a few notes.) Now consider that mental model with new eyes. Ask yourself the above questions.

Notes

1 This builds on the idea of developing emotional aperture to better recognise diverse emotions in a collective (Sanchez-Burks and Huy, 2009).

2 The phrase is often attributed to the economist John Maynard Keynes, but others attribute it to British philosopher Carveth Read.

3 As we saw earlier, the shadow side comes from Jungian psychology, reflecting unconscious aspects of our personality that we may not want to admit to having. Patricia Shaw (1997) wrote about shadow systems in organisations, which I refer to as the informal aspects of organisational life.

4 An unfortunate side effect of focusing too narrowly is inattentional blindness (Mack and Rock, 1998). We miss what we are not looking out for.

5 Post-truth was named Oxford Dictionaries Word of the Year in 2016 following a spike in its use in a political context in the UK and the US. For more information see: https://languages.oup.com/word-of-the-year/2016/ (accessed 12/08/2020).

6 There is more detail in the Power of Questions blog post: https://www.hsdinstitute.org/resources/the-power-of-questions.html (accessed 12/08/2020).

7 Researchers will recognise that I am referring to Grounded Theory.

8 After Action Review (AAR) is a structured de-brief process commonly used in knowledge management. It typically asks: What was supposed to happen? What actually happened? Why was there a difference? What would you do differently next time?

Chapter 5
Noticing what is changing

It all starts with noticing

Now that we have adopted a complexity thinking orientation, we are ready to activate learning informed leadership. It all starts with noticing (see Figure 5.1). Without it, we will inevitably be learning about the past, rather than learning from the emerging present. The traffic light theme highlights the importance of stopping to notice weak signals about what is changing.

In a dynamic world where things are inextricably entangled, events can quickly escalate. Better noticing helps us in spotting the vital signs of changing, before the change itself becomes obvious, before it gets more widespread, more entangled, and more ingrained in the patterns of life.

Being on the front foot means paying close attention to small changes in the dynamic patterning of organisational life. Noticing weak signals about what is changing gives you the opportunity to *choose* your actions and words carefully as you play into the dynamic patterning that you are co-creating with your words and actions. Noticing weak signals about what is changing also helps you to *learn* how your words and actions are playing out as they combine with everyone else's words and actions in forming emerging patterns of continuity and change (see Figure 5.1).

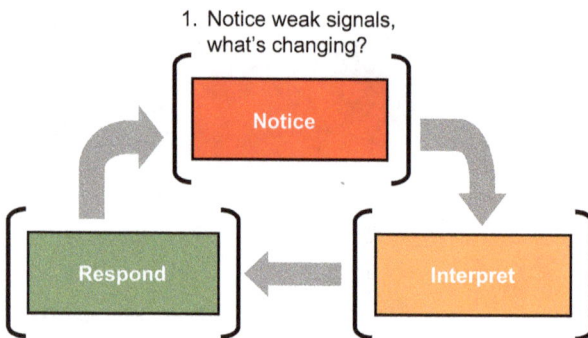

Figure 5.1: Complexity learning cycle – notice.

This chapter invites you to break the habit of assuming that small changes will not make much difference and can be safely overlooked. It begins by highlighting the value of noticing. Next it considers what it means to be a better noticer and explores three barriers that often get in the way. It encourages you to rethink your orientation to data by valuing small, human-scale data that is freely available but is often ignored. It encourages you to develop the habit of noticing more broadly and more

https://doi.org/10.1515/9783110713343-005

deeply to pick up weak signals about what is changing. The final sections outline strategies and practical tips to help you to enhance your noticing.

Why noticing is so important

Heading off problems sooner

The well-known proverb 'For want of a nail' is a reminder that small issues can escalate in unforeseen ways. Something minor and easily resolvable becomes worse and worse. Like the proverbial 'a stitch in time saves nine', the message is that timely intervention may head off something that would be more time consuming or problematic to deal with later.

For want of a nail
For want of a nail the shoe was lost.
For want of a shoe the horse was lost.
For want of a horse the rider was lost.
For want of a rider the message was lost.
For want of a message the battle was lost.
For want of a battle the kingdom was lost.
And all for the want of a horseshoe nail.

Why do problems escalate? In a stable world, things would stay as they are. Shirt buttons do not fall off by themselves. Hems do not come down under their own agency. The shirt button falls off, or the hem comes down as the clothing is being worn, or washed, or pulled out of a suitcase; there is movement and interaction with something or someone else. Even this remarkably simple example is dynamic and relational.

Similarly, a horseshoe falls off as the horse moves. In this proverb, however, we see more of the complexity of the situation. The story's setting is not a child's Sunday morning riding lesson, it is warfare. In this context, the missing horseshoe nail is part of a complex system with multiple interacting parts. There is a horse and a rider and a message. Indeed, there are probably many of each, and many other things besides, that do not make it into this story. There is complex interaction through a battle. Furthermore, we learn that the stakes were exceptionally high. The loss of this particular message turns out to be pivotal in the battle being lost and in the consequent loss of the kingdom. The problem of lacking a horseshoe nail escalates and the pattern of interaction that is 'the battle' turns on a specific event that does not even happen (the message was not delivered).

In dynamic patterning, things do not stay still. You cannot safely park a problem – and if you solve it, it may not stay solved. The effects of dynamism and entanglement means that problems readily escalate and often have knock-on effects in other areas. Issues have an inconvenient habit of turning into something more complex and more difficult to head off while your back is turned.

Better noticing here is about positioning us to head off emerging problems sooner, while they are relatively small. For example, noticing gripes about a proposal to introduce new car parking arrangements might be a clue in a developing story that 'they' don't care about 'us' (see Box 2.2). You might therefore take early action to avoid aggravating existing tensions and reinforcing divisions.

Of course, there are no guarantees in uncertainty, so this is about increasing our chances. What we are trying to do is to tip the balance in favour of noticing emerging issues sooner, rather than against it. Where noticing is concerned, chance favours the prepared mind.[1]

Grasping opportunities earlier

Problems are not the only problem. In a dynamic world, opportunities may open up, but they do not simply remain open. For example, there used to be lots of internet search engines, some better than others. I remember using different search engines for different things. Now, Google is dominant in much of the world. The invitation to 'Google it' is synonymous with web search, even though other search engines exist.

In the past, the door was more open in this area than it is now. It might well open up again, with new technology, or if Google falls from grace through acts of commission or omission. The challenge is spotting emerging opportunities, in real time, when they are small enough to exploit. Stories of missed opportunities are typically told with the benefit of hindsight. *If only* the now defunct video rental giant Blockbuster had bought Netflix when it was offered to them . . . and so on.

Spotting opportunities is not just an entrepreneurial endeavour. It is a broader leadership challenge in complexity and continuous changing. We may want to grasp emerging opportunities to land planned change with people, to enable the strategy, to develop better ways of working, and so on. As we know, it is easier to push on an open door. We want to find sparks of opportunity and take early action to fan the flames.

So, better noticing here is about positioning ourselves to grasp emerging opportunities earlier, when they are still in reach. For example, noticing a ripple of excitement during a meeting might indicate an opportunity to build staff engagement. Again, there are no certainties. What we are trying to do is employ better noticing strategies and skills to help tip the balance in our favour.

Valuing weak signals

Emerging issues and opportunities rarely arrive with a fanfare. Instead, they appear as weak signals. Weak signals are small pieces of data in the 'here and now' that indicate a potentially emerging issue or opportunity in the future. These weak signals are important indicators of change, and, in an unpredictable world, they are extremely valuable.

Weak signals are ambiguous. They do not come with their meaning attached . . . until later. Often their full value becomes clear only when issues have escalated – sometimes irreversibly – and when opportunities have passed by. Hindsight frequently judges those in charge harshly. Post-mortem accounts of disasters and missed opportunities tend to make it painfully clear that managers and political leaders had the data they needed to make different decisions. Looking back, it is obvious what they should have paid attention to back then, because we know how things *actually* turned out. Indeed, everything is obvious, once you know the answer (Watts, 2012).

Detecting weak signals is not straightforward. Signals are often weak because they are hidden in small pieces of data and they may appear trivial (like the horseshoe nail). They often seem random and disconnected and they frequently disappear into a flood of background noise (Schoemaker and Day, 2009). For these reasons, potentially valuable weak signals may go unnoticed.

Of course, there are no guarantees that we will not miss things that later turn out to be important. Clues do not come with labels attached. However, by understanding the huge value of weak signals and attuning ourselves to noticing small cues, rather than filtering them out, we are trying to increase our chances of detecting weak signals earlier.

Becoming a better noticer

Powering up your noticing

If you want to become a better noticer (and I hope you do), then it is helpful to understand what we are aiming for and the kinds of barriers that often get in the way.

Better noticing means picking up *more signals* about what is changing. By paying attention to noticing, we are trying to detect more early warning signs of change than we otherwise would. In an entangled world ripple effects are common, so we are aiming to enlarge our noticing aperture to pick up the signs of changing from *more domains* than we otherwise would. This involves a broadening out from what is immediately in front of us, like using a wide-angle lens to see a bigger picture. Powerful noticing includes spotting what is not happening, such as the dog that did not bark (Bazerman, 2014).[2] We are also trying to go deeper by sensitising our noticing to pick up *more nuances* in what is changing than we otherwise would. It is like using a zoom lens to see more detail.

Bazerman (2014: xviii-xix) advises managers to power up their noticing by "noticing important information in contexts where many people do not" and by "noticing more pertinent information from your environment than you would have otherwise". If we knew ahead of time what would be important and pertinent, this would be fairly straightforward. The challenge is that we can only know which specific pieces of information turn out to be important or pertinent with hindsight.

Our overall aim, therefore, is to develop a *general disposition* that is attuned to noticing what is changing. Doing so will increase our chances of noticing weak signals that later turn out to be important and pertinent. There are a few barriers to overcome if we want to achieve that.

Overcoming conceptual barriers

First, we must overcome the conceptual barrier of assuming the working world is stable and composed of separate things. If we believe that it is manageable, then we are unlikely to bother looking for weak signals. The mechanistic assumption is that small things have small effects, so weak signals are too small to be worrisome and we therefore filter them out. However, as we learned from the Complexity Conundrum (Figure 2.1), small differences can make a big difference.

At this stage of the book, I trust you are already making good progress in overcoming this conceptual barrier. If so, you will understand the importance of noticing what is changing to inform your responses in a dynamic world.

However, there is a second conceptual barrier here. Unfortunately, many managers and professionals have been conditioned *not* to pay attention to weak signals. They have been encouraged to overlook and undervalue small, qualitative, human-scale data in the pursuit of objective facts, hard metrics, and big data sets. If you want to become a better noticer, you will need to understand the value of small data. We will consider small data's power in the next section.

Negotiating practical barriers

Many common working practices get in the way of better noticing. Individuals are expected to focus on achieving specific objectives – the SMART-er they are, the worse it is![3] People are recognised and rewarded for delivering limited outputs such as projects, programmes, roadmaps, rollouts, initiatives, and so on. They may be promoted on the back of those narrow successes to positions of seniority within the formal hierarchy. It becomes a self-reinforcing cycle, which reduces the likelihood of spotting weak signals about emerging issues and opportunities beyond our immediate gaze.

The busier we are, the more likely we are to focus attention on narrow priorities and to discount data outside our immediate focus as noise. Indeed, that is the point of focusing attention, to avoid distractions and put all our energies into the task at hand. Unfortunately, it is like wearing blinkers.

We already know from Part I that being insiders in complex human systems means we only see part of the picture. But this habit of focusing our attention on what is immediately in front of us narrows the picture even more. The price we pay for this focus is that it inhibits our ability to notice critical information (Bazerman, 2014: xvi).

If we want to become better noticers, we must negotiate these practical barriers to avoid self-imposed blind spots. That means allocating time and dedicated effort to deliberately broadening our perspective beyond our own projects, areas of work, and communities. We will consider some strategies and practical tips to help you with better noticing later in this chapter.

Understanding perceptual barriers

The third challenge is that our brains filter our perceptions (Starbuck and Milliken, 1988), so we do not see a true picture of the world. Executives, and everyone else, have perceptual filters that influence what they notice (Starbuck and Milliken, 1988, Bazerman, 2014).

Moreover, change brings its own perceptual challenges as we saw in Chapter 1 when we considered 'the invisible gorilla experiment' (Simons and Chabris, 1999). This experiment showed that, during dynamic events, individuals may fail to perceive specific objects (inattentional blindness) or to notice changes to objects and scenes – even large ones – over a period of time (change blindness).

Other perceptual barriers include selective perception and confirmation bias, where individuals tend to actively notice information that accords with their preexisting views (e.g., younger workers are more tech-savvy) and to overlook information that challenges those beliefs. Some of those biases may be unconscious, such as taller people are better leaders. This is clearly nonsense when we stop to think about it. But how often do we do that? When we respond automatically, we are therefore likely to be more affected by the many biases that restrict our noticing (Bazerman, 2014).

If we want to become better noticers, we must understand that we all have a vast array of blind spots and cognitive biases and make efforts to compensate for those perceptual filters. The strategies and practical tips for better noticing later in this chapter will help you.

The power of small, human-scale data

Why we love data

Many managers love data. They particularly like things they can count. They like data that lends itself to statistics and trends, charts, and dashboards. I like those things too.

We like these kinds of data because they give us a sense of knowing something. That can feel very comforting when we are faced with perpetual uncertainty and ambiguity. Charts give us the feeling that we really know what has happened. Trends give us a sense that we know where we are going. We can imagine a future that is based on solid data about the past. Statistics demonstrate some ability in manipulating data and make us feel that we have some mastery in the underlying situation. Clever statistics can help us to feel very clever indeed. Dashboards can be particularly beguiling. Seeing green lights in a RAG (Red-Amber-Green) dashboard makes us feel that we are on top of things. Where we see amber or red lights, we assume that we have clarity on where we are now, and where we need to focus attention going forward.

Another reason that we like things we can count is because knowledge can now be more easily shared and compared. 'Knowledge' has been separated from the knower(s) and made "explicit" (Nonaka, 1994).[4] We can readily see how we are doing compared to last year, for example, or in comparison to other departments or institutions. We can collect and publish numerical data to show stakeholders such as employees, shareholders, regulators, and customers how the business is going or how the institution is performing against key targets or benchmarks.

Having these kinds of explicit data – along with the array of charts, trends, statistics, and dashboards that illustrate our mastery of that data – increases our sense of control. It shows, to ourselves and to others, that we know what is going on. It gives us a sense that we know where we are heading. Feeling more in control can help us to feel better. Basing our actions on that kind of data helps us feel justified in what we are doing. Of course, we now know that feeling of control is a mirage.

Thinking critically about data

When we gather numerical data, we must examine it critically using complexity thinking. Like the models we looked at in Chapter 4, charts, trends, statistics, and dashboards are always wrong, even when rigorous procedures have been applied. They are wrong because they are simplifications of a more complex reality. We can never know in advance whether we have captured the aspects of complexity from the specific situation that will turn out to really count in what happens.

We must be provisional about what we know and understand that it will never be fully right. We must recognise that explicit knowledge, while it looks objective because it has been separated from the knower, can come laden with biases. There will be biases arising from what was included and excluded, as the machine learning example below clearly illustrates. Furthermore, information only becomes knowledge if there is a knower.

The bias of machines

As Melanie Mitchell explains in 'Artificial Intelligence: A guide for thinking humans', machines learn through multi-layer neural networks. Rather than categories being programmed by humans, they are learned directly from vast amounts of online training data. Therein lies the problem.

In facial-recognition tasks, machines are generally trained using online images, which are biased towards famous and powerful people. Some widely used data sets contain images that are 77.5% male and 83.5% white, reflecting biases in society. No wonder, then, that some commercial face recognition systems are more accurate on white male faces than on female or non-white faces.

Machines observe and learn by making statistical associations. What they are learning is not necessarily what a thinking human would expect them to learn. Unfortunately, they may pick up biases without us knowing. Deploying AI based on machine learning with hidden biases reflects, magnifies, and perpetuates those biases. Even small differences in accuracy between racial groups may have damaging repercussions in the real world.

Source: Mitchell (2019: 123–126)

Big data

Big data refers to the vast amounts of digital information now available and the smart analytics used to find patterns in that data. Data got big from a combination of the stratospheric growth in interconnected devices and reductions in storage costs. The scale of data created by individuals and organisations every day is vast. Moreover, it is growing – fast!

Previously data was retrospective, so it only told us something about yesterday. The potential advantages of big data come from its real-time ability to tell us something about today.

What makes big data clever?

Big data is underpinned by massive data sets, but *volume* alone does not make data clever. Big data also has *velocity*: the proliferation of mobile devices combined with more bandwidth and increases in processing power, has enabled fast streaming of large volumes of data. The ability to integrate a huge *variety* of organisational and social media data sources available (e.g., text, audio, image, video, sensor data, metadata, and so on) is what makes big data insights really useful. The clever part comes from the analytics used to interrogate those vast and disparate internal and external data sources in close to real time.

> Fortunately, the massive improvement in backroom analytics has been accompanied by massive improvements in the *visualisation* of data, using graphical, dashboard-style displays. Advances in mobile technology enable users to access big data insights on mobile devices, so insights can be utilised at the point of need. That accessibility is what makes big data most *valuable*.

However, bigger is not necessarily better. As data itself has proliferated, so have the Vs of big data. The additional Vs of big data – *veracity, validity, variability, volatility,* and *vulnerability* – remind us to exercise caution; we must not believe it too much.[5] We must continue to apply complexity thinking in being tentative about what big data can tell us.

Big data applications tend to support business activities that offer commercial advantage, rather than supporting leadership practice. That may change, but big data applications are not necessarily available to support everyday decision making. Furthermore, the value of big data comes from asking the right questions. But if we do not know what is changing, how do we know what questions to ask of big data? That is where small, qualitative, human-scale data comes in.

Small data

Rather than big data, I talk about small data. Small data refers to qualitative, human-scale data. It is plentiful, comes free of charge, and is a valuable resource for leadership. Yet we often dismiss data that we cannot count and leave it on the table.

Small data lives in the kind of information that we all pick up, every day, in the normal course of our work. It might take the form of a conversation that suddenly galvanises people into action; an increasing frostiness in the dealings between two teams; a story that catches people's attention; or a ripple of excitement in a room. Small data is human data that we can all notice, *if* we know what to look out for.

Small data can be powerful; it can challenge what we know. After all, you only need one black swan to show that swans can be black. Small data is also the best data we have about how an organisation is changing, until after the fact. Importantly, small data can offer an *early warning* of emerging problems or completely new opportunities. It can signal important twists and turns in change, heralding the kind of surprises and unintended consequences that you just cannot plan for. The sooner you notice those weak signals, the sooner you can choose how to respond to any emerging opportunities or problems, by either fanning the flames or dousing them out.

Small data's enormous value comes from its ability to provide us with clues about what is changing that we can use to inform and adapt our leadership responses. Without small data, leadership is either based on out-of-date assumptions or, worse still, simply guesswork.

By asking 'what is changing?', you might notice increasing conflict between groups, or people developing informal coalitions. You might notice people becoming more focused on the internal workings of their team and taking their eyes off other things. You might notice more negative emotions, such as worry or withdrawal. None of these observations would be surprising in a change situation, but they could provide important clues about a perfect storm brewing. If you notice patterns sooner, you can choose a response sooner. As you play into the patterning of behaviour, you may influence what happens because your behaviour forms part of what is emerging.

The secret with using small data is to combine multiple, local insights and to then ask searching questions about what it might mean. We will explore this in more depth in Chapter 7. When you are making sense of small data in change, you want to avoid jumping to conclusions or accepting the most obvious answer. Conditions might be changing, so ways of making sense about yesterday's data might also need to change.

Looking in a rearview mirror

I am not against data. Far from it. In fact, gathering data and making it explicit is at the heart of Part II of this book. But we need to understand more about what kinds of data we have at our disposal and what they can and cannot do for us in complexity and continuous change.

Data can be past, present, and future facing - see below and Table 5.1.[6] We need to understand this temporal orientation because it illustrates that increasing certainty about hindsight does not give us foresight.

- **Data about yesterday** often takes the form of pre-structured, quantitative data. Traditional measurement tells yesterday's story, often from a single perspective, such as staff turnover; achievement against pre-set targets; or financial performance. Yet "retrospective understanding may not help executives who are living amid current events" (Starbuck and Milliken, 1988: 35).
- **Data about today** is distributed across multiple sources and must be quantified to bring it together. Big data advances allow us to ask more sophisticated business questions of more sophisticated data sets. For example, do my best people intend to stay? What is the best induction process to maximise productivity? While the data examined is current, the selection and structure of data sources is not.
- **Data about tomorrow** is small data that helps us anticipate how the future might be different from the past in some important aspect. It arises in human interaction in specific contexts and is qualitative. Small data offers clues about how the prevailing patterns in an organisation, in the wider working world, or across society are changing.

Table 5.1: Orientation of data.

	Data about yesterday	**Data about today**	**Data about tomorrow**
Data types	– Databases – Limited sources – Quantitative data – Lagging data	– Big data – Diverse, distributed – Quantified data – Lagging/leading	– Small data – Diverse, local sources – Qualitative, human – Leading data
Key question	What happened?	What's happening?	What's changing?
Orientation	*Measurement* offers a precise interpretation, but tells yesterday's story	*Analytics* aid human interpretation to decipher today's story	People consider *meaning* to anticipate and influence tomorrow's story

Source: Adapted from Varney (2015).

The unbearable lightness of evidence

Small data may signal large changes; a reminder that the things which really count in this world cannot always be counted. Yet small data has a 'lightness' to it, since everything in the world happens just once (Stake, 2010).

Compared to the colourful displays and eye-catching graphics of big data dashboards, small data may be hazy and indistinct. Signals are weak and may take the form of snippets of information hidden in a torrent of data.[7] Small data is widely distributed. Its meaning is uncertain and different people are likely to have differing interpretations. Weak signals often live in the things unsaid and undone. For example, a 'gut reaction' of a new opportunity brewing, or that something is amiss, might be a valuable bodily clue to pay attention to noticing what is changing.

The lightness of this evidence means that small data is easy to overlook. We may miss what is not in front of us, or we may filter out small data as noise. Rather than sharing uncertainties, and working together to explore meaning, people often keep quiet until there is greater certainty. Yet delays may mean that opportunities are missed and that problems escalate.

We are immersed in this potentially valuable small data every day, both at work and in our lives. The good news is that people are much better than computers at noticing and interpreting small data, which is qualitative, indistinct, and very human. If we want to make leadership count in complexity and change, we must develop our skills in noticing valuable small data about what is changing.

Strategies for better noticing

Overcoming 'agilitis'

Imagine responding to every new trend, adopting every new technology, trying to influence every conversation. You would be incredibly busy, and you might be feeling a buzz, but you would soon be exhausted. Yet, as we saw in Chapter 1, you would never be on top of things. Instead, you would be stuck in a punishing loop of activity that has no end, rather like Sisyphus.[8]

Now imagine that kind of repeating pattern magnified in scale across an organisational system. There would be no business as usual beyond continuous upheaval; no cultural norms beyond constant activity; no way to judge between alternative courses of action; just constant movement from one idea to another.

You may be thinking that is a fairly good description of your own experience. Pressure to do things faster and faster, to change direction at speed and to learn in ever smaller loops (if at all) is becoming normalised in many work settings. I call this 'agilitis' (Varney, 2019). Agilitis is an overreliance on agility to solve the problems of a dynamic world. It comes from a tendency to confuse speed with adaptability.

The paradoxical nature of complex systems means that they are both adapting and enduring *at the same time*. Viable systems develop a balance between responding to every fluctuation and resisting some of the dynamics in the environment (Cilliers, 2006). Without some level of resistance to fluctuations, an organisational system would have no coherent structure and no coherent identity. It would not survive in any recognisable form.

Speed is never going to catch up with complexity because it is the wrong response. Remember requisite complexity from Chapter 2? It is internal complexity that gives us the capacity to adapt to external complexity, not speed. If we want to adapt our responses, we need to slow down.

Slowing down thinking

Cilliers (2006) argues that "slowness" is a more appropriate response to complexity than speed because it helps us to cope with the demands of a complex world "in a *better* way". He explains:

> The argument for slowness is forward looking: it is about an engagement with the future as much as with the past. Slowness is in itself a temporal notion, and in many ways the opposite of the notion 'static.' In point of fact, it is actually an unreflective fastness that always returns you to the same place.
> (Cilliers, 2006: 106)

Unless we deliberately slow down thinking, the "lazy controller" of fast System 1 thinking is likely to be more influential on us than we think (Kahneman, 2012).

When this happens, we act automatically out of habit (Kahneman, 2012), by going round in a single loop (Argyris, 1977) which returns us to the same place (Cilliers, 2006). If you have ever found yourself stuck in a familiar loop over and again at work, or in life, you will understand what Cilliers means.

Paying attention to noticing helps to break that cycle. Deliberately noticing what is changing enables us to take over from the lazy controller of habit and engage System 2's slower thinking (Kahneman, 2012). It enables us to rethink our responses into the dynamic patterning (double-loop learning), rather than habitually deploying the same responses (single-loop learning). In turn, engaging in slow thinking helps managers to broaden their perspective and unlocks the "power" of their noticing (Bazerman, 2014).

Inviting diverse perspectives

As insiders in a complex world, we can only see part of the picture. Our view is shaped by our position in the system, which shows some aspects and obscures others. For example, being in the management hierarchy includes us in some conversations, but it leaves us out of others. Furthermore, how we see and experience the world is shaped by our personal history. It is a partial and filtered view. We are primed to notice some aspects and to overlook others.

If we want to notice more, then actively inviting other perspectives can bring us more diverse noticing data, as Susan's story in Box 5.1 illustrates. She used the 'vital signs' of change tool (more about that in Chapter 6) across a network of change champions to learn about the nuances in the dynamic patterning across a large organisation. The insights from those collective 'noticings' helped Susan to energise a major change programme by creating local pull for the mandated technology solution.

Box 5.1 Developing a noticing network
Susan is the project lead for an Office 365 rollout in a large, non-departmental public body. Like many programme leads, she created a group of change champions to support the change process.

Unlike many other programme leads, however, Susan did not use the network of change champions to push out the change programme through a traditional, structured roll out. Instead, she took the opportunity to engage 30 people with different views, perspectives, and antennae in helping her to extend her noticing about what was changing.

Over several weeks and months, the change champions network regularly shared perspectives and pooled their noticings. They used their insight about emerging needs in specific areas to identify local hooks for the technical solution. They also used their learning to shape ongoing communication so that it resonated with the people involved and created more pull for the technology.

Susan described her experience as "absorbing complexity". What she was doing, although she may not have realised it, was developing requisite complexity. By complexifying the points of noticing within the programme team, Susan and her network were able to better match the complexity of their institutional context.

Noticing at multiple levels

I worked with ten managers and professionals from six large organisations in a Henley Forum action research project: 'Engaging with Complexity'.[9] Over several months, they each practiced noticing in their own organisational context and regularly gathered noticing data in an electronic diary. When I analysed this data, I discovered they were variously noticing what was changing at different scales:
- **Individual**. Noticing what was changing for themselves, for example, their own thoughts, feelings, impactful events, relationships, and so on.
- **Team/project**. Noticing what was changing in their immediate team, or project, for example, changes in the emotional energy and in the frequency of meetings.
- **Organisational**. Noticing what was changing across their wider organisational context, for example, changes in the top management team, changes in the tone and content of communications.
- **External world.** Noticing what was changing in the wider world, for example, changing industry norms and stock market fluctuations.

Reflecting together on these emerging findings, we likened these entangled levels of scale to an orchestra. An individual player, such as cellist Sheku Kanneh-Mason,[10] must simultaneously notice his own playing, whilst also paying attention to the string section, the orchestra, and the wider context of the audience and auditorium. When an orchestra performs well, musicians – including the conductor – are not simply following the notes on the page, they are adapting and responding in the moment to one another and the wider context.

Jazz bands are often used as a metaphor in complexity to illustrate the improvisational aspects of organisational life. A jazz band makes that point well. However, most of the managers I work with are working in contexts with many more players than in a jazz band, with more defined sections, and a more formal hierarchy. So, the orchestra metaphor is a better fit than a jazz band for their lived experience.

The 'organisation as orchestra' metaphor provides a useful prompt to notice the dynamic patterning at and across different scales. It invites us to zoom in and out with our noticing and to make connections between levels (Ibarra et al., 2005).

Real-time noticing

We have slowed down to pay attention to noticing small data. We have invited others to bring their diverse perspectives to enhance the breadth of our noticing. We have also extended our collective noticing across many levels. Now we must turn our attention to the frequency of our noticing.

Chris' story (Box 5.2) highlights the potential opportunities and challenges of real-time noticing. Noticing in the moment provides the opportunity to engage with emotional and other nuances within the fluidity of the dynamic patterning of change. Once particular patterns of change have become "irreversible", as we see in this story, it is rather harder to nudge things along to capitalise on emerging opportunities and to head off emerging issues. However, the challenge of close to real-time noticing, as Chris discovered, is that it reveals the vast amount of data that is available. This can be overwhelming, in a practical sense, as well as emotionally.

Box 5.2 Noticing regularly

Chris works for a national retailer. He wanted to understand "broader perspectives" from other people's experience of change over the previous six months, so he sent a survey to 100 people from various areas of the business.

Chris discovered that around 30% of people believed the business had *irreversibly changed* over the previous six months. He concluded that "it became clear the opportunities and challenges of a paradigm shift of the old normal has opened up a world of creativity and opportunity".

When it comes to noticing, Chris reflected that "it's more effective when done in the moment". Yet he also explained, "I was shocked at the vast amount of data that I come into contact with on an ongoing basis". He summed up the issue by concluding:

> You can spend a lot of time noticing everything and seeing nothing ... there is a risk of both going too small and too wide; if you focus on noticing occurrences in isolation then you can miss the opportunity to see links between them. But if you try to attempt to compare everything you note it is easy to become overwhelmed.

There is no easy solution here. Real-time noticing will help you to engage with the *dynamics* of dynamic patterning, whereas retrospective noticing will help you to engage with the *patterns* of dynamic patterning. Making your leadership count means doing both. Once again, leadership in complexity and change means grappling with a paradox.

Practical tips for better noticing

Noticing your noticing

You are probably noticing all the time, without even being aware of what you are noticing. As adults, we rarely remark on our noticing. Children are different, as Lola's story (Box 5.3) illustrates.

Box 5.3 Noticing our noticing

I was waiting on a station platform with my four-year-old niece and reminding her *never* to step over the yellow line until the train had stopped. She skipped around quite happily while I kept a very close eye on her. Whenever she strayed near the yellow line, she stopped and she looked up at me to show that she had heeded the warning. I acknowledged and reinforced her good behaviour. The message was understood.

Suddenly she looked up, eyes open wide, and cried out at the very top of her voice; "Look!" Everyone on the platform duly looked at her. "Look at that man!!", she screamed, pointing at a commuter who was rocking on his heels. Everyone on the platform turned to look at him as he froze, mid-rock (how did he do that?). "He's *over* the yellow line!!!"

At that moment I became aware that I had already noticed it. But I had not remarked on my noticing, even to myself. As a regular commuter, I had seen this kind of minor overstepping the boundaries (here, literally) on every journey. I did not notice my noticing because it reinforced existing mental models I held, and probably some unconscious biases (he thinks the rules don't apply to him; he's arrogant).

Yet, this man was rocking *backwards* on his heels with his *back* to the track. This was much riskier than the norm of a toe over the line. It would not have taken much to turn that action into a fatal incident; a momentary loss of concentration, someone's wheelie case clipping him as they rushed down the platform for the approaching train. Thanks to Lola's vigilance, disaster was averted.

In health and safety terms, the incident in Box 5.3 was a near miss. In complexity terms, the rocking man was far from equilibrium. Under those conditions, an accumulation of small events in a system (here the system centred around the station platform) can create a chain reaction that has much larger consequences (the 'butterfly effect').

Becoming aware of what you are noticing is an important first stage. For most adults, our brains quickly jump to conclusions (Kahneman, 2012). We fail to notice our noticing because we have already made sense based on our mental models of how things normally work. We conveniently overlook slight changes to the picture because we assume that small changes will only make a small difference. Yet in complex systems that are far from equilibrium, that is a risky assumption to make.

These sweeping generalisations are only true for neurotypical thinkers. Neurodiverse thinkers can offer valuable perspectives when it comes to noticing small data about what is changing. It is another reminder of the value of diversity for leadership in complexity and change.

Mindfully noticing

If we want to become powerful noticers, then we must pay attention to what we are noticing. The aim here is to elevate noticing from being a subconscious activity by bringing it into our conscious minds. Being more mindful helps us to notice things that we might otherwise overlook.

Anyone who has tried mindfulness for meditation will understand something about what that involves. In mindful practice, you actively notice your thoughts; bodily sensations like your breathing, heart rate, and any areas of tension; along with any sounds and sensations from the outside world. In mindfulness, the aim is consciously noticing *without* becoming attached to what you are noticing. You notice your thoughts and feelings and let them go without interrogating them or judging yourself for having them. If you are a busy-minded fidget, like me, it does not come naturally. Meditative mindfulness is considered a lifelong practice.

Mindfulness is a useful analogy for three reasons. First, it encourages us to pause and consciously notice. Second, it invites us to notice what we are noticing *without* jumping to conclusions. Third, it reminds us that we can get better at noticing with practice.

Bracketing time

Consulting firm McKinsey suggests that weak signals are strategically important enough to demand top management attention.[11] They propose allocating management time and attention to paying attention to diverse sources of data and deliberately noticing weak signals.

A good way to get better at noticing what is changing in the mass of small, qualitative, human-scale data that surround us is by doing it regularly and intentionally. So – and this must be the easiest tip in the whole book – put it in your diary!

Putting it in your diary provides an important reminder to look beyond the focus of your immediate work to notice what is changing in your team, project, division, organisation, industry, and beyond. It also invites you to look inwards, to your own experience of being part of the organisational system, and to pay attention to small, qualitative, human-scale data that you may otherwise overlook.

Simply block out a regular time to deliberately activate your noticing. It does not have to be long. Try blocking out 15 minutes on a Friday to reflect over the week and asking yourself:
- What is changing this week?
- What is new or different this week?
- What is there more/less of this week?
- What is puzzling, surprising, or unexpected this week?

You might be tempted to take longer, and that is fine at the beginning. However, do not give yourself too long, or you will be tempted to do more than just notice. You might start analysing prematurely, or the 'lazy controller' will take over again and jump to habitual conclusions (Kahneman, 2012). So, just notice and note. When I introduce the vital signs of change to people (which I will do in Chapter 6), I often give them just two or three minutes to note down as much as possible about what has been changing. People are amazed how much they can jot down in such a tiny amount of time.

It can be hard to stop our brains from racing ahead when that is normally what we expect them to do. If you want to change what is going on in your mind, a good tip is to change what is going on in your body. Try going for a 15-minute walk to change your state, and then spend 15 minutes noticing what has been changing over the week and noting it all down.

The kind of conscious noticing that we are trying to cultivate does not *just happen*, although we can get better at it. It takes time and effort, often scarce resources in organisational life. Clock time is probably the only linear aspect in a complex world, so it makes good sense to regularly bracket time in our busy working lives for important activities such as noticing. Practice will help you to become a better noticer, so that you become more attuned to picking up weak signals about what is changing.

Being systematic and structured

Some people assume that leadership in an emergent world is all about spontaneity and being in the moment. They assume there is little value to planning or deliberate action in processes of emergence. I disagree. Planning, along with other forms of intentional action, are not separate from emergence. In human systems, they are *part of* that emergence.

Being systematic by regularly bracketing time for noticing makes it easier to pick up changing nuances in the dynamic patterning over a period of time. Being systematic about collecting our noticing data adds some rigour to the noticing process and helps us to make small, qualitative, human-scale data count. For example, Lichtenstein (2000) used regular diaries to pick out pattern amid the chaos of transformative change.

As well as bracketing regular time for noticing, we can be deliberate and structured in our approach. We saw that in Susan's story (Box 5.1) where she deliberately developed a noticing network, and in Chris's story (Box 5.2), where he surveyed 100 people to broaden his noticing. Like many managers, Chris acknowledged that the process of noticing small data felt alien as he came from "a world of KPIs" (Key Performance Indicators) and the kind of data you can count or measure. You can see his preference for structured data in his decision to use a survey.

The continuation of Chris's story (Box 5.4) shows how he turned his preference for a structured approach into an asset in the noticing process. He used open questions in the survey to systematically gather a wealth of small data from a range of sources. It opened his eyes to the value of small data that he might normally have overlooked, which he found "extremely helpful".

Box 5.4 Noticing systematically

Chris's change survey included open questions. He asked people about their personal responses to the change they were experiencing, and he invited them to share their thoughts for
the future. He received a flood of replies. The wealth of small, qualitative, human-scale data included valuable signals about the patterning of emotional energy (excerpts below):

- this year has been very much about . . . keeping hearts and minds in a positive state, this
  has at times been exhausting
- optimistic for the future but weary of further change and its impact
- it felt pretty exciting dealing with the challenges of the change
- we have had to completely rethink the way we operate and work, which has been both
  exciting and daunting

In looking at the data, Chris reflected on how the emotional responses were intertwined with what
had been happening over the period. It became clear to him how people had felt and reacted differently to what had been happening, with some managers responding in more practical ways.

Noting your noticing

Regular noticing should be accompanied by regular noting. Noting is an important
activity because it means that you can revisit your noticings at a later date. This
gives you the chance to review them and pick out emerging patterns. There are various practical ways you can do this, such as:

- **Jot it down on a desk planner.** In the action research project on engaging with
  complexity, we developed an A3 desk planner to help people capture their noticings.[12] The idea is to take a new planner each week and use it to jot down words
  or doodles to capture noticings as they arise. We structured the planner around
  the four vital signs of change (see Chapter 6) and the four levels of noticing to
  invite a broader focus for noticing and noting.
- **Use your phone.** The advantage of using an app on your phone to capture your
  noticings is that you can do it anywhere. It also gives you the opportunity to collect your noticings as voice notes. Depending on the app you select, you can
  also get a detailed date and time log.
- **Divide up your meeting notes.** One manager from a large consulting firm used
  this method to great effect. Inspired by Chris Argyris's (1980) left-hand column exercise, he divided his meeting notes into two columns. In one column, he wrote
  the meeting notes. In the other, he noted down his noticings about the dynamics
  playing out in the meeting.
- **Create a spreadsheet.** Alternatively, you could capture regular noticings on a
  spreadsheet. You can pre-structure the spreadsheet, as we did with the desk
  planner (above) and use different tabs to record each set of noticings. Susan
  used this method with her noticing network (Box 5.1). While it can facilitate a
  later analysis, try not to look back before you note your new noticing as that
  might narrow your focus.

When it comes to systematically noticing and noting it down, there are many approaches you can take. I would encourage you to experiment and find an approach that works for you.

Key insights
- In dynamic patterning, small issues or opportunities can rapidly escalate beyond our grasp
- Noticing what is changing increases our chances of picking up useful clues sooner
- Weak signals about the emerging future are hidden in small, qualitative, human-scale data
- Small data is plentiful and freely available, but its value is often overlooked
- Slowing down thinking and bracketing time to notice helps us to pick up valuable small data
- Inviting diverse views and zooming in and out adds valuable nuances to our noticing
- Being systematic and noting it down helps us to make our noticing data really count

increase our chances
slow down thinking useful clues
small qualitative human-scale data
noticing what is changing
weak signals hidden bracketing time
small data zooming in and out
diverse views noting it down
dynamic patterning

Noticing and noting
It is your turn to try it out. Before you move on, take a few minutes to reflect over the past month and ask yourself, what has been changing?
- What is new or different?
- What is there more/less of?
- What is puzzling, surprising or unexpected?

Note it all down, as quickly as you can. Do not worry about whether you have got it quite right. You can come back to it later.

Notes

1 The original quote "chance favours only the prepared mind" is attributed to French scientist Louis Pasteur.

2 The dog who did not bark comes from a short story by Sir Arthur Conan Doyle featuring fictional detective, Sherlock Holmes, who is famous for his skills of observation.

3 When it comes to objectives, SMART usually stands for Specific, Measurable, Achievable, Realistic, and Timebound.

4 As Nonaka (1994) explains, explicit knowledge is the tip of the iceberg. Beneath it lies a wealth of potentially valuable knowledge that is tacit.

5 George Firican from the University of British Columbia highlights the 10 Vs of Big Data https://tdwi.org/articles/2017/02/08/10-vs-of-big-data.aspx (accessed 25/08/2020).

6 I originally discussed some of these ideas in a 2015 Croner-i article: 'Change – why "small data" is HR's best friend' (Varney, 2015).

7 This comes from a 2014 McKinsey Quarterly article 'The strength of "weak signals"' https://www.mckinsey.com/industries/technology-media-and-telecommunications/our-insights/the-strength-of-weak-signals (accessed 25/08/2020).

8 In Greek mythology, Sisyphus was condemned to the eternal punishment of rolling a boulder up a hill in the depths of Hades. Each time he neared the top, the boulder rolled back down, and the cycle began again.

9 The Henley Forum is an applied research centre at Henley Business School, part of the University of Reading www.henley.ac.uk/henleyforum (accessed 25/08/2020). The action research project 'Engaging with Complexity' was conducted in 2017–2018.

10 Sheku Kanneh-Mason won the 2016 BBC Young Musician Competition and became better known for performing at the wedding of the Duke and Duchess of Sussex at Windsor Castle in 2018.

11 See endnote 7.

12 See endnote 9.

Chapter 6
Spotting the vital signs of change

The vital signs

Trying to notice everything, all the time, would be totally overwhelming. So, in Chapter 5, I invited you to pay particular attention to noticing small data about the dynamic patterning of change. I offered you some key questions to help you in developing your noticing skills: What is changing? What is new or different? What is puzzling, surprising, or unexpected?

You can enhance your noticing to the next level by using the vital signs of change. These new insights into the dynamic patterning of change come from my doctoral research (Varney, 2013).[1] The vital signs of change will help you to notice more broadly *and* more deeply. So, they are valuable lenses for anyone trying to spot the vital signs of change sooner.

In the medical world, the four vital signs are body temperature, heart rate, respiratory rate, and blood pressure. There are others, such as oxygen saturation, weight, and so on. Healthcare professionals regularly measure the vital signs when someone feels unwell. They are looking for signs of change, any deviations from normal patterns of activity. Change from the norm does not tell them precisely what is wrong with you, but it does offer some important clues.

The vital signs of change work in the same kind of way. They invite you to notice deviations from the normal patterning in a particular setting. There are four vital signs of change (see Figure 6.1):

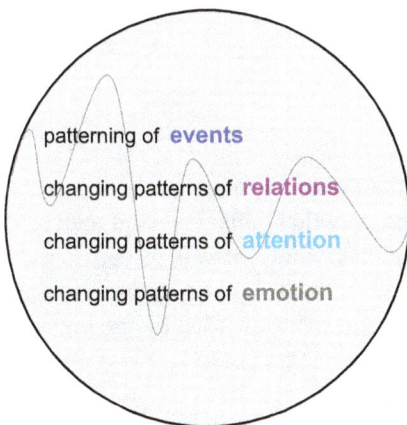

Figure 6.1: The vital signs of change.
Source: Adapted from Varney (2013).

https://doi.org/10.1515/9783110713343-006

I introduced the term dynamic patterning in Part I to highlight the constant motion of the working world and beyond. It draws attention to the vitality in organisational life – the power of enduring and changing – that is created and re-created by the everyday interaction between people. The vital signs (Figure 6.1) keep our attention on the vitality of changing as we focus on the dynamic patterning of events, relations, attention, and emotion.

There are at least five good reasons to apply the vital signs of change to enhance your noticing:

1. **Applying multiple perspectives.** Each vital sign of change offers a different lens on a complex reality, so they help you to apply multiple perspectives.
2. **Going beneath the surface.** The vital signs of change invite you to notice more deeply, so they sensitise you to noticing more clues about what is changing beneath the surface.
3. **Opening up thinking and conversation.** The four vital signs are broad domains, not narrow categories, so they open up thinking and conversation.
4. **Making noticing data count.** The vital signs provide a structured way to collect small, qualitative, human-scale data, so they help you to make that potentially valuable data count.
5. **Aiding practical judgement.** The vital signs of change provide clues about what is changing, so they serve as a valuable aid to practical judgement, they do not replace it.

This chapter introduces the vital signs of change and explores each of the lenses in more detail. It concludes by putting it all together and considering how to use the vital signs in leadership practice.

Patterning of events

Events in changing

If you ask someone about a period of change, their response often starts with something along the lines of, 'well this happened and then that happened, and then . . . ' and so on. They naturally provide an account of the events that took place.

In my doctoral research, I asked managers to tell me what had changed in their organisation since our previous meeting. Many of them responded by tracing a series of events as a backbone for their story. As one manager put it:

> Then of course two things happened almost half-way through the year: first of all, a few days after opening the [new building] . . . the Chief Executive announced that he was leaving . . . and, of course, there was an economic crisis in the country and elsewhere. And we were told in no uncertain terms that there were going to have to be major economies.

In this short quote, there are four distinct events: opening the new building; the chief executive's announcement that he was leaving; an economic crisis in the country and elsewhere; and the announcement of major economies. Each event is situated in a particular time and place.

Events, as I define them, happen *at* or *over* a period of time. Events can be very brief, like a remark or a gesture. (As we now know from the butterfly effect, small events can be immensely powerful when they are amplified by positive feedback.) They might last a bit longer, like an announcement or a leadership programme. Or they might take place over a more extended time span, like a period of consultation, or an economic crisis. Events are embedded in context as well as time: they happen in specific places, with specific people, and specific things.

In my doctoral research, I found many middle and senior managers were attuned to noticing events in change (Varney, 2013). It provides empirical support for the claim that "people are likely to notice more events and to engage in more sensemaking while they are adapting to changes" (Starbuck and Hedberg, 2003: 334).

Going deeper

When there is greater volatility, such as in large transformation projects, people can become overly focused on the events in working life. The formal and informal conversations can become dominated by what happened, what people think about what happened, what they think should have happened, and so on. People can get stuck chewing over the same things in the same ways. When people are lulled by the familiar patterns of repeating conversations, they often act out of habit. Rather than activating their deeper noticing, engaging their interpreting, and *choosing* their best response into the dynamic patterning, people often jump to conclusions and leap into action. (We will look at how we can avoid these two unhelpful habits in chapters 7 and 8, respectively).

Habitual responses can keep people very occupied in change. Unfortunately, it can also leave them stuck in repeating patterns. The vital signs of change provide an important reminder that events are just part of the picture. While events are often the first things to come to our notice, there is a lot more going on beneath the surface. This is illustrated by the vital signs iceberg in Figure 6.2.

Rather than getting caught up in the content of events, we are trying to build a fuller picture of how things are changing. That means paying attention to the *patterning* of events and to the changing patterning of relations, attention, and emotion.

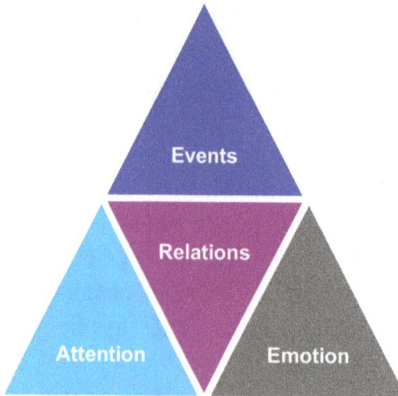

Figure 6.2: The vital signs iceberg.

Why events matter – a lot!

In complexity terms, events matter. As we saw in Part I, the detail of the specific things we say and do, at specific times and places, with specific people and artefacts form the raw material for emergence. Actual events contribute to shaping the dynamic patterning of organisational life:

> [At] the heart of complexity theory, is the way forms, *patterns*, and institutions *emerge* and become established and are then constantly challenged and potentially invaded by the particular *events*, variances, decisions, shocks, and so on that *take place in particular places at particular times.* (Boulton et al., 2015: 29, emphasis added)

As Boulton et al. (2015: 29) vividly describe it: "the future is a dance between patterns and events". They are highlighting that patterns and events are entangled in a nonlinear and dynamic relationship.

In complexity terms, macro patterns (e.g., organisational culture) and micro events (e.g., a specific conversation) co-evolve. Events may reinforce familiar patterns of continuity. For example, a conversation about trying something new, or doing something differently, may reinforce a cultural pattern of supporting innovation. When events reinforce patterns, we know roughly where we are. Of course, we must always be vigilant in our noticing to check that we are not being misled by a false sense of familiarity.

Importantly, events may also act as triggers for unfamiliar patterns of change. Events may trigger transformation (Lichtenstein, 2000), radical change (Plowman et al., 2007), or new approaches and behaviours (Higgs and Rowland, 2005). Small variations in the micro detail of specific events have the potential to radically change the trajectory of the organisational system. For example, a meeting where people feel really listened to by their manager may alter those relationships and trigger much wider effects.

It is this ability to affect the balance between continuity and change that makes events so valuable as a 'vital sign' of change.

The dance between patterns and events

Events shape patterns. Organisational culture does not arrive in your inbox alongside the articles of incorporation of a business. Organisational culture is shorthand for a recognisable pattern – 'the way we do things around here'. Such cultural patterns emerge from specific events, that is, things we say and do. That is why organisational culture is different from place to place. Specific events then serve to reinforce cultural patterns or to change them.

Patterns shape events. Patterns of legal, institutional, cultural, and social norms shape events. The prevailing patterning makes some events more likely and others less likely. For example, the focus on behavioural safety in the oil and gas sector makes it *more likely* that someone will remind you to hold the handrail when you walk down the stairs in their offices. Yet, that would be much *less likely* in a law firm. The way that patterning shapes events is a bit like tipping the floor by a few degrees. You could walk uphill if you really wanted to. But it takes less effort to walk downhill.

The dance. Events and patterns shape one another *at the same time*. As people interact, they act in ways that reinforce or challenge prevailing patterns. That is why events and patterns co-evolve.

Noticing events

Life is punctuated by events. We tend to notice those events that stand out from the patterning in some way. Specific events may stand out for being unusual – new, different, unexpected, puzzling, or surprising – or for being particularly important. In my doctoral research, managers highlighted events that were 'unanticipated' and those that were 'major' in some way.

Managers and professionals notice a wide variety of events, such as changes at the top of the hierarchy, opening new office buildings, picnics, social media postings, and so on. Table 6.1 gives some real examples extracted from diary entries submitted as part of the Henley Forum research project 'Engaging with Complexity'. The event types were added afterwards. In line with the complexity thinking from Chapter 4, these event types are not offered here as a definitive list of event categories. Instead, they are designed to be useful prompts that help you to open up your own thinking and broaden your noticing of events in the continuous flow of dynamic patterning.

Individuals pick out events which are salient, for them, from the overall flow of their experience. So, once again, it is extremely helpful to invite multiple perspectives by encouraging other people to share their noticings. Some managers do this formally, by sharing the vital signs of change and working through it in a workshop. Others do it informally by asking questions such as, what has been changing in your world? What key events stand out for you?

Table 6.1: Salient events.

Event type	Diary excerpts
People events	One of the directors was suddenly re-deployed; I resigned from my role; new executive board leader announced; several swift senior departures; new group head of transformation; CEO is on a 3 month 'sabbatical'; colleague celebrated 20-year anniversary; lots of farewell drinks; more adjustments to team structures; new ministers
Financial events	Additional money released; new pressure on year-end budgets; budgets are being locked down; new budgets released ahead of time to fund rapid start; monies ear marked 'not spent' are now lost; share price fall; share price lifted; pay award accepted
Operational events	Won case at Supreme Court; voicemail not working; phase 2 goes live; several incidents; ISO9001 audit actions; senior management have just endorsed a series of policies
Physical events	New office building, relocation of staff; lack of space; digital services team will be moving out; now working from home; people not attending meetings or declining at short notice
Communication events	Leadership offsite meeting; EXCO off site this week; a company-wide email regarding [system] being down; increase in mental health awareness and well-being events across the business; increase in video messages posted on Yammer; diabetes day
Seasonal events	Summer picnic; not very summery . . . but exciting weather; Christmas decorations going up in office; holiday next week

Source: Henley Forum Research (2018).[2]

You can also use the vital signs of change framework to help you in noticing the dynamic patterning within and between groups during a meeting or workshop. When I do this, I tend to ask about 'moments' rather than events.

Patterns of events

Events are not isolated happenings. Managers often describe chains of events in chronological terms (this happened, then that happened) and in causal terms (this led to that, which led to something else). They are probably wrong, or at least not completely right, in attributing cause and effect. Yet, they are correct in thinking that events are often related to one another.

For example, extending a hand when you meet someone is likely to invite a similar response in terms of a handshake. (This pattern changed in 2020.) Such gestures and responses are events which are entangled, albeit in a nonlinear manner. Stacey (2001) refers to this entanglement of gestures and responses as the complex responsive processes of relating (CRP).

Noticing changes in the patterning of events might be more important than the individual events. For example, in safety terms, noticing an increase in near misses in a particular area might be a sign to look more deeply into what is changing in that area. More events, a greater range of events, or change in the normal pace, pattern and rhythm of events might be useful to notice. For example, an HR manager in a retail business observed:

> It's normally busy at this time of year, but it's ridiculous at the moment, beyond the pale. It keeps everybody very occupied, running furiously in the hamster wheel, But I don't have time to stop and think.

What she was noticing was a change in the pace and the rhythm of events in her organisational system. "It's normally busy at this time of year" references a familiar seasonal pattern. If you work in the retail or travel sectors, for example, you expect seasonal ebbs and flows in the pace of events. Finance professionals may experience increases in the pace of events around end of year. Project professionals may experience increases around the start and end of projects. Acute hospitals expect to be busy over the winter period. We get used to the normal rhythms in our own context. When those patterns fluctuate, we take note. "It's ridiculous at the moment", suggests the intensity is greater than the normal seasonal high. Not just that, but it is beyond the bounds of acceptable behaviour ("beyond the pale"), suggesting that it is an abnormal pattern.

Going back to the vital signs metaphor, it is a bit like noticing an increase in your pulse rate. Your pulse rate fluctuates depending on what you are doing. When you exercise, your heart rate rises. When you stop exercising, it should return to a resting level. A continuously elevated pulse rate may be a cause for concern, particularly over the longer term. As we saw in Chapter 1, an organisation is not a special person, so there is no 'it' or a pulse rate. Yet, changes to the rhythm or pulse of events might offer vital signs about emerging patterns of change.

Major events are hard to miss. Yet smaller events may go unnoticed, until they accumulate. That is why we are actively looking out for changes in the patterning of events.

Changing patterns of relations

Relations and why they matter

In the dynamic patterning of organisational life, individuals are not separate parts. We are bound together within a complex whole. Since relationships affect what emerges, it is vital to understand more about their patterning.

A colleague told me a story that illustrates the importance of relational dynamics rather well (see Box 6.1). Yet this mini case also highlights how easy it is to miss unspoken weak signals.

> **Box 6.1 A quiet disconnection**
>
> A city-based charity working with troubled teenagers was growing, so they set about expanding their team of youth workers. Managers decided to recruit for complementary knowledge and skills to boost the team.
>
> The original youth workers had gained their expertise through direct experience; they worked on the streets, engaging directly with troubled teenagers, and they cared strongly about them. These youth workers formed a close-knit community, with strong, supportive relationships. The new generation of youth workers who joined them were highly trained social workers who had plenty of theoretical expertise, lots of psychological tools and were full of potentially useful ideas. Yet they lacked hands-on experience with the young people.
>
> The original youth workers began to feel irrelevant as the new generation of youth workers brought in their new ideas. Although they could see some of the practical pitfalls, they did not comment because they did not have the 'glossy qualifications'.
>
> Rather than having a fruitful exchange of knowledge and perspectives in the expanded team, it gravitated into two informal communities with little exchange between them. There were few outward signs of this beyond the original youth workers becoming more tightly knit as a group and things left unsaid in their relationship with the newcomers.

If we spot vital signs of change in the patterning of relations sooner, we can use this data to make more-informed responses into that patterning, either by attempting to head off emerging issues before they escalate, or by building on emerging opportunities before they pass us by. For example, in the mini case in Box 6.1, we might develop a buddy system to build relationships and foster collaboration. It reminds us of the importance of actively paying attention to the second vital sign of change: the changing patterns of relations.

Formal and informal relations

In social groups, we tend to fall into recognisable patterns in how we relate to others. As we know from family life, for example, these patterns show up in how close we are, physically and emotionally, to those in our immediate and more distant family. They might be reinforced by material things such as the space we have available, or access to transport and technology. Repeating relational patterns also show up in the kinds of informal roles we take in the family system: carer, breadwinner, joker, challenger, conciliator, educator, free spirit, organiser, etc.

Hierarchies and power dynamics within family systems affect who gets 'a say' in decisions, whose needs are prioritised, and how much freedom individuals have to make their own choices. This might also be influenced by material things, such as direct access to resources. I use the family example to illustrate these relational dynamics because sometimes we fail to recognise that similar informal dynamics are also at play in organisational systems.

In the working world, we tend to focus attention on formal relationships, such as the hierarchies denoted in organisational structures and the formal authorities set out in various policies. These formal relations help to regulate who controls valuable resources, who can make decisions, and so on. Yet, they become entangled in a web of informal relational dynamics as people interact in the normal course of their work. When we are considering the patterning of relations, we must take both formal and informal relational dynamics into account.

Considering structural patterns

We considered one aspect of the structural patterning of relationships in Chapter 3 when we talked about changing the physical distance between people (social distancing) to slow the spread of Covid-19. Formal organisation structures and policies also serve to pattern relationships. For example, they denote who is part of the formal organisation; how people are formally related through reporting lines or other contractual arrangements; who gets a formal say over other people's decisions and action; and who is in/out of a particular team.

There are also important informal structural dynamics at play. In the mini case in Box 6.1, there were two relatively clear-cut groups: the original youth workers and the new recruits. In that situation, if you are paying close attention to the vital signs of change, you could notice changes to that social structure directly. However, the informal structural patterns of relations between people may themselves be more complex and harder to detect directly. Social network mapping tools can be useful in helping to reveal more of the informal relational structures at work.

Mapping social networks

In my doctoral research, I surveyed the top 100 people in the organisational hierarchy and asked them; who do you go to when you want to influence change?

The resulting mapping[3] of the informal social networks showed that some, but not all, of the executive team were central to this network. Importantly, it also revealed some people from *outside* the executive team who were pivotal in change because they informally connected different groups.

You would not be able to see that from the formal organisation structure. Key individuals may not know the crucial role they take in the network. Network mapping can reveal crucial connections that direct observation or questioning would not reveal.

Social mapping tools are useful for revealing structural connections that are difficult to see directly. Yet we are looking out for what is *changing*, so spotting the vital signs of change in small, qualitative, human-scale data remains vitally important.

Noticing qualitative patterning

In the 'Engaging with complexity' research from earlier, managers and professionals noticed changing patterns in various qualitative relational dynamics, as illustrated in Table 6.2 (labels added). As with the event types, this is not a definitive list of categories. Think of them as useful prompts to open up your thinking, helping you to augment your own noticing.

Table 6.2: Patterning of relations.

Relational dynamic	Diary excerpts
Cooperation and conflict	Pace of change has brought conflict and cooperation; initial reaching out between groups to establish better collaboration; conflict between certain members more apparent; conflicting personalities becoming more obvious; a warm front is developing in our relationship with [team name]; cooperation remains a challenge as networks have been broken through recent changes
Power and politics	Becoming clear who are supporters and who are blockers; new senior team players like to exert power and ensure people recognise their arrival; support from senior management for the team; a good ally . . . feels he's lost power and influence in moving to a new role; interesting alliances being formed across leadership and management teams; team focused on getting into a good position
Communication and engagement	Greater engagement with [team name] and teams outside; lots of engagement around ISO9001 remediation; high level of engagement this month; emphasis on external communications – still an internal gap; limited comms at this stage . . . head down . . . missing the bigger picture; more sarcastic references about the dictatorial leadership style
Structures and hierarchies	More staff movement – sometimes challenging to track down the right person; reorganisation at the top of the shop; more change at the top with new appointments; more adjustments to team structures; roles and responsibilities are being adjusted; changes in senior staff; continued new senior players – in Division and at Group
Group dynamics and in/out groups	New Executive Committee members settling in; quiet asides between individuals within group; very noticeable lack of trust in me by boss; unaligned and unchecked behaviours (particularly alpha male); relations becoming more tense; a little tension due to lack of involvement of key team members; tensions within team as participants . . . start to butt up

Source: Henley Forum Research (2018).[4]

Spotting the vital signs

Patterns of relations are formed and reinforced through interactions. As people tend to interact with one another in similar ways, familiar patterns are likely to emerge from the process of dynamic patterning. These deep structural patterns of relations are often relatively enduring which reinforces the status quo. Some are so pervasive, we even give them names, for example, 'patriarchy'. No wonder we often feel stuck in repeating patterns of relations.

Sometimes the patterning of relations is so entrenched that changes in personnel, for example, have little effect. Informal roles and relations are particularly difficult to shift. Even big re-organisations, which have the appearance of major change, may effectively be neutralised by the patterning of informal relations. Such is the power of relational dynamics, that families, teams, institutions, and so on can find themselves stuck in repeating patterns.

These patterns of 'stuckness' give the appearance of being unchanging. As we learned in Chapter 1, however, the opposite is true. Enduring patterns are being dynamically re-created through our everyday words and actions. That repetition reinforces the patterning and makes it even harder to shift. Once patterns of relating are repeated and reinforced, they become much harder to influence.

Spotting the vital signs of changing patterns of relations early has a huge advantage. While new patterns are forming, a few nudges can make all the difference in what emerges.

Watching out for cues

Relational events such as new arrivals, moves, departures and restructures can have a profound effect on families and teams. But even the joyful ones can feel very disruptive. As we saw with the youth workers (Box 6.1), new arrivals may create significant change in the patterning of relations. The good news is that relational events are relatively easy to spot. Some are heralded by formal announcements, so we know to watch out for potential changes in the wider pattering of relations.

However, the patterning of relations is also changed by everyday interactions which are more likely to go unnoticed. Everyday interactions may accumulate over time to create significant change in the qualitative dimensions of relations, for example, patterns of power and politics; inclusion/exclusion ('us and them'); patterns of cooperation, collaboration, and conflict; patterns of communication and engagement; and so on. These qualitative changes in the patterning of relations may be harder to spot. We must actively look for weak signals of emerging change in these relational dynamics, or we may miss the opportunity to nudge them along.

Change events provide useful cues. In times of rapid or major change, there may be more fluidity to the patterning of relations. Yet, in times of rapid or major change, our focus is often on dealing with the change events themselves, so we may miss the vital signs of changing patterns of relations.

For example, in the mini case in Box 6.2, senior managers were under pressure to deal with several difficult issues over a short period of time. That is not unusual. What is particularly interesting in this case, and especially difficult for those involved, was the subsequent fragmentation of relations in the top management team (TMT) which rippled out across the organisation.

Box 6.2 Changing relations in change

A convergence of difficult things: "What's been changing here since we last met?" I asked. I heard about "a convergence of difficult things", in terms of internal and external events, with many senior managers "really under pressure". One senior manager commented that "from the point of view of leadership and management . . . we've had our biggest challenges really for many years".

Managers under pressure: According to one of its members, the impact of this pressure on the TMT was the "exposure, really, of some of the leadership and management issues that would have remained dormant, or not been challenged". Over that period, senior managers noticed more "arguments", "confrontation", and "fights" within the TMT, with people being caught in the "crossfire". They noticed "games being played" and greater levels of "open competition" between TMT members, with "different groupings" forming. Under pressure, they described pre-existing divisions in the TMT being exacerbated and trust being eroded.

Ripple effects: Senior managers outside the TMT noticed an increasing "sense of fragmentation of the unity of senior management" and people beyond that team becoming "a little polarised" in who they supported. They noticed people becoming "more engaged in the internal departmental politics" and spending more time "justifying their own existence".

This mini case illustrates changes in the group dynamics within the TMT which rippled out across the institution. Those changes included more conflict in the TMT; more political behaviour of TMT members, and beyond; fragmentation of the TMT into sub-groups, along preexisting divisions; erosion of trust, and so on. The issues were not new, but they became more pronounced.

What happened in this case was not a deliberate attempt to disrupt. Rather, it was an emergent pattern that no one wanted. As issues escalated, attending to the relational dynamics took up a huge amount of time, attention, and emotional energy, diverting much-needed resources away from dealing with the initial challenges.

It is a sobering reminder of two things. First, as an organisational system moves beyond the bounds of its familiar patterns (far from equilibrium), we might well notice more out-of-the-ordinary events happening together. Second, with the entangled nature of complex systems, we should expect to find direct and indirect effects in other domains. When we are under pressure, regularly noticing the vital signs of change beyond the scope of our immediate work becomes more important than ever.

Changing patterns of attention

Attention and why it matters

Attention is selective. When we pay attention, we are concentrating our minds on some things rather than others. We are "isolating . . . what information is important and what is given attention from an endless stream of events, actions and outcomes" (Osborn et al., 2002: 811). Effectively we are bringing some things into focus and screening other things out. You are doing that right now as you read this book.

Attention is a cognitive process, so we cannot see it directly. However, we can pick up important clues about the patterning of attention in what people are saying (i.e., what they talk about and how they talk about them) and doing (i.e., how they spend their time).

Attention is a scarce resource. So, giving attention to certain things inevitably means not giving attention to other things. This is important because the ways in which attention is distributed in an organisational system has been linked to different outcomes for businesses. For example, in Nokia, the focus on short-term product development was at the expense of long-term innovation (Vuori and Huy, 2016). At Novo Nordisk, a world leader in diabetes care, not attending to signs of danger resulted in a damaging interruption to its ability to sell insulin in the United States (Rerup, 2009). In multi-national enterprises, the attention of corporate executives is typically divided across the various units around the world in ways that do not give an equal hearing to all parties (Bouquet and Birkinshaw, 2008).

Attention is important for leadership because it plays a role in explaining organisational adaptation and change (Ocasio, 2011). Managers may deliberately structure attention through sensegiving in strategic change (Gioia and Chittipeddi, 1991) and in the leadership of emergence (Lichtenstein and Plowman, 2009). Setting organisational priorities, targets, and metrics are common ways of formally structuring attention by bringing certain things into focus. However, important issues and opportunities may be emerging in those areas that are out of focus, so we must pay careful attention to the third vital sign of change; the patterning of attention.

Paying attention to talk

When I introduce the vital signs of change to managers, many of them find that noticing changing patterns of attention is more challenging than the other vital signs. So, I invite them to start by noticing what gets airtime. Talk often betrays what is getting attention. Many businesses have learned to their cost that when the talk is all about gaining new customers, it may be at the expense of keeping existing customers. Equally, when the conversation is focused on speed or cost cutting, quality may suffer in ways that damage reputation.

The patterning of attention tends to ebb and flow because balancing competing demands for attention is not easy. For example, in the UK's National Health Service (NHS), staff and policy makers must continually balance the attention paid to funding and efficiency issues; clinical and compassionate care for patients and service users; staff recruitment, training, retention and engagement; prevention and treatment, and much more. I use this example because NHS staff and policy makers are doing this in the glare of public attention, so omissions tend to hit the headlines.

Other ways to pay attention to attention are by listening carefully to what is changing in terms of the stories told, rumours circulating, metaphors in use, and questions asked:

– **Stories:** The stories people tell offer clues about how they are focusing their attention. Box 6.3 recounts a story of quality that was proudly told to me by the founder and owner of a medium-sized manufacturing firm. In this case, the actions matched the words.

  When I hear stories like that in Box 6.3, I actively listen for competing stories and actions. Over time, and with changes in personnel, familiar stories may start to lack conviction in the telling, or in the supporting actions. It gives us a clue that the patterning of attention may be changing.

> **Box 6.3 Paying attention to quality**
> As part of a talent management project in Singapore I went to visit Mr Wang (a pseudonym), the founder and owner of a specialist manufacturer with locations across Asia. Over 25 years, his firm had established a valuable reputation for quality with its clients. "Success", he told me, "is about finding why we fail and how we can improve".
> As we toured the site, Mr Wang pointed out a large stack of carefully engineered aluminium pipes. He proudly told me that, while the client had accepted the installation, his engineering manager was not satisfied, so they dismantled the structure and replaced it at their own cost. As a private company, that action had a direct financial impact on its owner.

– **Rumours:** Stories from those in charge help us to consider the formal patterning of attention, but rumours play into the informal patterning of attention. Rumours may or may not be true. Often, they are a mixture of truth and untruth, which gives rumours just enough credibility to be spread. In times of uncertainty and change, people tend to want information for reassurance. When those in charge fail to provide certainty because such information is not available or shareable, it is common for people to fill in the gaps. Box 6.4 highlights how and why one senior manager tuned into the patterning of rumours.

> **Box 6.4 Listening to the rumour mill**
> During a period of disruptive change, a senior manager in a university told me that he was spending more time in the coffee bar chatting informally with students and staff and carefully tuning into the rumours that were spreading.

Many of the rumours were quite outrageous, so other managers simply discounted them as rubbish. This manager was interested in the rumours for two reasons. Firstly, he was in a position of seniority and trust, so he wanted to counter misinformation with information. Secondly, he was interested in the patterning of rumours, the "rumour index" as he called it. He explained how increases in the number of rumours, the more outlandish their content, and the rapidity of spread gave him valuable data about "the level of anxiety of the troops".

– **Metaphors:** Metaphors are powerful attention directors; they simultaneously highlight some aspects of our complex reality and obscure others (Morgan, 1997). The metaphors people use offer useful cues about the patterning of attention by indicating how they are thinking about complex issues. We considered the organisation as a machine metaphor and its limitations in Chapter 1. Box 6.5 highlights the common usage of warlike metaphors in the public talk about Covid-19 in national media. Warlike metaphors draw attention to combat rather than care. So, a key question is what are we *not* paying attention to when we use warlike metaphors?

Box 6.5 Fighting Covid-19
During 2020, many UK politicians and journalists employed warlike metaphors in relation to Covid-19. Talk about 'fighting' Covid-19 was commonplace, along with calls to defeat this deadly virus. Some described being 'at war' with Coronavirus, along with reports of 'embattled' medical staff 'on the front line' who are 'battling' this terrible disease. Even gentler words about Covid-19 as a 'threat', with attention drawn to 'winning' and 'losing' play into this metaphor.[5]

– **Questions:** Questions, like metaphors, can direct attention. 'Who's to blame here?' directs attention differently than 'what can we learn here?' Similarly, 'how can we address this?' signals collective responsibility, while 'what are you going to do about this?' signals individual responsibility.

Prevailing patterns make some questions taboo. In the cult of change (Hodgson, 2011), for example, it becomes difficult to question anything about change. As an IT manager in a large private sector company confided: "Everyone focuses on the 'why' of change. If you ask about the 'how', you're criticised for not being on board with change".

Paying attention to action

Clues about the patterning of attention can also be seen in action. We can spot the vital signs of changing patterns of attention by noticing what gets focus and time, and how that is changing:

- **Focus:** In one educational institution, managers regularly spent time scanning externally for opportunities, such as grants and other funds, to help them achieve their goals. At their regular Monday morning meeting, the TMT would then discuss the opportunities, fairly quickly make a go/no go decision, and then get on with it. They prided themselves in "punching above their weight" in bringing in these kinds of opportunities. Yet, under pressure from a series of events, their focus changed dramatically to internal concerns, and they lost sight of revenue generation.
- **Time:** Following a referendum in 2016, the UK government decided to leave the European Union (EU) after more than 40 years. During 2017, public sector participants in the 'Engaging with Complexity' project were fully absorbed by the UK's EU exit.[6] At that time, various government bodies were busily trying to plan for multiple, unknown scenarios in the absence of an agreed withdrawal deal. It was taking up enormous amounts of time and attention, there was little time for anything else. Yet that was not the case (at that time) for participants working in large private sector businesses.

Returning to the 'Engaging with Complexity' research, Table 6.3 illustrates diary excerpts from participants reflecting the patterning of attention (categories added).

Table 6.3: Patterning of attention.

Attentional dynamic	Diary excerpts
What gets airtime: – stories	Big story about losing two directors in one week. As of yet no official communications; more [formal] comms and [informal] talk about wellbeing and mental health; positive chat re: non-work-related achievements
– rumours	There have been rumours of splitting to create a new department; rumours continue about people who may be thinking about resigning, promotions etc; time wasted on rumours and 'what if' scenarios; future of wider team and pace of change questioned; the rumour mill was slow off the mark. No leaks on that one!
– metaphors	Time to get things off the runway and into the air; getting on board; on the path; be brave . . . grow a spine; two sides of same coin; hanging, waiting, going into a holding position
– questions	What will that look like?; who will fill the roles?; confusion and questions . . . ; questions about pay, nothing in particular about our project; when will the next round of redundancies come?; increasing [number of questions], mostly good ones and inquisitive; questioning around details of what new picture is; pace of change questioned

Table 6.3 (continued)

Attentional dynamic	Diary excerpts
What gets focus, for example, internal/ external, team/ organisation	Brexit is dominating; concentration on getting things done; constant fire drills cause loss of focus; in the India office the attentions, conversations, priorities very different to HQ in London; Agile initiatives kicked off but as buzz words rather than depth of attention
What people do and do not spend time on	There has not been time to break down stovepipes between the teams; less attention on the detail of thinking strategy-structure; less and less time to focus on details

Source: Henley Forum Research (2018).[7]

The dog that didn't bark

It is one thing noticing changes in the kinds of things that people are saying and doing and how they are spending their time. Once you start to pay attention to the patterning of attention, like many new things, it becomes easier.

However, attention is a limited resource. Inevitably if people are talking about some things more, other things will be getting less airtime. If they are emphasising some things more strongly, other things will be getting less emphasis. If people are spending more time than before doing some things, other things will be getting squeezed. Noticing waning patterns of attention is not easy. Sherlock Holmes may notice the curious incident of the dog that did not bark in the nighttime, but busy managers may not find it easy to notice things that did not happen.

I ran a series of change leadership masterclasses for a pharmaceutical firm. When I first visited their German office, my client and I met in a comfortable, light-filled social meeting space with some impressive coffee machines. While we were sat there, three or four people wandered through, grabbed a coffee and left. When I remarked on it, my client sighed. The area was designed to encourage informal collaboration, she explained, and it used to be well used. Now, she told me, everyone is worried about cost cutting and there have been rumours about closures. People are focusing on doing their own work and making sure they look busy, and no one uses the collaborative space.

Attentional choices are multi-dimensional. So, spending more time and attention on something, probably means less time and attention on a range of other things. Like Sherlock Holmes, we must pay attention to what is no longer happening, as it may be a source of emerging issues and opportunities.

Changing patterns of emotion

The unspoken dimension of change

In my doctoral research, I found that managers readily spoke about the patterning of events: this happened, then that happened, then there was that brilliant/awful thing that happened, and so on. Then they talked about the changing patterns of relations, describing changes to patterns of conflict and collaboration, and so on. They gave some indication of the patterning of attention through their language and by talking about the talk. But they did not talk about emotion.

I could *see* the emotion in people's faces and in their body language; it was apparent in a downcast look, a slump, a shrug, as they talked about some of the difficult things they were experiencing. I could see people brightening up, smiling and being more expansive with their gestures when they spoke about things that they felt excited about. I could also *hear* changes to people's emotional energy in the pace of their speech, their tone of voice, long sighs, laughing, and so on. Yet, they rarely put the emotional dimension of change into words.

When I went back to my written transcripts of the meetings, the emotional patterning was hard to find, as people did not talk about it. Yet, when I listened to the audio recordings, I could hear people's emotions in how they spoke about their experiences, and I could remember it from their faces and the feel of the meeting.

Curiously, emotion is a relative latecomer to the English language. Emotions were not "invented" until the 19th century, when the word came into more common English usage to reflect internal feelings and also caught the imagination of Victorian scientists (Smith, 2015). Physiologically, emotions are felt from the arousal of the body's nervous system in response to stimuli. However, as Sigmund Freud explained, felt emotions can be expressed or repressed.

Emotion and why it matters

Motion and emotion are entangled. The world emotion comes from the Latin movere 'to move'. Change always has an emotional dimension; it moves us. As we know from personal experience, change can be exciting, terrifying, and many things in between. Research bears that out. Change events can trigger positive emotions such as excitement, or negative emotions such as anger (Oreg et al., 2018).

Emotion is intimately connected with energy (Russell, 1980). The balance of positive and negative emotion (known as valence) creates the emotional tone. Positive and negative emotions may be higher or lower in energy (known as activation).[8] People's emotional responses in change are related to their energy for change (Bruch and Vogel, 2011, Oreg et al., 2018). Since we must expend more effort to do things differently than to act out of habit (Kahneman, 2012), emotional energy is a valuable resource in change.

Emotions are contagious as they ripple across organisations (Barsade, 2002), creating collective patterns of emotion such as 'the feel of the place', team spirit, morale, and so on. Collective emotional responses are emerging in the dynamic patterning of organisational life, triggered by change and other events. Patterns of emotion also affect what is emerging. For example, patterns of emotion may disrupt planned change efforts (Huy et al., 2014), or they may manifest in terms of productive energy (Bruch and Vogel, 2011) and change proactivity (Oreg et al., 2018).

Emotional states may be fleeting (Vuori and Huy, 2016), characterised by emotional episodes (Oreg et al., 2018). Since emotional energy is changeable, it provides a useful source of insight about emerging opportunities and issues within the dynamic patterning of organisational life. Furthermore, patterns of organisational energy are malleable so they may be influenced by deliberate action (Bruch and Vogel, 2011).

Noticing the patterns of emotion

Table 6.4 includes diary excerpts from the 'Engaging with Complexity' research (categories added). It includes individual emotions, for example, feeling irritated, and collective emotions, for example, good atmosphere.

Table 6.4: Patterning of emotion.

Emotional dynamic	Diary excerpts
Positive emotions, higher energy	Excitement as the 2018–2020 strategy develops and new programs of works are developed; excitement about new building; budget week 'buzz'; overall positive feel . . . good energy levels as people return from their breaks
Positive emotions, lower energy	People are looking forward to the festive break – good atmosphere; calm; positive attitude to mental health; my mood has lifted which I think has impacted on few people around me
Negative emotions, higher energy	A lot of needless activity; frustrations within the team as some not pulling weight and now showing; irritated
Negative emotions, lower energy	Change fatigue, with more to come; disquiet beneath the surface; frustration about how long [it] takes to get decisions; 'petty' resentment about travel policy and how interpreted across the organisation escalating; constant fire drills through poor planning sap energy and commitment

Source: Henley Forum Research (2018).[9]

Accurately recognising the composition of diverse emotions in a collective is challenging (Sanchez-Burks and Huy, 2009: 22). It requires us to notice a wider range of emotional cues from a wider group. This demands enhanced "emotional aperture", which is like a social emotional intelligence that helps individuals to capture diverse patterns of shared emotion (Sanchez-Burks and Huy, 2009). Developing emotional aperture involves *broadening* our noticing in the emotional domain.

We tend to notice emotions that erupt, such as a burst of laughter or anger. In Gestalt terms our perception focuses on the main 'figure' in the scene (e.g., the burst of laughter), and we may neglect everything else that forms the backdrop or context (the 'ground'). Gestalt suggests that emotion is continuous (Perls et al., 1994). So, a figural burst of laughter – an emotional 'event', if you like – comes from and forms the emotional ground, that is, the patterning of emotion. (It is another example of the dance between patterns and events that we considered earlier in this chapter.) What we are aiming to do here is pay close attention to the changing patterning of the emotional ground by *deepening* our noticing in the emotional domain.

Emotional patterning across groups is affected by the general culture and the specific context (Ashkanasy et al., 2017). In the working world, the culture of positivity has become almost cult-like (Oettingen, 2014), making it harder to express anything but positive emotions. However, all the positive talk may mask the underlying "emotional complexity" (Rothman and Melwani, 2017). Attending to a greater range of emotional complexity is very useful in planned change as it "provides leaders with rich and varied information about their environment, facilitating their ability to make adaptable decisions" (Rothman and Melwani, 2017: 260). In complexity terms, what we are doing here is developing requisite emotional complexity in the emotional domain.

Organisational energy

As we saw earlier, the language of emotion does not always come naturally. I was running a global leadership development programme for the top 100 managers in an engineering and construction company. In one workshop, we were discussing how people felt about where they worked, and we invited them to share some emotions. Stephane was unusually quiet. Normally he actively and enthusiastically participated in group discussions. I invited him in, but he remained silent. I caught up with him over coffee. You seem quiet today, I observed. Yes, he agreed, and explained, even though I have been working in English for more than 20 years, I don't have the English vocabulary to say how I feel. In French, Stephane joined the discussion with his usual enthusiasm.[10]

Even where English is your first language, the language of emotional energy may be hard to express in the business world. In some contexts, it is common to hear people say; let's take the emotion out of this. Emotion is not spoken about at all. It is undiscussable (Argyris, 1980).

In contrast, I find that people are much happier to discuss energy, particularly organisational energy. Organisational energy is activated energy across a team, division, or a wider group (Bruch and Vogel, 2011). Bruch and Vogel offer a useful tool, their 12-item organisational energy questionnaire (OEQ12©). It enables users to draw an energy profile for their team or unit relating to four possible energy states (see Table 6.5).

Table 6.5: Four organisational energy states.

Energy state	Quality	Intensity	What might this be like in change?
Productive energy	Positive	High	'I get it and I'm on it'
Comfortable energy	Positive	Low	'we could give it a go and see what happens'
Resigned inertia	Negative	Low	'you have to go along with it, there's nothing you can do about it'
Corrosive energy	Negative	High	'that's a stupid idea, it will never work'

Source: Adapted from Bruch and Vogel (2011), quotes added.

I often use this tool to open up conversations about the patterning of emotional energy in teams. I find it gives a language for people to talk about the emotional context of their experience. For example, I used it with a globally distributed team in an oil company when the team was being disbanded as part of a wider restructure. They found it really helpful in sparking conversations about how they were feeling and how they might generate more productive energy for themselves.

Putting it all together

Notice what comes naturally . . .

Most managers are attuned to noticing the patterning of *events* during change. Events are externally located. Our ability to 'place' events in time and space, with particular people and objects makes them easier to notice (see Table 6.6).

Some people readily notice changing patterns of *relations*. Organisation Development (OD) professionals, for example, are used to 'reading the room'. One OD professional told me he can "smell the culture" when he goes somewhere new (Garrow and Varney, 2011), and I knew exactly what he meant. A curiosity about people helps, but reading group and organisational dynamics is honed by practice (Garrow and Varney, 2011), more in Part III. Changing patterns of relations are embedded in behaviour, so many managers find they can notice relational dynamics when prompted by the vital signs to do so.

Paying attention to *attention* can be more challenging. One manager candidly admitted it was "a struggle" and she felt that she had neglected this vital sign. Of course, for communications professionals, social media influencers, and politicians, this skill might feel more natural. However, there is a good reason why you might struggle here. Attention is a cognitive lens (see Table 6.6). Thoughts happen in the internal world, so we cannot directly observe people's thoughts. We therefore need to look out for externalised aspects of attention which can be found in what people say, write and draw, as well as in how they spend their time.

Noticing changing *emotional* dynamics comes fairly naturally to some people and is harder for others. Some individuals are more emotionally open, more able to recognise and express their emotions. The cultural and organisational context also matters; in some settings talking about emotions is commonplace, in others it is actively or tacitly discouraged. Moreover, we are not detached observers. Our own emotions are entangled in the emotional patterning, making it more difficult to accurately read collective patterns of emotion (Sanchez-Burks and Huy, 2009).

Table 6.6 summarises and contrasts the four vital signs lenses. I have ordered them in terms of which ones people tend to find easier and harder to notice. However, this is a generalisation. Every person is different, so I encourage you to notice which lenses you find easier and harder to apply.

Table 6.6: Noticing the vital signs of change.

Vital sign of change	Lens type	Location	Noticing
Patterning of events	Temporal Artefactual	Externally located in time and place (people and things)	Easier
Patterning of relations	Behavioural	Interpersonal (behaviour)	
Patterning of attention	Cognitive	Inter/intrapersonal (talk and thought)	
Patterning of emotion	Affective	Intrapersonal (feelings)	Harder

Source: Adapted from Varney (2013).

... and work on the rest

The four vital signs of change offer diverse lenses on *one* complex reality. It is important to use all four vital signs because each lens helps you to notice different entangled aspects of the dynamic patterning. Greater proficiency often comes with practice (see Box 6.6).

> **Box 6.6 A valuable learning tool**
> When I introduce the vital signs of change to managers, I generally run a warm-up for two or three minutes. I encourage everyone to divide a sheet of paper into four quadrants representing the four vital signs and to reflect on what has been changing in their working world.
>   Having four quadrants is a useful learning tool because it provides managers with rapid visual feedback about their own noticing. They can easily see for themselves whether they have applied all four signs and if some boxes are fuller than others.
>   After the rapid warm-up, I invite people to share their noticings in small groups, so they can appreciate the different perspectives that others take. I also encourage them to reflect on which of the vital signs they found easier and harder to apply.

When managers first use the vital signs to help them open up their noticing, they often worry about "allocating themes" to the correct boxes. I encourage them to keep going, to continue noticing and noting, then to reflect on the process after a few weeks or months. Six months later, the manager who was initially worried about allocating themes had this to say:

> Having had time to reflect … I suspect I may have allocated some examples to the wrong part of the model however I don't feel that that has had a detrimental effect on my ability to interpret the emerging patterns of change, so perhaps I'm being too rigid in its application.

I fully agree with his sentiment. You will remember from Chapter 4 on complexity thinking that we are aiming to hold leadership and management models lightly, using them to open up thinking, rather than closing it down. That mindset still applies here. Consistently applying the vital signs of change and reflecting on the process will help you to develop your noticing skills, so that you get better at spotting a wider range of weak signals.

Deepening your noticing

Once you have practiced using the vital signs, I would encourage you to reflect on your noticing. You are looking to reveal any patterns in what you are noticing and, more importantly, what you are *not* noticing. For example, you may learn that you are noting larger, formal events and neglecting smaller, informal events. You may find that you are paying a lot of attention to the patterning of relations in your team, or the top team, but not elsewhere. You may discover that you are noticing your own emotions more than the wider patterning of emotions. Or you may find some areas where you are really well tuned into the patterning of attention, and others where you have no idea what the informal chat is about.

    Once you have identified some neglected areas, think about how you could extend and deepen your noticing capacity to pick up a more diverse range of signals. One manager developed a bullseye diagram (see Figure 6.3) to help him to notice at more levels: himself, his team, brand, organisation and externally. Another described using the vital signs to guide her "into the deeper and less obvious elements" at play in the dynamic patterning of organisational life.

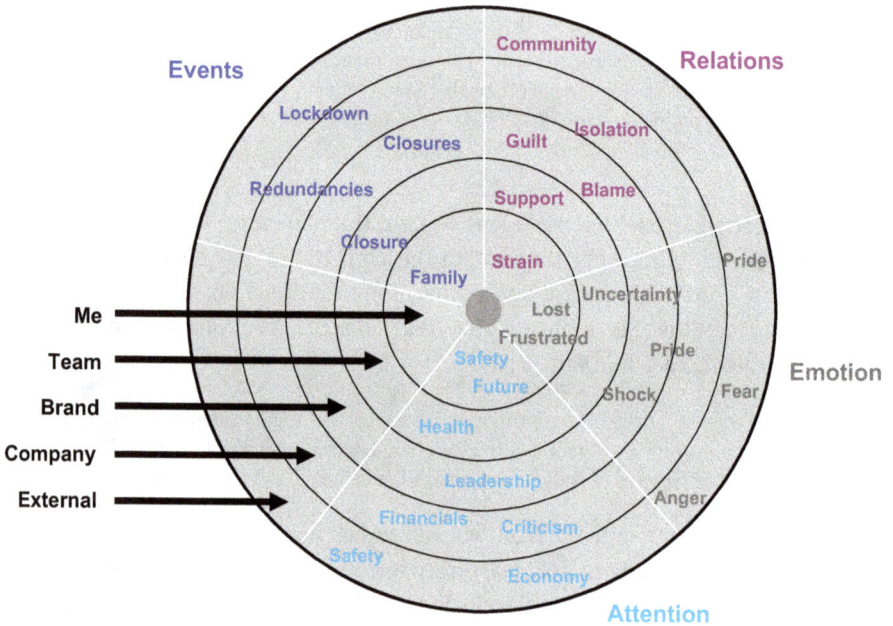

Figure 6.3: Extending your noticing.

Key insights
- The vital signs of change bring focus to noticing without narrowing it down
- They stimulate deeper noticing beyond the events in change
- Each lens illuminates a different aspect of the dynamic patterning:
    - the patterning of *events* (a temporal and artefactual lens)
    - changing patterns of *relations* (a behavioural lens)
    - changing patterns of *attention* (a cognitve lens)
    - changing patterns of *emotion* (an affective lens)
- Together the vital signs of change offer multiple perspectives on one complex reality
- The vital signs of change support learning for yourself by opening up thinking and conversation
- These useful tools provide an aid to developing practical judgement

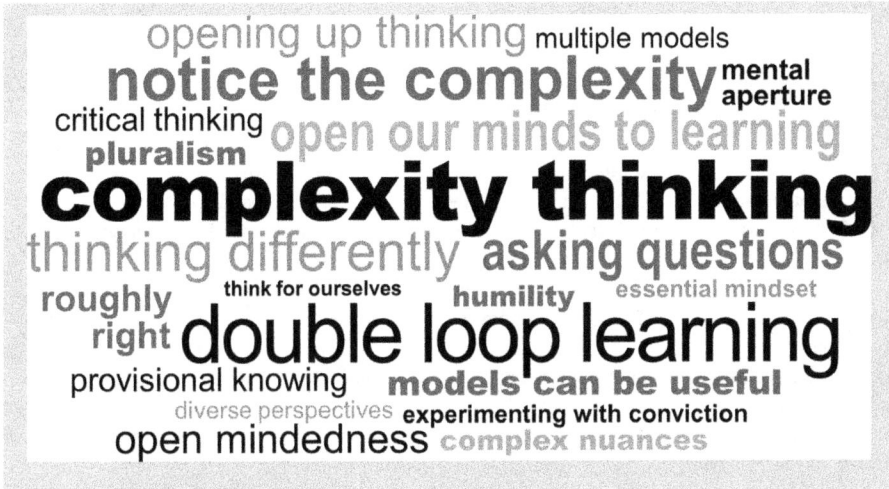

Noticing and noting
Take a few minutes to reflect on the past three months. Grab a sheet of paper and divide it into four quadrants: Events, Relations, Attention, Emotion. Use the vital signs of change to stimulate your noticing about what is changing. (What is new or different; more/less pronounced; puzzling, surprising or unexpected?)

Tips:
- Set a timer (15 minutes is good, but even 5 minutes will work)
- Jot down words and/or pictures to capture your noticings in each quadrant
- Work quickly and let your ideas flow
- Make sure you put something in *all four* boxes.

Key prompts:
- **Patterning of events.** Think about key events, big or small, any changes to the rhythm of your work life.
- **Changing patterns of relations.** Think about formal and informal relations, any changes in the harmonies between between people and groups.
- **Changing patterns of attention.** Think about changes in what groups of people are talking about, how they spend their time, and where attention is focused, any changes to the melody.
- **Changing patterns of emotion.** Think about emotions (positive/negative) and their intensity (high/low), any changes in the emotional tone.

Some reflective questions:
1. Which of the four vital signs were easier/more difficult for you to notice?
2. What does your answer to question 1 suggest to you?
3. How will you use the vital signs of change in your own leadership practice?

Notes

1 In my academic work I used the term 'domains of emergent change'. When I am working with managers, I refer to these domains as the vital signs of change; an analogy that signifies their value in sensemaking.

2 This data comes from an unpublished research project 'Engaging with Complexity', conducted at The Henley Forum in 2017–2018. The Henley Forum is an applied research centre at Henley Business School, part of the University of Reading https://henley.ac.uk/henleyforum (accessed 25/08/2020).

3 Thanks to Dr Ugur Bilge, an Agent Based Simulations expert (formerly with the Complexity Research Group at the London School of Economics), for his generous assistance with the mapping.

4 See endnote 2.

5 These references were taken from a range of articles in the UK national news.

6 Brexit (British Exit) was the popularised media term for the UK's exit from the European Union. 'Brexit' is not a neutral term. It directs attention to British Exit, rather than the alternative, and it sounds like a done deal.

7 See endnote 2.

8 This refers to the Circumplex model of affect (Russell, 1980), which underlies studies about emotional responses in change (Oreg et al., 2018) and organisational energy (Bruch and Vogel, 2011, Cole et al., 2012).

9 See endnote 2.

10 The word emotion entered the English language from the French émotion in the 16th century, where it has a longer heritage (12th century). Its current usage in English is more recent (19th century): https://www.etymonline.com/word/emotion (accessed 29/12/2020).

Chapter 7
Interpreting reality in flight

Developing insight

Over the past two chapters, I have invited you to pay close attention to noticing small data about what is changing. In this chapter we will be exploring how we might use that potentially valuable noticing data to enable learning informed leadership.

Let us remind ourselves what we are trying to do. Rather than acting out of habit based on data about the past, we want to interpret our noticings to develop insight. We aim to use that insight to inform how we respond into the ongoing processes of dynamic patterning (see Figure 7.1). This is a significant shift. Rather than acting based on hindsight (approximations of how things were), learning informed leadership uses *insight* (specifics about how things are) to help us in choosing context-appropriate responses.

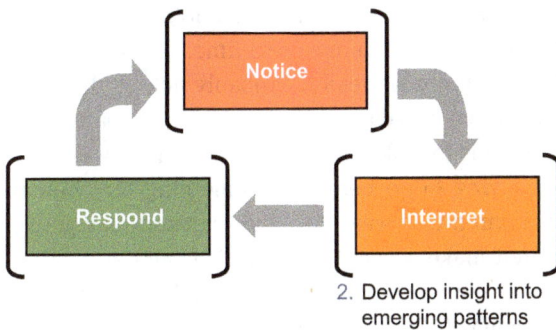

2. Develop insight into emerging patterns

Figure 7.1: Complexity learning cycle – interpret.

In dynamic patterning, nothing stands still, so we are aiming to 'catch reality in flight' (Pettigrew, 1992: 10). Interpreting reality in flight demands a delicate balance. We want to draw insight from our noticing data *without* imposing too much sense on emerging patterns, which are both changeable and changing.

That traffic light theme in Figure 7.1. offers a reminder to proceed with caution. If we want to develop insight in the midst of this dynamic patterning, we must break the habit of jumping to conclusions about what our noticing data means, such as, 'I have seen this before; I know what it means'. We must instead adopt more fruitful habits such as exploring connections, contradictions, and potential patterns in our noticing data; along with developing multiple interpretations, and holding them lightly.

https://doi.org/10.1515/9783110713343-007

This chapter begins by considering the assumptions and limits of interpreting in complexity and change. It continues by exploring the nature of patterns and non-patterns, then offers some thoughts about developing interpretive thinking skills and engaging the power of multiple perspectives. It concludes with a gentle reminder not to get too attached to our interpretations.

Conceptual foundations

Making too much sense

Later in this chapter we will look at some practical skills for interpretation. In order to use those tools and techniques wisely in complexity and change, we must first unpack some underpinning assumptions and subtleties about what we are doing when we are interpreting our noticing data.

We can do various things with data. When we have 'hard data' in terms of facts and figures, we can analyse it, manipulate it and display in many different ways. We have lots of tools to help us do this. As we saw earlier, technology now allows for rapid analysis of extremely large data sets in almost real-time, so it can appear that we are catching reality in flight. But are we really? Probably not, as the questions we ask to structure big data are often based on past experience and patterns.

Another thing we can do with data is to make sense of it. Sensemaking is a reasonable reflection of what we are trying to do here. It is something that human beings do naturally, our brains are wired that way. Machines can sort, categorise, and classify rapidly, but they cannot make sense. Karl Weick's (1995) and subsequent work on sensemaking can help us in understanding and developing our interpretive capacity. However, the problem with sensemaking is the word 'sense'.

When people think they have made sense of something, particularly something complex and ambiguous, they often become attached to the sense they have made. What then happens, they tend to talk about the sense made *as if* it is objective and unchanging. They no longer see reality as being in flight. Furthermore, they have glossed over their position as subjective insiders.

A further word of caution here. Complex human systems are characterised by *emergent coherence*, that is, the system forms a unified whole from the multitude of interactions between people, rather than from a top-down, rational design (Letiche et al., 2011). The implication is that the underlying structural patterning may not be obvious, and it may not make logical sense from the perspective of human beings caught within those patterns.

Ascribed coherence is what happens when human beings retrospectively apply categories and labels to their experience (Letiche et al., 2011).[1] When we make 'sense' of emerging patterns we are creating meaning for ourselves in human terms. The implication is that we must remind ourselves from time to time that things may not actually mean what we think they mean. We may simply be making too much 'sense' of emergence.

Interpreting data

However, paying close attention to the dynamic patterning in processes of emergence, as we are doing here, "may reveal trends, possibilities and opportunities" (Letiche et al., 2011). We are exploring emerging patterns in the present to help us in spotting nascent issues and opportunities sooner, so we can adapt our responses.

Rather than talking about analysing or making sense, I therefore prefer to talk about interpreting (from Goldspink and Kay, 2010). This helps us to retain the subjectivity, multiplicity, and changeability of our interpretations:

- Like sensemaking, interpreting is a human activity. However, it is easier to remember that interpretations are subjective because they remain attached to the person or people making them. We are more likely to ask, 'whose interpretation?', than we are to ask, 'whose sense?' or 'whose analysis?'
- It is common to talk about making interpretations, in the plural. It is therefore easier to think in terms of holding multiple interpretations than it is to think of holding multiple senses or multiple analyses. This helps us in retaining multiple perspectives in a complex reality.
- Finally, we tend to accept that interpretations are open to change, over time, with new data, and in relation to other interpretations. It is a reminder that reality is always in flight.

Stepping in and out

Interpreting requires a different type of attention to noticing. When we notice, we are metaphorically stepping in. We are paying attention to gathering perceptual data (Weick, 2011) from our "immersion" (Stacey, 2010) in the "flux" (Weick, 2011) of our experience. In contrast, when we interpret, we are metaphorically stepping out. We are paying attention to "abstracting" from our experience (Stacey, 2010) to develop conceptual "hunches" (Weick, 2011) about the meaning of our experience (see Box 7.1).

Box 7.1 Meetings

Stepping in. When we step into our direct experience in a meeting, we can gather massive amounts of first-hand perceptual data using our five sense *if* we pay attention to noticing.[2] For example, we might see where and how people are sitting or standing, what they look like and what they are wearing, we see eye contact and body language, we see surroundings and colours, we see movement and stillness, and so on. We hear what people say and how they say it, we may hear our internal thoughts and external background noises. We may feel the temperature, the sensation of the chair, the sensations in our bodies. We may taste the coffee or smell the air.

Stepping out. When we step out of our direct experience in a meeting, we can make interpretations about our experience. For example, he is not paying attention, she looks really energised, they have worked together before, I feel excited about this, here we go again, this chair is uncomfortable, and so on. These are conceptual hunches about what is going on.

We cannot literally step out or stand back from the flow of our experience to interpret what is changing. We cannot stop or pause the ongoing process of dynamic patterning to make sense of it. What we are doing, as Figure 7.1 illustrates, is *bracketing our attention* differently.

Attention is a limited resource. As we saw with the invisible gorilla experiment earlier, when people paid attention to counting the passes during a basketball game, many of them failed to notice the person in the gorilla suit (Simons and Chabris, 1999). When we metaphorically 'step out', during the course of a meeting, for example, we are paying attention to our interpretations about what is going on. We are therefore paying less attention to noticing what is *actually* going on. We may not notice the vital signs of change that can help us to develop insight, so our interpretations are more likely to be based on hindsight.

Catching reality in flight involves becoming more aware of how we are bracketing our attention between noticing and interpreting so we can engage in both. It is another paradox. Attending to noticing and interpreting together creates a liminal space where interpreting is "bracketed from yet connected to everyday action" (Howard-Grenville et al., 2011: 522). A liminal space is an ambiguous betwixt and between position which prompts an array of different interpretations (Swan et al., 2016: 781).

Gaining insight

In a changing world, hindsight is not particularly useful. In a complex world, foresight is impossible. What we are trying to do here is to gain *insight* by more deeply understanding what is changing in the here and now. Gary Klein (2013) has some useful things to say about gaining insight:

- Insight may arrive suddenly, as an 'aha' moment, or it may appear gradually. His research identifies 56% of insights as sudden and 44% as gradual.
- When we gain insight, it changes how we see the world: how we understand; our beliefs; how we see and feel; and how we act. As historical novelist Hilary Mantel puts it, in Wolf Hall; "The moment is fleeting. But insight cannot be taken back. You cannot return to the moment you were in before" (Mantel, 2010).
- Insight is not the same as intuition. Intuition is about using the patterns you have already learned, whereas insight is about discovering new patterns.

Klein defines insight as "the discovery of new patterns" (2013: 27) and "an unexpected shift to a better story" (2013: 24). Both are good descriptions of what we are trying to do here. We are trying to interpret our noticing data to discover new patterns as they are emerging. This involves looking across our noticings and developing a better working story about what is changing.

Patterns, meta-patterns, and false patterns

Discovering new patterns

Klein's (2013) five strategies for developing insight are connections, coincidences, curiosities, contradictions and creative desperation (see Table 7.1). When we are trying to catch reality in flight, four of those strategies are useful. *Creative desperation* is a last resort in extreme circumstances. I have included it for completeness.

Table 7.1: Strategies for gaining insight.

Strategy	Aim	Challenges	Action
Connections	Connecting dots by being exposed to different ideas and perspectives	Determining which dots to connect	Finding new ways of combining different sets of information that fit well together
Coincidences	Shaking people loose from their stories, providing early warning about new patterns	Testing out coincidences (they can be misleading)	Collecting evidence to make sure the coincidence is not spurious
Curiosities	Recognising a single event or observation that is notable	Following curiosities that do not lead anywhere takes time	Asking 'what is going on here?'
Contradictions	Focusing on differences rather than similarities; taking notice of outliers, anomalies, and doubts, not discounting them	Resisting temptation to discard anomalies and explain away contrary evidence	Developing a new story that can accommodate contradictions as well as connections (this may require a paradigm shift)
Creative desperation	Finding a way out of an impasse, a trap that seems inescapable	The pressure is real and intense; the platform really is burning	Finding and discarding a weak belief that is trapping us

Source: Adapted from Klein (2013).

When we are noticing, we are staying alert to *coincidences* and *curiosities* aided by the four vital signs of change. Once we have noticed something interesting, it is natural to want to jump to conclusions about patterns between coincidences (i.e., closing things down). It is also natural to want to pursue every interesting curiosity (i.e., opening things up). You might naturally lean to one or the other depending on your personality preferences.[3]

From time to time, curiosities and coincidences demand immediate attention. When they do not, I would encourage you to just hold them without closing them down or opening them up. Notice them, note them down and leave them. Then return to your noticing data and deliberately pursue the strategies of *connection* and *contradiction* together.

Connections and contradictions

Professor Jane McKenzie from Henley Business School highlights the importance of considering both connections and contradictions when learning in uncertainty and ambiguity. She has adopted "connections and contradictions" as a strapline for her academic work with managers and professionals involved in real world practice (e.g. McKenzie, 1996, McKenzie and Van Winkelen, 2004, McKenzie and Varney, 2018).[4]

Complexity practitioner, Dr Glenda Eoyang uses the term "pattern logic".[5] In a similar vein, she invites people to discover meaningful patterns in strange and unpredictable situations by looking out for connections, contradictions, and relationships. She respectively refers to them as containers, differences and exchanges in her CDE model (Eoyang, 2011).

A useful first step in taking both connections and contradictions into account is to ask questions of your noticing data. There are some useful prompt questions in Table 7.2. The next step is creating stories about what might be going on which embrace *both* connections *and* contradictions as a way of engaging with real-world complexity.

For example, if you find connections that suggest a developing pattern of people dropping out of meetings because they have too much work on, you might develop a working story that 'people are becoming too busy to attend meetings'. If you then look for contradictions, you may find some exceptions, for example, finance meetings. That might help you to develop a new working story that 'as people get busier, financial matters are being given more attention than non-financial matters'.

Table 7.2: Seeking connections and contradictions.

Connections	Contradictions
When you look back at your noticings, what connections can you see?	When you look back at your noticings, what contradictions can you see?
What patterns might be emerging?	What data does not quite fit the pattern?
What connections do you notice between your data from the four vital signs of change?	What differences can you detect between your data from the four vital signs of change? Are there any contradictions between them?
What connections do you observe across the different levels?	What differences do you observe across the different levels?
What connections can you recognise between your noticings over time?	What differences can you see between your noticings over time?
What connections can you see between your noticings and other people's noticings?	What differences can you see between your noticings and other people's noticings?

Meta-patterns

Just as ants have no sense of the emergent global system that is the ant colony (Sullivan, 2011), it is not possible for human beings to see or directly study the meta-patterns of behaviour across a wider scale. We are *insiders* in those systems, so we must accept that some meta-patterns are hidden from our direct view. Complexity theorist, John Holland (1995), refers to a hidden order in complexity. However, there may be useful clues within our direct experience because patterns, such as 'behaviour', may be similar across different scales.

Meta-patterns

Meta-patterns are patterns of patterns (Bateson, 1979) and may apply across different scales. For example, 'behaviour' is a pattern that arises from the interaction of neurons in a person's nervous system (Holland, 1995).[6] Yet behavioural patterns also manifest across a wider scale, for example, group, organisational, societal and human behaviour.

Patterns that repeat at different scales are known as fractals. Fractals are common in nature. If you look carefully at a fern frond, a smaller frond branching off that main stem, an individual leaf, and at each leaf segment, you will see self-similar patterns. YouTube is a good source of computer-generated fractal videos; they can be very meditative to watch.

A word of caution. In complexity science, the notion of fractals comes from deterministic chaos, a mathematical branch of complexity science. We must be careful in assuming that particular features of models from other domains are directly applicable to the human world. It is a timely reminder of complexity thinking.

Yet, if we use the idea of fractals as a metaphor to inform our search for both connections and contradictions in our noticing data across multiple levels of scale, then it can be particularly useful. For example, when faced with seemingly intractable problems, Glenda Eoyang invites people to try expanding and reducing the size of the container when they are looking for pattern logic.[7]

False patterns

Patterns are easy to find, perhaps too easy. We must remember Daniel Kahneman's warning that our brains are machines for jumping to conclusions (Kahneman, 2012: 79). Our minds naturally create a narrative that links cause and effect to explain what happened, even though direct cause-effect relationships are incomprehensible in complex systems (Sullivan, 2011: 90).

Over sensitivity to coincidences can lead us to see connections that are not real (Klein, 2013). Thereby lies the route to conspiracy theories. In early 2020, the emergence of a novel Coronavirus and existential fears around the Covid-19 pandemic coincided with the roll out of the 5G telecommunications network. Joining those dots, and a few others, led to some damaging conspiracy theories.

Joining the dots to interpret patterns is not as easy as it sounds. Difficulties include removing non-dots, clarifying ambiguous dots and grouping similar dots (Klein, 2013). We are working with uncertainty and the imperfect data of the emerging present, rather than the certainty of an already-emerged past. So, when we are trying to make sense of a potential pattern by connecting dots, we must stay alert to the risk of connecting dots from unrelated data to create a pattern that does not exist. Developing our interpretive thinking skills can help.

Developing interpretive thinking skills

Look out for black swans

We often rely on a weight of data to back up interpretations. Yet, we only need to observe one black swan to learn that not all swans are white. Anomalies are really interesting in complexity and continuous change. We are looking for early warning signs of change in the dynamic patterning of organisational life, so single instances may be really important.

If your noticing data suggests a particular pattern, look out for anomalous data that does not support that pattern. For example, rather than concluding that 'everybody thinks Jay is a brilliant leader', or that 'everybody thinks this change programme is a bad idea', look out for those people who do not think that Jay is a brilliant leader, and for people who think the change programme is a good idea. This is where surrounding yourself with people who genuinely think differently is particularly valuable.

If accepted wisdom is that *everyone* thinks something, then you might have to look very carefully to find people who do not, as they may well choose to keep their unpopular views to themselves. Or if everyone acts in certain kinds of ways, then those who decide to take another path may well choose to do that 'under the radar', rather than in full sight. As Taleb (2010) explains, an "absence of evidence" should not be mistaken for "evidence of absence".

Whatever you think, think the opposite

Developing your interpretive thinking skills means not taking your interpretations for granted and resisting the urge to jump to conclusions. We can do this by asking questions, testing our ideas, seeking out the counterintuitive, making our data strange.

In "Whatever you think, think the opposite", Arden (2006) argues that nothing is more dangerous than playing it safe. While he advocates risk taking in business, I am proposing taking risks in your thinking to develop your interpretive skills. A good way to avoid mistaking our favourite interpretations for truth is to hold them up to scrutiny by reversing them, and then giving equal consideration to thinking the opposite.

For example, a manager in a retail business interpreted his noticing data to suggest "our business has been more reactive to external events". In thinking the opposite, he could look out for examples where their business is being *less* reactive to external events. Reverse brainstorming is a practical way of thinking the opposite (see Box 7.2).

> **Box 7.2 Thinking the opposite**
> Brainstorming is a well-known creativity technique that encourages people to rapidly generate and voice ideas, build on other people's ideas, and note them all down without judging them. The next step explores the outputs and connections between ideas to generate creative solutions.
>
> We can use these techniques to help us in thinking the opposite. In a reverse brainstorming session, we would reverse our favourite interpretation of what is going on, then we would imagine all the ways in which that opposite interpretation is true. Like brainstorming, some creative licence is allowable. The aim is to rapidly generate alternative ideas, rather than to gather contradictory evidence.

Once you have brainstormed the opposite interpretation, those ideas are then available for you to use in reexamining your original interpretation. For example, by considering how the business is being less reactive to external events, you may generate ideas that help you to qualify or complexify your original interpretation. Actively considering the opposite might draw your attention to the kinds of external events that are prompting a reaction and those that are not, so you can make a more nuanced interpretation. Or it might lead to you revising your original working story.

The reverse brainstorm technique in Box 7.2 does not consider the ways in which the original interpretation was wrong. Instead, it gives credence that the opposite (or even multiple opposites) may be true. Importantly, both interpretations still stand. Doing it that way enables us to consider both views together to complexify our interpretation, rather than taking a simplistic either/or position.

Paradoxical thinking – both/and

Thinking both/and, rather than either/or is a valuable interpretive skill. Holding seemingly contradictory interpretations at the same time is not easy to do. Uncertainty and ambiguity, "equivocality" in Weick's terms, are triggers for sensemaking (Weick, 1995).

A good way of holding the paradox open is to bolt opposites together to create a "generative image" that holds them both (Bushe et al., 2015). An example would be 'sustainable development' that fuses together calls for environmental sustainability and calls for economic development – which are normally seen as opposing ideas – in a way that invites creative responses (Bushe and Storch, 2015). One of my favourite generative images is 'seismic nudges', which frames actions as being very large and very small at the same time. I am also playing with the idea of 'proactive reactivity' in learning.

By fusing opposing ideas, a generative image brings more of the complexity of the situation into focus (see Figure 4.1). So, it is a useful way to practice thinking paradoxically.

Power of other perspectives

Making differences sing

In Chapter 5, we explored inviting multiple perspectives to power up our noticing, because we all notice different things. Once again we are faced with the "vantage point problem" (Sargut and McGrath, 2011: 72) whereby we can only *comprehend* what is going on from inside our own perspective and position in the system. So, it is just as important to actively seek other views when we are interpreting noticing data.

Inviting different perspectives and maximising cognitive diversity will increase our chances of developing multi-faceted interpretations about what is going on. Yet, we often fail to do this. Managers may feel it is not their job to do it, or that time pressures mean they have no opportunity to seek other interpretations. But that short-term view will be counterproductive if we miss emerging issues and opportunities.

In the workplace we are often surrounded by people who are rather like us, with similar backgrounds and experiences. Most recruiters look for organisational fit, rather than organisational misfit, which is far more valuable here. The risk is that we find ourselves in an echo chamber, whereby other people's similar views reinforce our own views, giving us false comfort that we are right, so we fail to look further.

One mitigation strategy is to actively seek out "smart people who think differently" (Sullivan, 2011: 91), rather than lots of people who think like us. Smart people are not necessarily the most senior or the most self-confident. So, we should avoid being swayed by the interpretations of individuals who appear more authoritative (Sullivan, 2011) because they have formal authority or informal influence. Smart in this context is about seeing things differently to generate different interpretations of our noticing data.

Bringing diverse thinkers together is not enough if they only share what is common and fail to reveal the different perspectives and interpretations that make them so valuable. To maximise the benefits of diversity in collaboration, we need to bring people together in ways that create *just enough* connection for them to make their differences sing.

Creating dialogue

Dialogue is a way of thinking together (Isaacs, 2008). It is concerned with how thought is generated and sustained at a collective level (Bohm, 1996). Adopting the principles and practices of dialogue (Bohm, 1996, Isaacs, 2008) offers a practical way of bringing diverse perspectives into play when we are interpreting perceptual noticing data to generate insight.

The four practices of dialogue are listening, respecting, suspending and voicing (Isaacs, 2008). Learning to *suspend* our judgement whilst *listening* to others and *respecting* their different experiences and perspectives means avoiding the habitual reflex of jumping in with our own thoughts, questions, and views. That can be harder to do than it sounds because it means quietening our own thoughts before *voicing* what is emerging from the whole group.

Creating meaningful dialogue among diverse and divided groups involves creating a safe space (physically and psychologically). This creates a container for rich dialogue about complex problems. Dialogic principles have famously been used by Nelson Mandela, and others, in service of creating peace and reconciliation in post-apartheid South Africa. Here we are using dialogue to "uncover the undiscussed thinking of the people in your organization" and to "perceive new directions and new opportunities more clearly than we can on our own" (Isaacs, 2008: 11).

Enlisting rivals and crowds

Another way to enlist diverse perspectives is to create a team of rivals (Sullivan, 2011: 91). Here individuals with markedly different perspectives are tasked with bringing different points of view and challenging the status quo. Creating a team of rivals means putting group goals before self-interest. The aim, as with dialogue, is to use rival perspectives to generate new understanding of the situation, rather than to debate the relative merits of differing views. US President Abraham Lincoln famously surrounded himself by a team of rivals in his cabinet during the American civil war.[8]

Digital technology enables us to tap into the so-called wisdom of crowds. Crowds are not really wise. What this refers to is aggregating diverse perspectives on particular issues by extracting information from large numbers of independent individuals and putting it on the table to be considered. In prediction markets, large numbers of individuals put monetary values on their interpretations by placing predictive bets on the outcome of particular events. It is like the 'ask the audience' option in the TV programme Who Wants to Be a Millionaire, but with a lot more people.

Most companies fail to harness the wisdom of their people in any meaningful way (Mauboussin in Sullivan, 2011). One of the difficulties here is that the wisdom of crowds requires *independence*. This is problematic if we want to use the wisdom of crowds in organisations of interdependent people. Practical ways to address this challenge (from DeWees and Minson, 2018) include:

- team members should form independent opinions *before* coming together as a group
- the process for aggregating views should be agreed beforehand (who decides and how)
- the person who is responsible for making the final decision should not form their own opinion first.

Importantly, disagreement should be thought of as valuable information (DeWees and Minson, 2018) in avoiding the limitations of groupthink (Janis, 1972).

Storytelling

Telling stories is a particularly useful way of making interpretations in the midst of dynamic complexity (Boje, 2008, Colville et al., 2012). Storytelling enables us to move away from linear narratives to reflect the kinds of "multiplicity and difference" that is inherent in complexity (Boje, 2008: 27). It encourages a multi-dimensional approach to "storytelling-sensemaking", whereby many dimensions reflect one another and interact within a "polyphonic" story that can incorporate many voices (Boje, 2008: 40). We are back to the music metaphor again (see Chapter 5)!

The dynamic nature of organisational life offers particular challenges for traditional sensemaking. When we are faced with novel and changing circumstances, storytelling helps us combine the "requisite complexity of thought" with a simplicity of action, that is, telling a story (Colville et al., 2012: 6). Storytelling also helps to coalesce the past, present and future (Boal and Schultz, 2007).

Making sense of rare and unexpected events is particularly difficult (Beck and Plowman, 2009, Sargut and McGrath, 2011) using traditional methods because relevant data is in short supply. Stories may offer useful insights into complex systems because telling a story does not restrict the story teller to available data (Sargut and McGrath, 2011). Being in the midst of complexity and continuous changing becomes a distinct advantage. Middle managers can therefore play a valuable role in interpreting rare and unusual events richly due to their interconnections with a wide range of people across hierarchical levels (Beck and Plowman, 2009).

Visualising

I began this book by inviting you to visualise a murmuration of flocking starlings. It is a powerful visual metaphor for complexity and change. When managers are learning to use the vital signs of change, I often invite them to form small groups and to share their noticings with one another, then I ask them to create a picture that draws out the essence of their different perspectives. What they are doing is collectively interpreting their data.

Numbers and words both demand precision, which is only available with the certainty of hindsight. Pictures are superb vehicles for interpreting in uncertainty. Creating a picture enables people to convey ambiguous and paradoxical aspects of complexity in a concise way using visual metaphors to interpret their rich experience (McKenzie and van Winkelen, 2011: 138). Creating a picture stimulates creative thinking and invites people to interpret what they are noticing in a different way. Like questions, pictures often open up thinking and further conversations – both essential in complexity thinking – rather than closing them down.

Pictures often need little introduction. If you look at Figure 7.2, what does each picture suggest to you about the emerging patterns in this workplace? What does each suggest to you about the patterning of relations between people; the patterning of attention in this organisation; and the patterning of emotion? What paradoxes can you see in the pictures? (A paradox is where opposites co-exist.) What emerging issues and opportunities are you seeing in these pictures?

Take a look at the pictures in Figure 7.3. What does each suggest to you about the patterning of events? What questions do you now have?

Creating pictures is a great way to surface new ways of thinking about familiar situations, so I often use them in workshops. During a change masterclass in a pharmaceutical business, I divided participants into four groups and invited each group

Figure 7.2: Interpreting the vital signs of change.

Figure 7.3: The patterning of events.

to share their individual noticings about *one* of the four vital signs of change. Each group then drew a picture to capture their collective insight. When they posted their pictures on the gallery wall, there was a distinct pattern; three of the four pictures featured a house. In the discussion that followed, the emerging story was an impending family break-up. This interpretation was not something that participants had previously discussed because they had never put their deeper feelings into words. Using pictures helped to surface interpretations that had not been voiced before.

Triangulating

No single method of interpretation can ever hope to fully reflect a complex reality. So, triangulation is a particularly good way to develop fuller interpretations of what is going on in complex systems (Sargut and McGrath, 2011).

Triangulation
Triangulation is the process of determining a geographical location by forming triangles to it from known points. For example, the position of a mobile phone may be calculated by triangulating the signals from three mobile phone masts. While one signal will give you some idea of the territory, triangulating from three signals at the same time will provide a more precise estimate of location.

In Chapter 4, we discussed the benefits of using multiple models to open our mental aperture to more real-world complexity. Triangulation is powerful because bringing multiple methods together in the process of interpreting (along with multiple voices and perspectives) may help us to develop more multi-faceted interpretations that better match the complexity of real-world situations.

Provisionality, again

Informing action

We create interpretations to develop insight about what is emerging in the living present to inform our leadership responses into the dynamic patterning (more in Chapter 8).

Since what we say and do plays into what emerges ("reflexive emergence" Goldspink and Kay, 2010), we are under pressure to get our interpretations right. Yet, in complexity and continuous changing, we must accept that interpretations can never be completely right. Certainty about what things mean is elusive, until it ceases to count. Since we cannot act in the past, only in the present, we must aim for being 'roughly right', as we explored in Chapter 4.

That does not mean 'anything goes' when it comes to our working stories. Some interpretations are better conceptions of a complex reality than others, as Richardson (2008: 21) explains:

> Any perspective whatsoever has the potential to shed light on complexity (even if turns out to be wrong . . .), but at the same time, not every perspective is equally valid in any given context (try fixing your car with prayer rather than with a good mechanic).

A good story does not have to be probable, but it should be plausible given the data (Boisot and McKelvey, 2010). So, while we must always be provisional in our understanding, and be willing to hold multiple interpretations, we are looking for plausibility. For example, the general law of gravity applies independently of individuals' knowledge or opinions of it, or their views of Isaac Newton.[9] So stories that fail to take the laws of gravity into account would lack plausibility.

Learning in action

The aim of creating a range of plausible working stories is to test our interpretations in action. Academic research offers two contrasting ways to test our stories, see Table 7.3. Traditional scientific method develops a detailed story about what should happen, based on existing theory, then gathers more data points to statistically test that story. The original story is then refined and reinforced to make it a better story. In this view, a better story is a general one that predicts what will happen in a wide range of situations.

Another way to test our stories is to develop a story and use it to inform action, while continuing to notice and learn from what is happening in practice to modify the story. In this view, a better story is a specific one that informs action in a particular context. A good way of putting this approach into practice is through action research (Lewin, 1947b) with its iterative cycles of action and reflection.

Table 7.3: Contrasting ways to test our stories.

	Traditional	**Emerging**
Start point	Develop a story (a working theory)	Develop a story (a working theory)
Actions	then gather more data points to test (statistically) the 'fit' of the theory to the data	then hold it lightly and intervene (act) while continuing to notice, reflect, and being prepared to modify your theory
Outcome	and reinforce the story.	and change the story.
Purpose	Predictive	Informative
Method	Scientific method	Action research

Action research is a better fit for leadership in complexity and change than scientific method.[10] History and context both matter in action research, just as they do in complexity. The iterative cycle of action research offers regular points for reflection in the ongoing flow of action to inform action, just like the complexity learning cycle. Action research and learning informed leadership are both change orientated. The former is concerned with changing group dynamics in field theory (Lewin, 1947b), while our aim is to better understand the dynamic patterning of organisational life.

Interpreting regularly

Sensemaking is ongoing (Weick, 1995). It never starts or stops. People naturally move into a more heightened sensemaking mode when there are shocks that interrupt the ongoing flow of familiar patterns (Weick, 1995: 86). Shocks may arise from "novel moments", when something unusual happens, or when something expected fails to happen; shocks also arise in turbulence; in ambiguous and changing situations; and in greater uncertainty and increasing complexity (Weick, 1995: 86–88). It is clear that a VUCA world offers many occasions for sensemaking.

The downside of using shocks to stimulate sensemaking is that they provoke physical and mental responses in our bodies. So, if we are shocked into making sense, our bodies are already using valuable cognitive and emotional resources that are not available for interpreting. Under pressure and in uncertainty, it is a very natural human reaction to want to cling on to what we know, closing our minds to disconfirming data about newly emerging patterns of change. Therefore, what I am proposing in the complexity learning cycle is using a discipline of noticing-interpreting-responding as a normal part of leadership practice, rather than in response to shocks.

Holding interpretations lightly

When we apply complexity thinking, we acknowledge that interpretations are tentative, provisional, and incomplete. We can never know complex things completely (Cilliers, 2002), as we know from the Complexity Conundrum (Figure 2.1). It is a reminder that we should not be overly certain in uncertainty.

Once we have developed our working stories, we must continue to hold those interpretations lightly because, as we saw in Chapter 4, our conceptual models can only ever be roughly right. If we become too attached to the sense we have made, it becomes more difficult to see things in a different way.

We must be alert to the risk of self-sealing logics, where disconfirming information is used to elaborate and reinforce the original story (Weick, 1995: 84). For example, when an organisational restructure does not deliver its intended goals, it is taken as evidence that it was the wrong structure, not that restructuring was the wrong solution. When interpretations are similar across groups of people, their interpretive stories can become more durable in the organisational system as they are crystalised into 'common knowledge'.

We can mitigate those risks by considering our interpretations, however carefully made, as "hunches" (Weick, 2011) or "transitory outcomes" (Livne-Tarandach and Bartunek, 2009: 19) in an ongoing process of dynamic patterning. Weick (2011: 9) uses the word "hunches" to highlight "the provisional nature of concepts and the fact that they are substantial abridgements of perceptual reality". While thinking of "transitory" outcomes reminds us that patterns are temporary and "evolving throughout change" (Livne-Tarandach and Bartunek, 2009: 19).

Using this provisional language reminds us that interpretations are incomplete and changing. When we interpret a complex reality in flight, we are always learning.

Taking experience seriously

Interpreting is a human and subjective activity that takes experience seriously (Stacey and Griffin, 2005). The complexity learning cycle (Figure 7.1) helps you to take your experience more seriously by bracketing attention to ensure that [noticing] and [interpreting] each gets focused attention.

However, noticing and interpreting are mutually informing activities. So, our aim is to build proficiency in each and connect them in ways that help us to notice more fully and to interpret more fully. Weick (2011) calls this activity change poetics:

> Change poets create evocative images in the sense that their *words include more of the flux of direct experience* and fewer of the surface categories that reduce options ... Poets talk airy nothing into existence ... But a crucial role for the change poet is to *ensure that the 'names that identify objects forever,' do not*. Instead, the poet *continues to experiment with hunches* that incorporate more of the perceptual flux that shapes experience.
>
> (Weick, 2011: 9–10, emphasis added)

Noticing and interpreting tend to be taken for granted activities. They rarely get attention in leadership or leadership development, so it is hard to know how to develop them. I have therefore bracketed noticing and interpreting in the complexity learning cycle so that you can learn to attend well to both (and to responding, coming up in Chapter 8). Noticing, interpreting, and responding together will help you to develop a rich, multi-faceted experience for learning informed leadership.

Key insights
- Interpreting aims to catch reality in flight, while staying close to the action
- It involves exploring potential patterns and possibilities in our noticing data
- Looking for connections and contradictions may create insight; the discovery of new patterns
- In searching for patterns, we must stay alert to the risk of finding false patterns
- Black swans, thinking the opposite and embracing paradox make for richer interpretations
- We engage diverse perspectives through dialogue, enlisting rivals and crowds, and triangulation
- Storytelling and creating pictures reflect multiple perspectives and hold ambiguity
- Interpretations inform action. Learning in and from action help us to develop a better story
- Interpreting is a liminal activity that is bracketed from and connected to the flux of experience
- In complexity and continous change, we must interpret regularly and hold interpretations lightly

potential patterns better story
connections and contradictions
insight thinking the opposite embracing paradox
catch reality in flight
black dialogue rivals and crowds
swans close to the action
triangulation hold interpretations lightly
pictures storytelling

Noticing and noting
Take a look back at your noticing data from Chapter 6. Note down any *connections* in your data. Then note down any *contradictions* in your data.

Draw a picture that encapsulates the connections and contradictions in your noticing data. Discuss your picture with a colleague and explore their perspective. Note down any differences and use them to challenge your initial views.

Notes

1 For an in-depth discussion of ascribed and emergent coherence see Letiche et al. (2011).

2 There is so much available perceptual data in group situations that individuals who are extremely sensitive noticers can feel overloaded, distracted, and overwhelmed.

3 'Openness to experience' is one of the Big Five factors used to study differences in personality between people. It considers someone's receptivity to new ideas and experiences.

4 For more on connections and contradictions see https://www.henley.ac.uk/people/person/pro
fessor-jane-mckenzie (accessed 07/10/2020).
5 For more on pattern logic, see https://www.hsdinstitute.org/resources/pattern-logic-blog.html
(accessed 07/10/2020).
6 In complexity science terminology, 'behaviour' is an emergent aggregate, a whole (see Holland,
(1995)).
7 From the Roffey Park OD Conference, 22–23 June, 2006, Roffey Park Institute, UK.
8 'Team of rivals' is a reference to Doris Kearns Goodwin's (2006) prize-winning book on Abraham
Lincoln.
9 This is a critical realist statement. For more, see Fleetwood (2005).
10 There are many similarities between action research and the approach taken by Ralph Stacey
and his colleagues. While they are keen point out some fundamental differences between complex
responsive processes thinking and action research, there are many points of similarity. Richard Wil-
liams offers a deeper comparison of action research and complex responsive processes thinking in
Stacey and Griffin (2005: 60–63).

Chapter 8
Adapting leadership responses

Going slow to go fast

In Chapter 8, the habit we want to break is leaping into action. We must go slow to go fast in uncertainty to de-risk it.[1] Noticing and interpreting in the complexity learning cycle (Figure 8.1) has interrupted the Pavlovian stimulus-response mechanism. We now want to use that insight wisely by getting into the habit of *choosing* our responses into the ongoing dynamic patterning, so we can adapt our responses to changing conditions.

Equally, we want to use our responses to gain further insight about the dynamic patterning. We do this by staying alert to noticing the vital signs of change and interpreting emerging patterns, so we can continue to choose context-appropriate responses into the ongoing dynamic patterning. The complexity learning cycle is continuous. The traffic light theme in Figure 8.1 highlights the importance of responding into the world to learn from it.

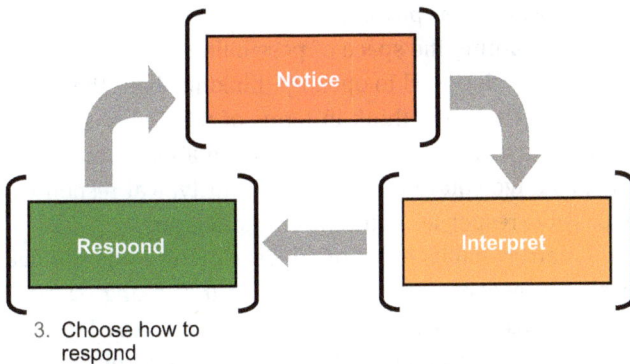

Figure 8.1: Complexity learning cycle – respond.

When we embrace the complexity of a world in constant motion, choosing how to respond may feel more challenging than before. Once we accept that we can never be certain how our words and actions will play out, how to be and act in the world no longer feels straightforward. Yet inaction is also a response. If you are feeling overwhelmed, I can offer some words of comfort. You have been living and working in complexity and continuous changing all your life, whether you knew it or not. So, you are not a complete novice and your life skills are valuable. This chapter encourages you to build on your life skills to better match the complexity in your working life.

https://doi.org/10.1515/9783110713343-008

The chapter begins by inviting you to creatively explore your space for action and to develop a wider variety of potential responses to choose from. The aim is to break out from narrow habits of action and to get into the more productive habit of adapting your responses to new learning about your changing context. The chapter continues by highlighting the importance of learning as you go in a changing world. It encourages you to think about leadership responses in terms of iterative loops, rather than straight lines, and in terms of questions rather than answers. Next it considers cultivating enabling conditions for 'learning as you go' to be absorbed into the ordinary practices of working life. The chapter ends with an encouragement to keep on keeping on in perpetual uncertainty and ambiguity.

Discovering your space for action

Exploring your possibility space

Once again, we are bracketing our attention. We have moved from the perceptual (noticing), to the conceptual (interpreting), and now we are concerned with the actionable (responding). Given the world as we understand it through our noticing and interpreting, the question is *what is now possible?*

I like to think about this as exploring the space of possibilities (Mitleton-Kelly, 2003, 2006). This spatial metaphor is designed to open up thinking about the broad territory for our responses. Games designers think in terms of possibility space to plot all the possible moves that players can make in a given situation.[2] I am using the term metaphorically to encourage you to think *beyond* your typical responses, to explore a wider range of possible responses to the specific situation.

The aim is to break out of narrow habits of action by developing a wider range of alternatives. When choosing a response, try broadening your thinking by mentally exploring "the landscape of possible paths of response" (Shotter and Tsoukas, 2014a: 224). Effectively we are applying complexity thinking to enlarge our mental aperture (Figure 4.1) and thereby increase the diversity in our range of potential responses. The aim is to complexify our range of potential responses to better match the complexity in our working world.

The "art" of leadership involves mentally "moving around within a landscape of possibilities" to help you engage your thinking in coming to a practical judgement about the actual response you will take (Shotter and Tsoukas, 2014b: 377). In other words, the art of leadership is about choosing a contextually appropriate response from a range of possibilities.

Stepping into the adjacent possible

If the landscape of possibilities feels too broad, try thinking in terms of the "adjacent possible" (Kauffman, 1995) to consider your territory of potential leadership responses.[3] Like others, I am using the adjacent possible as an evocative metaphor. I find it a useful way to bring both creativity and pragmatism to bear in choosing how to respond in complexity and change.

Imagine you are standing on a square in a large grid. From that vantage point, you can only see the eight squares that are immediately adjacent to you. Those eight squares represent your possibilities for action from where you are right now. Or you could opt to do nothing by staying where you are.

When you step onto an adjacent square, it will reveal some new possibilities for action. In Figure 8.2, if you move diagonally at Step 1, you will see five new adjacent possibilities for action. If you then move to the right at Step 2, you will see three new adjacent possibilities. For example, if you speak with someone different (Step 1), that conversation might offer a range of new possibilities, for example, different people to speak to, other actions, new ways of seeing the situation, etc.

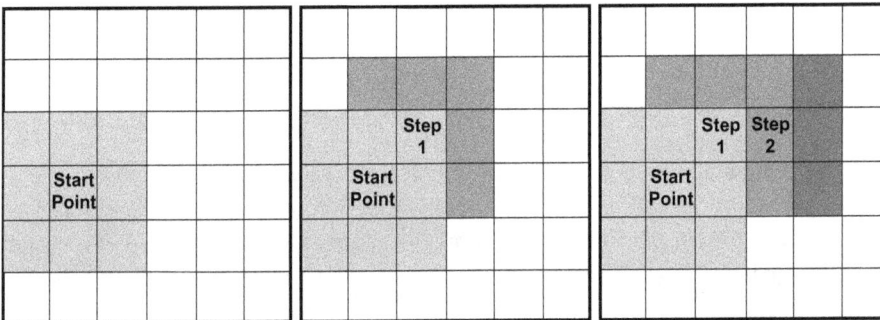

Figure 8.2: Exploring the adjacent possible.

This is a metaphor, not a literal walk. However, thinking about moving one step and reviewing the landscape from that new vantage point can free us up to act, especially if we are feeling overwhelmed by complexity. It is also a useful reminder that in the complexity learning cycle *responding* is a precursor to *noticing* (Figure 8.1).

I often use this idea to help people get themselves unstuck (see Box 8.1). Rather than leaving a leadership development workshop with a list of good intentions, I often encourage people to choose one step they will *actually* take and to discover where it takes them.

> **Box 8.1 Getting unstuck**
>
> When I was working with a senior HR team, I noticed they had fallen into a pattern of leaving each meeting with a long list of actions that were clearly not actionable, given their situation. Each week they regrouped having made little headway and spent the next hour or so revisiting and reprioritising a list of important things that was still unachievable. They were busy getting nowhere.
>
> Park the list, I suggested. Pick something you *can* make progress on given the current constraints, go and start it right now, then let us see where we are. When we regrouped the following week there was a huge sense of relief among team members that some things had gone from being on the list to being underway. Finally, there was movement in a rather stuck change project.
>
> The atmosphere in the room felt lighter. I noticed more light-hearted conversations, more humour, and that people were more animated. My interpretation was that team members might be feeling slightly better about the project, and about themselves. My first response was to check that out. 'How are you feeling?', I asked. With an affirmative reply, we then moved to exploring what was now possible.
>
> Later in the day, I discovered a positive unintended consequence: that sense of movement was also evident in the wider HR team. Normally the senior HR managers had lengthy follow-up meetings to communicate and cascade the long list of actions to their individual teams. A ripple effect was that HR team members had also been freed up to move things on.

Dynamic landscapes

Context is not static, so Figure 8.2 is little simplistic. As we know, context is dynamically co-created through all the interactions that comprise the organisational system. The territory in this metaphor (context) is changed by taking a step. We cannot simply step back into the world as it was before. Taking a step changes what is now possible.

Kauffman's (1993) work on rugged fitness landscapes brings that to life with a 3D model. The NK model is mathematical, but my use here remains metaphorical. The basic idea is that, in an entangled ecosystem, the landscape in the grid in Figure 8.2 would be represented as a rugged landscape of peaks and troughs, representing higher and lower levels of comparative 'fitness' for the various organisms. As an organism takes an adaptive walk across the landscape, it deforms the landscape, changing it for themselves and others. It is a reminder that what everyone is saying and doing across an organisational system co-creates the changing landscape for leadership.

I offer these complexity metaphors lightly, as it can be problematic to simply transfer concepts to different domains. However, I think they are of practical use because they help us to diversify our responses. Thinking in terms of the adjacent possible prompts us to think creatively about a range of responses (what is possible?) combined with a hefty dose of pragmatism (what is available?) on the verges of where we are now.

Exploring knowledge landscapes

Oliver and Roos (2000) conceptualise knowledge landscapes. Peaks here represent rich knowledge and expertise in the current environment. We might think of this as being fit for purpose today.

Troughs represent not knowing. However, in a changing world, there may be unlearning to do, so Oliver and Roos recommend taking a walk down into the valleys of not knowing which offer valuable opportunities for learning. We might think of this as preparing for tomorrow.

Chapter 7 offered some practical ways of interpreting which enable unlearning so that we do not become too attached to our knowledge, for example, searching for disconfirming evidence (black swans), thinking the opposite, embracing paradox, enlisting rivals, and holding interpretations lightly.

Starting where you are

A question that managers often ask is, where do I start? My advice is always start where you are.

The mistaken idea that you can start from anywhere other than where you are now assumes that you can map a path to your chosen future start point, without changing the landscape. You cannot. You might have a view of your intended path beyond step one, but you will need to hold that view lightly and learn as you go, using the complexity learning cycle to inform subsequent steps.

I am not suggesting stumbling forward without thinking ahead. Of course, we should anticipate and plan for *known* possibilities. If we embark on a change project without involving those affected, we know it is likely to be met with pushback. What is unknowable is the precise nature, source, and strength of that pushback. Will it be explicit or hidden? Will it come from those directly affected, or from elsewhere? This might guide you to adopt approaches that involve people in change, and to use that participation to surface emerging issues and opportunities sooner to inform your next step.

As we know, complex systems are entangled. Interdependencies mean that we may be able to influence other domains more indirectly. I like Meg Wheatley's advice: "Go inside. Start anywhere. Follow it everywhere" (Wheatley and Frieze, 2011).[4]

Following it everywhere

My liberal use of spatial metaphors in this section is deliberate. I am inviting you to reach beyond the bounds of your current experience and purposefully expand the range and variety of your potential responses.

Complexifying our *range* of responses in this way is about diversity. It is not the same as engineering overly complicated responses in a misguided attempt to control complexity. In a dynamic world, we are striving for "simplexity" by synthesising "requisite complexity of thought" with "appropriate simplicity of action" (Colville et al., 2012: 6). For example, my proposal to park the 'To Do' list and do something (Box 8.1) was simple to action. The complexity of thought came from noticing and interpreting the contextual nuances over the previous weeks which suggested that might be a good response in that particular situation, at that particular moment, with those particular people.

Being choiceful does not give us control of how our words and actions play out as they get entangled with other people's words and actions. So, we must be prepared to follow the ripples of our responses everywhere as we continue to learn in the dynamic patterning of organisational life.

Adapting as you learn

Loops not lines

Leadership is enacted through a wide range of everyday words and actions. There are no special recipes or tricks. What is distinctive here is that action is entwined with learning. In a changing world, we must learn as we go and adapt as we learn.

"Muddling through" (Rodgers, 2021) is a deliberately incremental approach to living life forwards amidst perpetual uncertainty and ambiguity (the Complexity Conundrum). It is not an aimless or careless way of acting; managers act with purpose, taking deliberate action to work through challenges, accompanied by a broad sense of direction and determination (Rodgers, 2021).

However, rather than following a plan, managers "keep chipping away" by "pursuing sought-after change incrementally, contingently and opportunistically" (Rodgers, 2021: 200). Essentially what Rodgers (2021) is pointing out is that in a "wiggly world" (his preferred term for complexity) we should be thinking about leadership responses in terms of loops rather than straight lines.

Responding in loops is exactly what we are doing with the complexity learning cycle (Figure 8.1). We continually loop around the cycle to choose our best learning-informed leadership responses in a changing context:

- We *learn to respond* in context-appropriate ways, that is, by noticing what is changing and interpreting that data to develop insight into emerging opportunities.
- We *respond to learn* by continuing round the loop, that is, by continuing to notice and interpret changing patterns to choose and adapt our next context-appropriate response.

These learning loops are iterative. We expect the world to be changing, so we pay close attention to learning how it is changing to *adapt* our response. This is vastly different to getting stuck in a loop going round in circles by doing the same things again and again.

Becoming agile

In my experience, managers often recognise the necessity of muddling through in an incremental way in uncertainty and ambiguity, but they feel uncomfortable with the phrase.[5] In contrast, the language of agility – also an incremental approach – has been widely embraced in business.

Many businesses have moved away from linear 'waterfall' approaches to delivering new IT systems through large projects, to embrace agile methodologies which take an iterative and incremental approach. The language of 'agile' with its focus on sprints and scrums has caught the imagination of many people in IT, project management, and change management.

The fundamental thinking behind agile approaches, which highlights collaboration and iteration, is congruent with learning-informed leadership. In both views, learning happens in context, based on empirical data about how developments are working, and conducted in collaboration with the people involved.

The problem is where agile has become sedimented as an ideology. When agility becomes synonymous with the routine activities, paraphernalia, and stock phrases used to enact agile methodologies, its potential is diminished. Individuals get caught up in repetitive activities of delivering the methodology. Their thinking, actions, questions, and learning become confined by the boundaries of the model (and, as we saw in Chapter 4, all models are wrong).

If we want to become agile, we must recognise that agility is not a set of methods. It is an ongoing process whereby people learn for themselves (although not by themselves) in the dynamic patterning of organisational life and use that learning to adapt as they go. That includes adapting the methods by which they learn and adapt.

Taking adaptive action

In the press of working life, we may feel overwhelmed by complex problems. When there are no simple solutions, it is easy to get stuck in repetitive patterns of action or inaction. Rather than trying to solve complex problems or, worse still, avoiding them, Glenda Eoyang, and her colleagues advise choosing your next "wise action" (Eoyang and Holladay, 2013).

Their "adaptive action" process (Eoyang and Holladay, 2013) asks three questions – What? So what? Now what? – while remaining engaged with real challenges in real situations. Asking 'Now what?' is designed to help you in choosing your next action. Thinking in this way can free people up to act (like the example in Box 8.1). Helpfully it sets action in the context of an adaptive process.

The idea of choosing a 'wise' action is a compelling call to action. However, it would be more accurate to talk about choosing our next action wisely, since we cannot know in advance whether a carefully chosen action will turn out to be wise, or not. Emergence is unpredictable because our actions and intentions get caught up in the interplay of actions, plans and intentions (Stacey, 2012).

If you apply complexity thinking, notice the vital signs of change, interpret your noticing data to develop insight about emerging patterns, and expand your range of potential responses, you will be well positioned to choose your next action wisely.

Probing first

David Snowden's Cynefin framework advises probe first, then sense and respond in complex contexts (Snowden and Boone, 2007).[6] By probing, Snowden is suggesting that action is deliberately experimental. In complexity and change, we can only know what will actually happen when it does happen.

Probing is an experimental way of learning that involves examining or enquiring closely into something. For example, we might ask probing questions, or we might try out small interventions to learn what happens. When we are probing a complex situation, we might try multiple probes in parallel to see how they work. We should expect some, or all, to fail. We are seeking to learn from action to adapt our responses.

Probing first makes a strong statement. Yet we must remember that in continuous changing, we are always 'starting' in the midst of things. In the real world, we can never start from a blank sheet of paper. There is *always* dynamic patterning for us to notice and carefully interpret to choose any probing actions wisely.

Experimenting and exploring

Addressing adaptive (i.e., complex) challenges means avoiding the grand gesture of sweeping new initiatives and instead running numerous experiments (Heifetz et al., 2009a). Heifetz and his colleagues highlight the danger of being pushed into action prematurely without doing the important diagnostic work, as they call it, of seeing the larger patterns (Heifetz et al., 2009b).

They advise those in positions of authority to get on the balcony above the dance floor to see what is really happening, rather than getting swept up in the party, then to move back and forth between the balcony and the dancefloor to continually assess what is happening and take midcourse action (Heifetz et al., 2009b: 7–8). We explored this stepping in and out in Chapter 7.

When I talk about experimenting and exploring, I am not limiting it to formalised experiments with controls. Instead, I am using the idea more broadly to encompass many moments of trying something different and, most importantly, *learning* from those moments to adapt your next response into the dynamic patterning.

Learning to respond

Learning informed leadership is intentional, but it is inevitably iterative as the complexity learning cycle (Figure 8.1) illustrates. Any plans for action must be continually revisited, re-understood, and adapted in light of what is changing. We adapt our next response based on our learning.

That means learning *in action* as we participate in the conversations and activities that arise as we work together. It also means learning *from action* because the ripple effects of words and actions may be felt much farther from the time and place in which they are said and done. The process of learning (noticing and interpreting) is similar, but the cycles of learning have a different pace.

When we learn *in action*, we are using rapid learning cycles. When we work 'live', we learn in the moment and from the moment, which has a spontaneous and improvisational quality to it (Shaw and Stacey, 2006). For example, we might notice interruptions, who is speaking more and less, changing relationships between people, changing energy levels, or the topic of conversation. We might make quick interpretations (e.g., I think people might be flagging) and respond in the moment (e.g. shall we take a quick break?). We might notice familiar patterns being reinforced in the room such as who is not speaking or who is not being listened to. We might make interpretations (e.g., I need to disrupt that pattern so that person can be heard) and respond in the moment (e.g., Alex, I would love to understand more about how you see things).

While the learning may be rapid, the thinking can still be 'slow'. We can avoid jumping to conclusions and leaping into action by using the complexity learning cycle to notice, interpret and then choose our response.

When we learn *from action*, we have the opportunity to employ longer learning cycles. This might enable us to develop insight into the larger patterns that are changing over longer timeframes, across different domains.

It is easy for busy managers to get caught up in 'doing' and for vital learning to get squeezed out. Regularly bracketing time for *noticing* what is changing, and for *interpreting* the emerging patterns ensures that these activities do not get neglected in the doing of leadership.

Throughout this section, I have drawn together various approaches that encourage you to adapt your responses as you learn in and from action. Each approach has its own language and flavour, but the broad message is clear: we must learn to inform our responses into the dynamic patterning.

Acting into the unknowable

Asking powerful questions

In uncertainty, asking questions is a powerful way of enacting leadership. Asking powerful questions holds the space for people to act with intention without leaping into action. You can even ask questions of yourself. It can also be really effective in groups. Using questions to open up thinking and stimulate learning can bring multiple perspectives to bear on complex issues and lead groups to discovery.

I encourage people to ask questions in the present tense to focus attention on where they are now, rather than where they have been, or where they might be going (see examples in Table 8.1). I find that managers tend to spend a lot of time picking over the past and envisioning the future, and rather less time in the here and now. The assumption is that the here and now is obvious to everyone. In complexity, it rarely is!

Table 8.1: Powerful questions for acting with intention.

Response	Example questions
Exploring assumptions	What patterns or signals are we not seeing? Which voices are we not listening to? What are we hearing underneath the opinions that have been expressed? What is *really* going on?
Exploring our own agency	Why are we finding this such a struggle? What are we contributing to this situation? What is enabling/constraining us in moving forward? Where does responsibility lie?
Exploring meaning	What does the opposite of this look like? What new connections are we making? What is emerging here for you? How has your view of the issue changed since we started?
Exploring possibilities for action	What possibilities exist now? What other options are there? How might we begin to move towards where we want to be? What might be our next best step?

In an uncertain and ambiguous world (remember the Complexity Conundrum) I prefer to ask questions with certainty, and to hold 'answers' more lightly. For example, when I ask, 'what are we *not* seeing?', I am fairly certain there will be something that has not yet surfaced, even though I do not know what that something might be.

Activating enquiry

Importantly, this state of enquiry is active, engaging, and generative of new possibilities. It is vastly different from asking questions to deflect attention or to avoid action. Posing powerful questions *is* action. As Professor Ralph Stacey once said to me in conversation; "when we think differently, we act differently". It is a reminder that separating thought from action is artificial. Thought and action (like many other things in this complex world) are entangled.

Questions are powerful leadership tools because they direct attention. For example, we might ask about problems of sickness absence, or we might ask about successes of attendance and wellbeing. Cooperrider and Srivastva (1987) invite us to enquire in the direction we want to travel by engaging in Appreciative Inquiry. The underpinning thinking is that enquiry is enactive of the emerging future and that asking positively framed questions moves us in that direction (see Box 8.2).[7]

> **Box 8.2 Appreciative Inquiry**
> Rather than asking problem-based questions (e.g., what is going wrong here?), we would ask positively framed questions (e.g., what is going right here?). The positive framing is designed to catch people doing things well and to elicit aspects of the current situation that are working. The aim is then to fan the flames of those bright sparks to amplify the pattern so that the best of the way things are becomes the norm.
>
> Appreciative Inquiry has been developed into a large group intervention, whereby large, diverse groups of people representing the whole system, come together in enquiring together about the best of what is, and to co-create their destiny.

The Appreciative Inquiry approach has been developed over many years as a methodology for action in change (Cooperrider and Whitney, 2005, Bushe, 2011). The process fits well with the complexity learning cycle because it invites multiple perspectives in *noticing* the here and now, in *interpreting* what is working, and in *responding* to amplify those patterns.

However, there are some 'watch outs' for managers in applying Appreciative Inquiry as a methodology. The 5 Ds (Definition, Discovery, Dream, Design, Destiny)[8] can be enacted as a rather linear process. Practically, the enquiry aspect is often front-loaded, particularly when it is employed as a large group intervention. When that happens, it becomes a participative approach to planned change, rather than an enabler for learning informed leadership in emergence. For a world in constant change, discovery (noticing and interpreting) must be continuous. It is a reminder to apply complexity thinking in action, so that we use methodologies as a stimulus in thinking for ourselves.

Responding to learn

There are two ways we can think about activating learning informed leadership through the complexity learning cycle (Figure 8.1):
- **Learning to respond.** Here we notice what is changing and interpret emerging patterns to use that insight in making more informed choices about our response. Essentially, we use our learning to continually adapt our responses into the dynamic patterning. The goal is to improve our responses.
- **Responding to learn.** We respond into the dynamic patterning to learn how it plays out by noticing what is changing and interpreting emerging patterns. Essentially, we use our responses to enable better learning. The goal is to improve our learning.

The 'responding to learn' aspect of leadership has been given different names by different people. Judi Marshall (1999, 2016) calls it "living life as inquiry". Glenda Eoyang and her colleagues refer to it as "standing in inquiry" (Eoyang and Holladay, 2013: 39). Ron Heifetz and his colleagues call it "living life as a leadership laboratory" (Heifetz et al., 2009b: 43).

Whatever you choose to call it, responding to learn makes a stronger statement about learning. Better learning is not just a means to an end in leadership. In continuous changing, there is no end. So, the means (i.e., better learning) *is* the goal of leadership.

Responding to learn enables a double loop of learning (see Figure 8.3). In the first loop, we respond to learn about the changing world to guide our next action; this is the experimental stance that we have been discussing. The double loop of learning (Argyris, 1977) comes from reflecting on our assumptions, values and beliefs about how the world works, and adjusting them in relation to new data. (We will explore learning about ourself in the world in more detail in Chapter 9.)

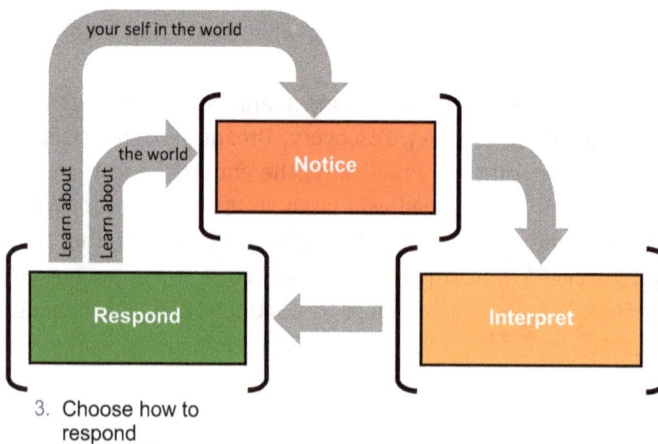

Figure 8.3: Complexity learning cycle – double-loop learning.

Cultivating enabling conditions

Setting the stage

Utilising the diversity of multiple perspectives has been a repeating refrain as we notice and interpret. It applies here too, as we respond.

Think about it. If we cannot know how things will play out until they do (emergence), then chance will always play a part in whether our actual responses will turn out to be the best ones, or not. So, rather than backing some people (e.g., those in charge) over others, leadership responses here must be partly about cultivating enabling conditions that encourage everyone to get involved in noticing, interpreting, and choosing adaptive responses into the dynamic patterning. This increases the requisite complexity in the system and thereby increases our chances of success in a changing world.

Managers sometimes worry that empowerment will create a free-for-all. However, the earlier financial services case (Box 1.1) shows how many people rapidly adapted their working practices to keep things running smoothly. Managers were part of this process. They too were adapting and responding. They played their individual parts in setting the intention – work from home safely and keep the business running smoothly – and in responding and adapting to what was emerging as thousands of people conducted mini experiments to find ways of doing that together.

I have been encouraging you to activate learning informed leadership by getting into the habit of noticing, interpreting, and choosing your responses. If you have authority and/or influence within and across communities, you can actively set the stage for others to work in these ways too. Setting the stage for learning informed leadership practices to grow involves some behind the scenes work and some active stage management.

Enabling adaptive space

Let us start behind the scenes. Mary Uhl-Bien, and her colleagues argue that the job of leaders is to enable the adaptive process (Uhl-Bien et al., 2007, Uhl-Bien and Marion, 2009, Uhl-Bien and Arena, 2018, Uhl-Bien et al., 2020). Enabling leadership, as they describe it, is facilitative and focuses on creating the conditions for adaptation. It is therefore "much less hands-on and much more behind the scenes than traditional leadership" (Uhl-Bien and Arena, 2018: 100).

This work conceptualises an "adaptive space" that connects an operating system (i.e., delivering today's work) with an entrepreneurial system (i.e., innovating for tomorrow) to support future viability (Uhl-Bien et al., 2020). Adaptive space is not a literal space or a separate business unit. It is a conceptual idea that embraces the learning-performance paradox (Smith and Lewis, 2011) by enabling both.

Enabling leadership is enacted through behaviours such as "brokering, connecting, facilitating, and energizing to trigger and amplify emergence of creativity, innovation, learning and growth" (Uhl-Bien and Arena, 2018: 100).

This idea of adaptive space is also helpful in another way. Many businesses and institutions have hierarchical structures. Practically, it means that attention is drawn up and down (vertically) through reporting lines. Connections across the verticals often receive much less attention. Uhl-Bien and Arena (2018: 98) encourage formal and informal leaders to "enable . . . the adaptive process by creating structures and processes . . . that effectively engage conflicting . . . and connecting" pressures for operational exploitation and for entrepreneurial exploration. This is an open invitation to give leadership attention to the important issue of horizontal connections, such as knowledge creation (Nonaka, 1994) and organisational learning (Fahy et al., 2014) through partnerships.

Partnering for change

Creating boundary-spanning partnerships is too important to be left to chance. Deliberately creating networks to support innovation involves *finding* the right partners beyond existing networks; *forming* productive relationships; and *performing* to meet the goals of the various partners (Birkinshaw et al., 2007). The collaborative endeavour here is to create enough *connection* for the respective *differences* between the various partners to sing.

In a Henley Forum action research project, we took this challenge seriously (see Box 8.3).[9] Applying the framework in practice demonstrated that the finding, forming, performing process is not a simple, linear progression. Developing successful partnerships across internal boundaries involves a complex negotiation around the three elements. Sometimes you need to go back and renegotiate to move forwards. Project team members likened their experience to navigating a continuously evolving maze.[10]

Box 8.3 Partnering for change

Managers and professionals from nine large organisations applied the Find-Form-Perform framework (Birkinshaw et al., 2007) over several months to progress planned change initiatives in their own organisations. They discovered that:

- **Finding the right partners** is like creating a line of sight through a continuously changing maze.
- **Forming productive working relationships** involves clarifying mutual purpose by understanding the benefits that each partner is looking for, as a way of bridging across internal boundaries.
- **Performing to meet goals** is about using opportunities as they arise, based on the network they have formed, and making the most of the diverse perspectives that the partners bring to navigate the changing maze together.

Creating space for learning

I set up my business 'space for learning' in 2007 having just conducted some re-search to discover how other practitioners were applying complexity science ideas in practice (Varney, 2007). I found they were creating enabling conditions for learn-ing in complexity (see Table 8.2 and Figure 8.4). In summary, they were bracketing *space*, which legitimised and set the stage for learning. They were also activating learning by bringing *stimulus* and holding the learning space through conscious use of *self* (more about use of self in Chapter 9). This shows a balance between behind-the-scenes work (creating the space) and actively managing the stage (bringing stimulus and self into the space).

Table 8.2: Creating enabling conditions for learning.

Perspective	Enablers	Leadership practices
space	context	Paying close attention to local context to decide when and how to intervene in a way that makes sense for those involved
	container	Creating notional boundaries to enable learning in complexity, for example, dedicating time; setting a place; creating psychological conditions to hold contradictions and differences
	connections	Fostering connections with diversity; fresh connections can bring fresh perspectives
stimulus	content	Helping people give voice to their own issues; the best learning content is what is real and important to those involved
	catalyst	Offering people something different to help catalyse their learning, for example, if they are too busy, slow down; if it's lack of urgency, speed up; if people are too certain, help them consider uncertainty; if they're too confused, help them find some clarity
self	confidence	Managing our own anxieties from working with complexity; holding creative tension and living with paradox

Space, stimulus, and self are entangled in practice. There is always much more in complexity than we can ever name, as illustrated by the blank space in Figure 8.4. However, my intent in highlighting these six conditions is to draw attention to some aspects within a complex reality that we might influence.

I would encourage you to use this framework to explore your own context for learning in complexity. Notice what you have, interpret what you need, and respond by building on what you already have to create more of what you need. See Box 8.4 for an illustration.

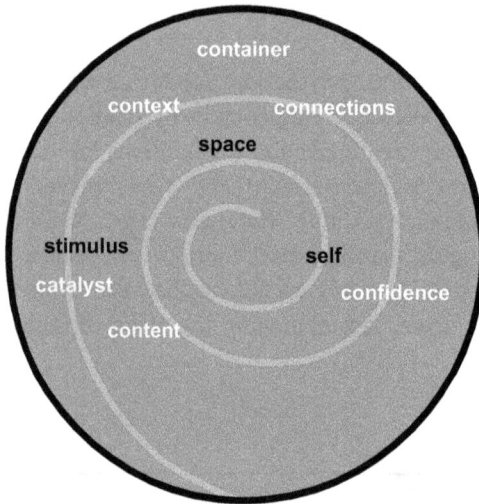

Figure 8.4: Enabling conditions for learning (Varney, 2007).

Box 8.4 Leadership development as a space for learning

Leadership development is a legitimised space for learning that is common across private, public, and not-for-profit sectors. It therefore offers huge potential for learning in complexity. However, much of that potential may be left on the table unless the enabling conditions are activated. For example:

Notice what you have. Traditional leadership programmes often provide well-designed *containers* for learning and frequently foster horizontal *connections* between people. The more developmental ones are delivered by skilled facilitators who have the self-*confidence* to hold the space for learning.

Interpret what you need. However, the *content* of leadership development programmes is commonly directed to create alignment rather than to explore contradictions. *Connections* tend to be horizontal, but they rarely serve to connect people across hierarchical levels. Often containers are divorced from *context*, rather than bracketed in context. Many leadership development programmes offer a much-needed *stimulus* to slow down; but adopting a familiar format may not promote deeper learning.

Respond by building on what you have. In this fictitious, but not uncommon example, I would be looking for opportunities to bring a different *catalyst* and to foster more diverse *connections* across hierarchical levels, embedded in the *context* of everyday work. Something like reverse mentoring might be useful here as part of the overall approach to leadership development.

Amplifying action

As we and others respond into the dynamic patterning, we are continuously noticing what is changing. When we spot the sparks of emerging issues, we may choose
responses designed to damp down the flames. When we see the sparks of new opportunity, we may choose responses designed to fan the flames. We can make the
latter sound a bit grander by calling it taking "amplifying action" (Lichtenstein and
Plowman, 2009).

What those in charge are doing here is amplifying action by using their authority and influence to legitimise experimentation. They encourage novelty by saying
that it is okay to try new things and to interact in different ways. Amplifying action
is supported by deliberate sensemaking and sensegiving behaviours (Lichtenstein
and Plowman, 2009). The idea is that, when you find adaptations that you want to
keep (through sensemaking, i.e., noticing and interpreting), you encourage them so
that they become established in the new normal that is emerging (through sensegiving, i.e., the words and actions you choose in responding).

This sensegiving might consist of saying things like:
- well done, carry on coming up with those new ideas
- good idea, let us try it
- the way the team pulled together around this crisis was great. How can we bring
  the best of that into the everyday?
- I am delighted to hear you are working collaboratively with your external partners. May I connect you with some people who are trying similar things, so you
  can share your stories?

Or doing things like:
- adopting new ways of working
- allocating resource to support new initiatives
- promoting people who try new things.

The aim is to encourage more of certain kinds of behaviour to infuse the dynamic
patterning by using influence or authority to "certify" emergent change (Weick,
2000). As Weick (2000: 238) explains it; "the job of management is to author interpretations and labels that capture the patterns in those adaptive choices". Doing
this means paying close attention to learning what is actually happening (noticing
and interpreting) to choose your response into that patterning.

Lichtenstein and Plowman (2009) provide a model for leadership of emergence.
Like all models it is wrong: it is an oversimplification which tells a linear story of
success by looking backwards.[11] Yet managers often wonder what to do with their
formal power and authority because they worry that complexity and continuous
change has effectively rendered it toothless. (Actually, it has not because the world
was complex and changing anyway.) This model reframes how those in charge in

hierarchical systems may use their power and authority in processes of emergence. So, what Lichtenstein and Plowman are usefully doing here is focusing on the actions and activities of formal leaders and managers in processes of emergence.

I am not suggesting that relabelling old roles is enough. However, if this model helps people to think for themselves in reframing their role – that is, they use it to aid practical judgement, not to replace it – then it is useful.

Involving people

Actively fostering a culture of deliberate learning and adaptation in the ongoing process of dynamic patterning is good for the system and good for people (see Table 8.3). From a complexity perspective, important system benefits arise from widescale participation because it builds adaptive capacity in the system. Participation can also be 'a good thing' for human beings, depending on the quality of that involvement, and may also encourage adaptive behaviour.

Table 8.3: Benefits of widescale participation.

Who/what benefits?	Enabler	Illustration
system	diversity	Large-scale involvement increases diversity in upstream responses, so multiple perspectives are built-in rather than added post-hoc, or not at all. More internal diversity (variety) builds adaptive capacity (requisite complexity) of the system.
	context first	The many people involved in ground-up experiments are immersed in the particulars of their local context, so responses are *contextualised* first, rather than being retrofitted to the various situations encountered in the real-world.
	increasing returns	With large numbers of local experiments, many fail quickly[12] and fewer will start to get ahead. That which is ahead tends to get further ahead through positive feedback (increasing returns, Arthur, 1996).
humans	more autonomy	When individuals have more autonomy and degrees of freedom in which to respond, they may feel more trusted and valued. Freedom to take risks and being trusted may encourage creativity, i.e., adaptive behaviour.
	engagement	When individuals have active involvement (and freedom not to be involved) they generate meaning and purpose for themselves. If people develop an intrinsic buy-in to what they are creating, they may be more disposed to make it work, i.e., adaptive behaviour.

As an organisation development (OD) practitioner, humanistic values shape how I work and how I believe that 'organisations' should work, so I support Burnes's (2009b) call for a return to Lewinian values[13] of participation in organisational change. But I agree with Morrison (2010) that we should avoid using complexity science as "disguised ideology". Using complexity science to legitimise a more humanistic approach to management is problematic because it risks undervaluing the potential contribution of both the science and the values.

Complexity science and OD

Complexity science and OD each offer good reasons to prioritise participation in organisational change. Many OD practitioners have therefore gravitated towards complexity. While they can be complementary, we need to understand what makes complexity science and OD practice distinct.

Complexity science is explanatory. It tells us how things work. You do not need to *believe in* complexity science, or to subscribe to a particular set of values, for there to be value in applying complexity science insights to leadership and management practice.

OD takes an ethical stance on how we should act because it is the right thing to do. You do not need to scientifically *prove* the efficacy of humanistic values for them to have value.

Keep on keeping on

Acknowledging anxiety

When things are unclear, we get scared.[14] Experiencing the perpetual uncertainty and ambiguity of a volatile and complex world (the Complexity Conundrum) makes people anxious. As we saw in Part I, for managers, that existential anxiety may be magnified when they recognise they are in charge and accountable, but they are not in control of what happens (Streatfield, 2001).

Those in formal positions of authority may also be under pressure to alleviate other people's fears:

> People put enormous pressure on you to respond to their anxieties with authoritative certainty, even if doing so means overselling what you know and discounting what you don't ... People clamor for direction, while you are faced with a way forward that isn't at all obvious.... Yet you still have to lead.
> (Heifetz et al., 2009a: 62)

People employ various strategies to avoid those feelings of discomfort. They invoke the language of certainty ('I have no doubt in my mind') in an uncertain world. They revert to management doctrines that assert individual autonomy in a relational world. They rely too heavily on familiar managerial tools, procedures, and practices in a dynamic world. They pose simplistic either/or questions in an entangled and paradoxical world. Or they outsource challenging and controversial management decisions to large, expensive consulting companies in an ambiguous world. These common defences against anxiety (Stacey, 2012) are perfectly under-standable. We want to make other people (and ourselves) feel better.

Unfortunately, these defences offer false comfort because they merely paper over complexity and the anxiety it provokes. Therefore, a key task for leadership is to *acknowledge* anxiety. Get it out in the open. Talk about it. We need to understand and voice our anxieties. Counterintuitively, we need to give them space and airtime, not suppress them (see Box 8.5).

Box 8.5 Acknowledging hopes and fears

Eddie Obeng encourages people to actively acknowledge hopes and fears at the outset of any meeting, then start with the fears. His advice is "in uncertainty, lose the fears as soon as possible, to get to the hopes".[15] This is good advice.

Asking people to take a few moments to individually note down their hopes and fears helps them to acknowledge their own anxiety. Inviting people to share their fears and their hopes, and writing them up for everyone to see, means they are acknowledged by the whole group. It is even more powerful when those in charge, including facilitators who are in charge of the process, also share their hopes and fears.

By acknowledging anxiety, we can begin to hold it. Holding anxiety means resisting the emotional pull to keep reacting to people's anxieties, including our own. By noticing our own and others' feelings of anxiety, and interpreting them as fears, we are interrupting the Pavlovian stimulus-response mechanism. This pause gives us the opportunity to bring learning informed leadership into action by choosing our best responses into complexity and continuous changing.

Learning continuously

Given where we are, in the midst of complexity and continuous changing, the key message from Part I is to reframe leadership as active participation in the dynamic patterning of organisational life.

Throughout Part II, I have been inviting you to adopt a learning informed approach to leadership, where understanding the dynamic patterning is just as important as shaping the patterning. It is the kind of learning where we use various tools and techniques of leadership and management to help us in thinking and learning for ourselves and we learn to think for ourselves in considering the benefits and limitations of the various tools and approaches that we employ.

The complexity learning cycle that we have been exploring in Part II, is designed to help us to learn in and from experience to inform our responses in the midst of complexity and changing. It is an aid to developing practical judgement, not a replacement for it.

As we have seen, in the complexity learning cycle, we bracket time and concentrate our perceptual effort on noticing what is changing in the flow of our experience.

We actively look out for the small, qualitative, human-scale data that offer vital signs of change in the patterning of events, relations, attention and emotion at multiple levels. We build noticing into our regular leadership practice so that we become better noticers and because we will never know in advance when we will need it. We avoid jumping to conclusions about what our noticings mean by bracketing attention and focusing conceptual effort on developing multiple interpretations, holding them lightly as we use them to help us choose our responses into the dynamic patterning. When we choose our responses, we avoid leaping into action by bracketing attention to deliberately explore alternatives. Then we act with intention, including the intention to learn in and from action (noticing and interpreting), so that we might adapt our responses into the dynamic patterning.

Leadership in complexity and continuous change is not a solo endeavour. We actively seek multiple perspectives to enhance our own noticing, interpreting, and responding. We use authority and influence to set the stage for everyone to be actively learning in and from complexity and change and by creating the connections for people to share their learning to inform their next responses. We keep on keeping on in the face of the perpetual uncertainty and ambiguity of the Complexity Conundrum by actively holding anxiety to maintain the space for learning.

Key insights
- Actively explore your landscape for action, expand your range of potential responses
- When you take a step, pay attention to noticing the new possibility landscape
- Start where you are, follow it everywhere
- When acting into the unknown, start with a powerful question
- Maintain active enquiry, learning as you go, adapting as you learn
- Cultivate the conditions and connections for others to explore and learn in action
- Keep on keeping on by holding the space for learning in the face of tension and anxiety

take a step
expand your range
learn in action cultivate the conditions
adapting responses
new possibility start where you are
active landscape for action
enquiry
powerful question

Noticing and noting

Think about a complex challenge that you are facing. Given your current context, imagine eight responses you might make from where you are now (your ninth response is 'do nothing').

TIP: It often gets harder after the first two or three, so be creative

TIP: Try using a grid or a mind map to create your landscape of possibilities (not a list)

Complexity response generator:

1	2	3
4	5 Do nothing	6
7	8	9

Notes

1 This comes from Eddie Obeng's Keynote at The Henley Forum Conference 'Building Dynamic Capabilities', at Henley Business School on 07/03/18.

2 Possibility space draws from the construct of probability space, where you might map out, for example, all the possible moves in a game of Noughts and Crosses (Tic-Tac-Toe) and their probabilities in a grid.

3 The adjacent possible comes from evolutionary biology, where complexity scientist, Stuart Kauffman (1995), used it to conceptualise the evolution of amino acids into complex proteins. It draws attention to the range of possibilities available at a given point in time (Björneborn, 2020).

4 "Start anywhere and follow it everywhere" is often attributed to Myron Kellner-Rogers (https://www.margaretwheatley.com/articles/lifetoschools.html accessed 26/10/2020).

5 The notion of muddling through comes from Lindblom's (1959) paper, The Science of 'Muddling Through', which proposed incrementalism as an approach to making complex public policy decisions, in contrast with the more linear approach to strategy of analysis-choice-implementation.

6 More about Cynefin at https://www.cognitive-edge.com/the-cynefin-framework/ (accessed 02/07/2021).

7 We are talking about social constructionism, a philosophical view that contends everyday life is subjectively created by people through their thoughts and actions and is then taken for granted as objectified reality (see Berger and Luckmann, 1969). Readers who are familiar with academic philosophical constructs of ontology and epistemology may have questions about the coherence of the ontological stance that I expressed in the introduction, the world really is complex and dynamic (a realist stance), and my adoption of social constructionist language here. Briefly, complexity suggests that the world is not simply 'out there' or 'in here', micro and macro are co-constitutive and entangled across levels (see Varney, 2013).

8 For more on Appreciative Inquiry, see the AI Commons site (https://appreciativeinquiry.champlain.edu/learn/appreciative-inquiry-introduction/5-d-cycle-appreciative-inquiry/ accessed 02/11/2020).

9 You can download a summary of this project: Knowledge in Action - Issue 34, Developing partnerships for change at https://s3-eu-west-1.amazonaws.com/assets.henley.ac.uk/legacyUploads/pdf/research/research-centres/henley-forum/Knowledge_in_Action_-_issue_34.pdf (accessed 30/10/20).

10 A second phase of the action research project created 'The Collaboration Maze', a board game designed to stimulate collaboration, see www.collaborationmaze.com (accessed 31/01/21).

11 I prefer leadership *in* emergence, a processual perspective. Tourish (2019), also a processualist, warns against depicting the theory and practice of leadership in relatively non-complex terms.

12 Many 'experiments' will fail fairly quickly as negative feedback in the dynamic patterning of organisational life serves to re-create continuity. This is different to the 'fail fast' mantra of agile development which is about learning to succeed through iteration.

13 Kurt Lewin's work at NTL in the US, along with socio-technical systems work at the Tavistock Institute in the UK served to create the OD movement. For more about the history of Organisational Development and the underpinning values system see Varney (2019) at https://st5.ning.com/topol ogy/rest/1.0/file/get/2578922817?profile=original (accessed 27/10/20); and Garrow et al. (2009) at: https://www.employment-studies.co.uk/resource/fish-or-bird-perspectives-organisational-development-od (accessed 27/10/20).

14 See endnote 1.

15 See endnote 1.

Part III: **Leadership in person**

Part I painted a picture of the landscape for leadership, where being in the midst of complexity and continuous change is a normal state of affairs. It reframed leadership in complexity and change as active participation in processes of emergence. Then it invited you to think of yourself as an insider, equipped with valuable first-hand experience of what is changing in the dynamic patterning of organisational life, poised to make your leadership count through your everyday interactions.

Part II actively encouraged you to take a learning approach to leadership. It offered some practical tools and techniques to help you notice the vital signs of change, to interpret your noticing data, and to choose your responses into the ongoing dynamic patterning. It encouraged you to complexify your thinking by utilising multiple perspectives and staying open to learning.

In Part III, we will explore the more personal aspects of leadership in complexity and change. I will invite you to adopt an orientation to leadership practice that takes experience and continuous self-development seriously.

Chapter 9
It all starts with you

Leadership is personal

Leadership in complexity and continuous change is intensely personal. We use ourselves as the main instrument for leadership. Any models, tools, and techniques that we employ are supporting acts. They help us to learn for ourselves, to keep our thinking open, and to challenge our mental models as we develop the craft of leadership.

However, the 'self' we use is not a given. Instead, our 'self' emerges in the situation through our relations with others (Perls et al., 1994). It grows as we learn to reflect and take in more of the complexity of the world (Kegan, 1982, Garvey Berger, 2011). The self we use as an instrument develops through practical experience where we learn to engage our contextual judgement (Stacey, 2012, Shotter and Tsoukas, 2014a).

This is good news. We are trying to engage with a world that is in constant motion, so it is reassuring to know that our main instrument can also evolve and change. Developing our self as an instrument for leadership means owning and refining our instrumentality (Cheung-Judge, 2012, Cheung-Judge and Jamieson, 2018). We will explore that further in this chapter.

As is often the case in complexity, our self and the wider system are entangled. One important consequence of that entanglement is that neither our inner world, nor the outer world are fully knowable. As Figure 9.1 illustrates, we get to learn more about them both, in practice, by engaging in social interaction. Through interaction, we potentially change the outer world and ourselves.

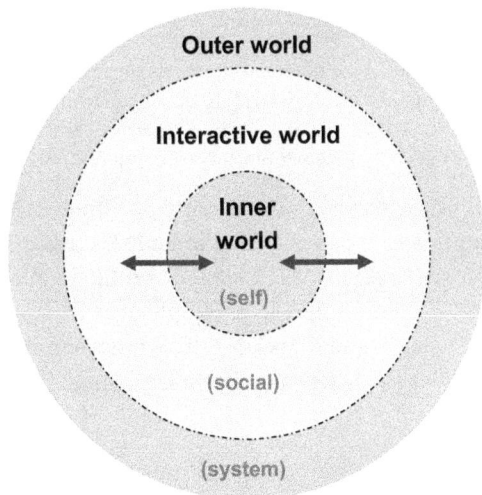

Figure 9.1: Inside-out, outside-in approach to developing leadership.

https://doi.org/10.1515/9783110713343-009

The interactive world in Figure 9.1 is the site of *both* leadership (how we bring our self into the social world) *and* leadership development (how we bring the social world into our self). It is a rich space for learning and change (represented by double headed arrows).

This chapter will help you to explore two key questions:

1. How do I consciously bring my inner self to engage with real-world complexity?
2. How do I develop complexity in myself to better match the real-world complexity?

We will begin by considering why use of self is important and what it really means. Next, we will take a stand on ethical practice before considering the courage required for leadership in complexity and change. We will then explore deepening skilful leadership practice as we grow our capacity to take on more complexity. We will finish by talking about power and considering how we might step into our power to bring leadership *in* complexity and continuous change into mainstream leadership practice.

You are the instrument

Use of self – why it is important

Since we are the main instrument for leadership – not the tools and trappings we use – then we need to understand and use ourselves effectively. There is a body of work around 'use of self' that we can tap into here. Mee-Yan Cheung-Judge has brought a wide range of thinking together in exploring use of self as an instrument in OD practice (Cheung-Judge, 2012, Cheung-Judge and Jamieson, 2018).

Effective use of self is equally important in leadership practice. In the quote below, I have replaced 'OD practitioners' with leaders:

> To be effective [leaders] need to be able to trust their own inner resources, making discerning judgment in the 'here and now' moment, staying choiceful in deciding how to show up and behave, and what interventions may work better in a particular context to achieve a particular outcome.
> (Cheung-Judge and Jamieson, 2018: 22)

Put simply, use of self is concerned with how we *consciously* bring our inner self into our outer work in the interactive world (see Figure 9.1). Our inner self turns up anyway. It brings values, biases, preferences, insecurities, feelings, and filters into our interactions – whether we are aware of them or not. In a complex world, tiny nuances can have large effects. So, when we talk about 'use of self', what we mean is increasing our awareness, and therefore our scope for making choices, about how our inner self shows up in our outer work.

Understanding yourself

In Part II, we employed the complexity learning cycle of notice-interpret-respond to get to know more about the patterning of outer world. We can also use it here to get to know more about the patterning of our inner world.

Practically that means *noticing* more about the nuances of how we show up and how that affects ourself and others in real-life situations in the interactive world. It involves *interpreting* that perceptual data to understand more about what is serving us and others well, and how we are getting in our own way, or in other people's way. We can use that insight to help us in developing a range of *responses* and in making *choices* about how we deploy our inner cognitive and emotional resources in the interactive world through our bodies.

Use of self is not self-centred. It is concerned with developing self, other and contextual awareness, and how we *apply* our awareness, technical knowledge, and practical skills in the moment (Cheung-Judge and Jamieson, 2018) in the interactive world. This explicit connection between the inner and outer worlds of individuals – "seeing self, other and context interacting" (Cheung-Judge and Jamieson, 2018: 29) – provides a good illustration of the entangled nature of levels in complexity. It is also an invitation to develop objectivity in our subjectivity.

The term 'use of self' is not commonly used in leadership circles. We are more likely to talk in terms of authenticity, for example, being yourself with more skill (Goffee and Jones, 2006); working with emotional intelligence (Goleman, 2009); demonstrating leadership presence and regulating distress (Heifetz and Laurie, 2001); or the broader self-efficacy (Bandura, 1977). I have decided to stick with 'use of self' in a leadership context because it is more multi-faceted and multi-level than some other terms. The multi-dimensional nature of the 'use of self' concept makes it a good match for complexity.

Developing yourself

Importantly, we can consciously hone our use of self by developing lifelong learning habits (Cheung-Judge, 2012). Cheung-Judge and Jamieson's research (2018) extracts key dimensions from the literature to identify nine clusters that comprise use of self (see Table 9.1). These clusters and dimensions provide helpful guiderails that practitioners can use to inform their personal development.

The sample dimensions I have included in Table 9.1 closely relate to the mindset and skillset that we explored in Part II. They highlight how we can employ our perceptual acuity and conceptual dexterity to better understand our inner world as well as the outer world. Some of the language is a little abstract, so I have included practical examples to bring it to life.

Table 9.1: Bringing use of self to life.

Cluster	Sample dimensions	Examples
Cognitive	Perceptual insights of situational dynamics Able to separate data from interpretation	Do notice what is happening (e.g., that person is tapping his/her foot) Do not jump to conclusions (e.g., he/she is frustrated)
Affiliative/ Emotional	Paying attention to emotional reaction (self and others) Able to sense level of safety people need to do the work	Notice what is happening (e.g., I feel tense, he has gone red) Make it okay for people to raise opposing ideas without feeling judged
Courage	Sense of self-agency Courage to put self on the line	Understand the control you have over your own actions Act even when you are not in control
Character	Relationship centric – build good connections with others Have patience to stand still to watch the unfolding of events	Develop trust and two-way respect Do not leap into action. Choosing to wait *is* a response
Skills	Able to work with ambiguity without rushing . . . to pre-mature decision Able to do experiments on the go	Manage your own anxiety, help other people to hold their anxiety Try things and learn from them
Values	Appreciation of diversity In a learning and developmental stance	Bring in marginal voices and views Use interaction to learn and develop
Self-work	Do work to deepen one's sense of awareness of self and others Knowing how to stay choiceful and intentional	Learn what you and others are contributing to situations Avoid automatically reacting to people's behaviour, choose your response
Self-management	Cultivate those habits that will increase the ability of generative thoughts Continue to seek feedback and learning opportunities	Regularly expose yourself to new situations and people Ask people about your impact on them
Continuous growth	Continuous development to increase cognitive, perceptive, affective capacity Track how behaviours/habits impact on others	Broaden and deepen your ability to notice and interpret a range of signals Continually learn about your impact in the interactive world

Source: Sample dimensions extracted from Cheung-Judge and Jamieson (2018), examples added.

One aspect of use of self that we have not talked about so far is the importance of doing 'inner work' to help ourselves in being more effective in our outer work. Inner work includes developing greater self-awareness, being able to separate our own needs from other people's needs, and continuing to work on unresolved issues in our own lives, to help us in staying non-reactive to challenging people and in challenging situations (Cheung-Judge and Jamieson, 2018: 26). In other words, we learn to intentionally bring our self into our work in a wider range of situations.

Taking care of yourself

Using our self as the main instrument for leadership in complexity and change requires a personal investment. There is a greater cognitive and emotional load involved in working in the ways I have outlined. Acting out of habit is less effective in a dynamic world, but it is also less demanding.

The demands of intentionally staying alive to what is happening inside and out, continually adapting and employing oneself in the moment, are not insignificant (Cheung-Judge and Jamieson, 2018). Rule number one for agents in change is "stay alive" (Shepard, 1975). There is no heroism in burn-out or self-sacrifice. If we are the instrument for leadership and other challenging organisational work, then we must commit to self-care (Cheung-Judge, 2012).

Like other instruments, our 'self' requires regular maintenance to stay in good shape, physically, mentally, and emotionally. Practically that means regular time 'off', including planning and making time for reflection to recharge ourselves (Cheung-Judge, 2012). The message from research with practitioners is to do what works for you.[1] That may include physical or creative activities, social connection, reflective or spiritual practice, learning and developing oneself, or simply doing nothing. Whatever you choose, you must commit *time* for self-care (Cheung-Judge and Jamieson, 2018).

Ethical practice

Unintended consequences

Leadership in complexity and change demands attention to ethical practice. When outcomes are uncertain, we cannot guarantee the positive effects of good intentions, so we must find other ways to make 'good' judgements about the right way to proceed.

One of the challenges is that, although we can choose our responses carefully (inputs, if you like), we cannot choose outcomes across an organisational system. Cause and effect get entangled in interaction, so we should expect unintended consequences. Yes, we can plan and schedule projects, and we can manage the manageable aspects of those projects in ways that deliver some intended outcomes. Yet, even intended outcomes may be accompanied by unintended consequences that ripple out from the things people say and do.

A note on unintended consequences

As we saw earlier, unintended consequences may be positive – an emerging opportunity, or an unexpected success – as well as negative. Indeed, they may be both. For example, unexpectedly becoming market leader may generate some unwanted attention from competitors. Helping someone may leave them in a better place and it may also leave you in a better place.

The internet is a good example of how unintended consequences emerge over time. When Tim Berners-Lee enabled the World Wide Web in 1989 he could not have anticipated the numerous positive and negative unintended consequences that are so familiar to us today.

As we saw in Part II, the impossibility of controlling ripple effects does not mean that anything goes. Everything we say and do plays into the dynamic patterning. Unfortunately, the ethical dimension of leadership in change has been neglected by many of those who concern themselves with emergent change (Burnes and By, 2012). If we cannot simply choose outcomes, I would argue that it is even *more* important to take an ethical stance in how we work.

Taking an ethical stance

We have lots of choices open to us. We can choose the ways we work with people, how we listen, how we empathise, how we treat others with respect, how we bring in marginalised voices, and so on. Our choices here affect the quality of the experience of working together. The benefits are embedded in the experience and are not contingent on specific outcomes. As I argued in Chapter 8, humanistic practices have value in their own right.

Ethics are beliefs about what is right or wrong that help us to judge the appropriateness of behaviour (Burnes, 2009b: 360). Values are "intimately connected" with ethics and "provide criteria for judging what is *good* in action" (Stacey, 2012: 31–32, emphasis in original). Deliberately taking an ethical stance by making our values explicit therefore offers us something else to use in informing our responses in complexity and change.

Being clear about the values we are using to judge the good in our responses is important. It enables us to scrutinise our decisions and actions through critical reflection. Being clear about our values also allows us to revisit and revise our values to take on more situational nuances as we learn in complexity and change. (This is complexity thinking in practice.) If we are clear about our values with other people, we can hold our decisions and actions open to wider scrutiny from diverse perspectives, just as we did with our interpretations in Chapter 7.

Cult or culture

Talking about our own values sets the tone. It may help us in fostering a culture where people feel safe to voice their values, so we can learn what holds us together, the values we have in common. This is a ground-up process where we collectively notice, interpret, and talk about the emerging patterns of values that are arising between us. Like the complexity learning cycle, it is an ongoing process, not a one-off exercise.

Importantly, we can also make it safe for people to express differences. As we saw in Part II, having people who think differently helps us to complexify our responses. This is rather different to conventional wisdom about people aligning behind organisational values. Take alignment far enough and the organisation's espoused values may become cultish (Stacey, 2012).

Just think for a moment about the idea of 'living the organisation's values'. One way of understanding this is as an invitation to explore the diverse ways in which those values are expressed, as I proposed above. Another way of understanding the idea of 'living the organisation's values' is that individuals are expected to suppress or modify their own values at work to live and perpetuate the given values of the organisation (as if 'the organisation' is a special person). The latter is cultish, as Stacey (2012) describes it. It is the shadow side[2] of strong organisational values.

Open to questioning

The issue here is not whether having written values is good or bad. The problem comes when written organisational values become idealised so they cannot be questioned, challenged, or modified. When something becomes undiscussable in that way, it effectively becomes unchangeable, so it holds us in familiar patterns of action. We create norms that resist change.

We may do this inadvertently, and with positive intent. Strong charitable or brand values may do a useful job in helping to focus collective attention and energy. Yet they may also be used to create in-groups that work as cliques and serve to stifle questions and dissenting voices (e.g., those deemed not to be 'on message').

While holding tightly onto espoused values may feel comforting, a dynamic world demands more adaptability, and a complex world demands greater complexity. We must learn and adapt, for example, through probing the boundaries of the values in practice and using that learning to develop a more nuanced understanding, revising them when necessary. Rather than stifling questions about values and norms in our patterns of action, we must actively encourage them.

Undiscussability is not just about values. It relates to all kinds of norms and ways of groupthink that shape the patterning of behaviour in organisational life (Argyris, 1980), such as the constant push for change mentioned earlier ("the cult of change" Hodgson, 2011). It is a way of acting that hides troublesome problems beneath "layers of issues that [are] undiscussable, and their undiscussability [is also] undiscussable" (Argyris, 1980: 205).

Courageous practice

Discussing undiscussables

Discussing undiscussables takes courage. Speaking out means going against entrenched group norms of behaviour. It is a challenge to group cohesion and may surface conflict that has remained dormant. It is socially risky behaviour, even if you are in charge.

We need to muster our courage to surface difficult issues that are hidden beneath undiscussables (examples in Box 9.2) because they influence the dynamic patterning. We see this when they erupt under pressure. Toegel and Barsoux (2019) suggest starting by tackling the things we think but do not say, by engaging in straight talk, rather than the more adversarial fight talk. Developing your use of self will help you in judging when and how to do this.

Hidden problems

Emerging problems become buried in all the things we do not say in formal meetings. These include:
- things we think but don't say (e.g., nodding to proposals without raising our objections)
- things we say but don't mean (e.g., saying yes and just going through the motions)
- things we feel but can't name (e.g., frustrations with other team members)
- things we do but don't realize (e.g., excessive dependency on the team leader)

Source: Toegel and Barsoux, interviewed in Sterling (2019: 13)

If you have power and influence in a group, then you can use it to manage the stage (as we discussed in Chapter 8). You can create a safe container for people to speak up. You can actively encourage dissent and recognise people for raising difficult issues. Regularly engaging in these kinds of conversations sets the tone and helps to normalise them, so it gradually becomes OK to voice more difficult issues and to face them together.

Acting into uncertainty

As Figure 9.1 illustrated, neither our inner world, nor the outer world are fully knowable. The interactive world is a space of both knowing and not knowing. We must act without being certain of the effects of our actions and knowing that we cannot step back into the world as it was before because dynamic patterning is a one-way street.

Acting into uncertainty is like letting go of the known without being able to grasp onto what will be. Bridges (2003) likens this psychological transition to swinging through the air from one trapeze to another. The trapeze metaphor is useful (and slightly terrifying) because it brings movement back into change. It is also a useful reminder about commitment. You cannot be half-hearted about flying through the air on a trapeze. You must develop the courage to fully commit to it.

We must carry on creatively (Stacey and Mowles, 2016) by continuing to take the next step into the emerging future and encouraging others to do the same (Rodgers, 2021). It sounds easy. Yet, if those around and above you in the organisational hierarchy are still talking and acting as if they can control what will happen, it takes courage to dance to a different tune (see Box 9.1).

Box 9.1 It feels like jelly

James, an experienced OD manager, wanted to have a chat about a large work change. "[It] feels like a massive jelly", he explained. James admitted that he was struggling "to put it into order" as people expected him to do.

Well done, I reassured him, you are in the right space! Jelly is a brilliant metaphor for complex change. Jelly acts like a solid *and* a liquid. It holds its shape and changes its shape at the same time. But, if you are working with jelly, 'putting it in order' is a rather strange thing to want to do.

James knew what he needed to do. With a bit of encouragement, he developed the courage to do it.

When we do not get the desired results, which will happen from time to time, it takes courage to keep on keeping on. It is not that traditional ways deliver better results. They do not. But they do provide layers of managerial talk and prescriptive actions that make us feel better about not knowing (Stacey, 2012). We can always blame the tools or blame the consultants. Here we are employing tools, models, and consultants to help us in thinking for ourselves as we act into uncertainty. It is much harder to hide. Essentially, we go into the leadership arena naked.[3]

Holding doubt

When I hear someone declare 'I have no doubt in my mind', I often think, what a lack of imagination! I realise it is the kind of certainty that people often want to hear in uncertainty. When I talk about courage, I am talking about inner courage, not outer bravado. That inner courage means embracing doubt. As Kahneman (2012: 80) explains:

> Conscious doubt is not in the repertoire of System 1 [fast thinking]; it requires maintaining incompatible interpretations in mind at the same time, which demands mental effort. Uncertainty and doubt are the domain of System 2 [slow thinking].

Doubt, here, is about maintaining multiple and conflicting possibilities at the same time (Kahneman, 2012). It is central to the complexity thinking that we explored in Part II. Courage comes into play because we learn to hold doubt, not to suppress it or to let it stop us, while continuing to act into uncertainty. Box 9.2 considers some practical ways to hold doubt open. Doing that with conviction requires courageous humility, rather than the bluster of cloaking our actions in the rhetoric of certainty.

Box 9.2 Holding doubt

During an away-day session, the digital team in a large UK government department decided to introduce some practical tools to help themselves embrace doubt in relation to their change plans.

They bravely decided to challenge the cult of change by brainstorming ten good reasons not to do each change project. They also introduced a premortem into the planning phase for each change project that got through that process.

In a premortem, those involved imagine themselves in the future faced with the disappointing scenario that the change has been a disaster. Then they creatively generate plausible reasons for the failure, first individually, then as a group. The aim is to use that thinking to adapt and strengthen the change approach.[4]

Premortems help people to avoid being over optimistic about their change plans and overconfident in their decisions (Kahneman, 2012). Additionally, the "prospective hindsight" generated sensitises team members to pick up early signs of emerging issues once the project is underway (Klein, 2007).

Courageous conversations

When I talk about having courageous conversations, I am referring to bringing this inner courage into the outside world. When someone in charge says, 'I have no doubt in my mind that this is the right way to go', the implicit invitation is 'trust me'. Trust me because of who I am, or the position I hold, or my body of expertise, and so on. They are taking on the role of heroic leader and expecting you to blindly follow, without thinking for yourself.

As I explained in Chapter 8, this is the opposite to what is needed in complexity and change. We should encourage people to think for themselves to help in developing more nuanced (i.e., complex) responses in complexity. This is a more adult-to-adult way of working, which invites those involved to share in absorbing the complexity. Compare it to the more parent-to-child approach of the would-be hero who glosses over the complexity of doubt to make people feel better in that moment.

You may recognise my reference to transactional analysis (TA) in this parent/adult/child language (Berne, 1961). In TA, the parent and child ways of acting import behaviours, thoughts, and feelings from past experience. In contrast, acting as an adult is focused in the present: "behaviour, thoughts and feelings . . . are direct responses to the here-and-now" (Joines and Stewart, 1987: 12), which is what we are trying to do in order to learn what is changing and to choose our responses.

A more courageous way to approach this conversation would be to share why you think this is the right way to go, given what is currently known. You could acknowledge the uncertainty (what is not known) and make it clear that you will learn and adapt the approach as you go. You would hold the doubt while speaking with conviction. If it is a conversation, rather a broadcast, you might create space for people to work through what it means – including expressing dissent – and work through some of the nuances relating to how they can make it work in their local contexts.

Skilful practice

Broadening and deepening

Skilful leadership practice in complexity and change does not rely on special tricks. What we are aiming for is to complexify our practice to better match the external complexity demands (requisite complexity). That means evolving our behaviour and developing our skills to enhance the quality of our engagement in the interactive world (Figure 9.1). I encourage you to think in terms of deliberately *broadening* and *deepening* your range to absorb complexity into your leadership practice.

It may help to think of yourself as a neo-generalist:

> Encompassing rather than rejecting, the neo-generalist is both specialist and generalist; a restless multidisciplinarian, who is forever learning. (Mikkelsen and Martin, 2016)

In the rest of this section we will explore how we might develop more skilful practice by broadening and deepening our use of self, our practical judgement and our complexity of mind.

Advancing use of self

Skilful use of self means being *intentional* in how we use our inner resources in the interactive world. It requires conscious competence. This involves "the conscious use of one's whole being in the intentional execution of one's role" (Jamieson et al., 2010: 5) and "staying choiceful in deciding how to show up and behave" (Cheung-Judge and Jamieson, 2018: 22).

The aim is to deepen first, for example, by developing deeper self-awareness, so that we understand where our actions, preferences and biases come from. We also seek to deepen other-awareness by developing a more acute social sensitivity and an enhanced ability to read the environment in the moment (Cheung-Judge and Jamieson, 2018).

We want to deepen and broaden our noticing aperture and to illuminate any blind spots. We can apply the vital signs of change to help with this noticing. The vital signs tool (from Chapter 6) invites you to pay attention to affective, cognitive, and behavioural responses in yourself and in your immediate interactions with others (see Box 9.3).

Box 9.3 Applying the vital signs of change

Events: What is going on for you that is notable? What things or happenings have triggered something in you? What have you said or done that has created a reaction in others?

Relations: How engaged and involved are you with what is going on right now? How is that changing in the moment? How is the quality of relations between yourself and others changing?

Attention: Where is your attention? How is your attention balanced between self, other and context? How is that balance changing? What is absorbing your attention? What is being neglected?

Emotions: How are you feeling in your body? How are your bodily sensations changing? For example, feeling more relaxed, sensing a tightness in your jaw, or in your gut, feeling more energised or more tired.

In using yourself as an instrument, the aim is to work live, using reflection in action, that is, noticing, then interpreting and choosing your best response in the moment. If you are new to these ideas, try giving yourself some reflection space immediately after a meeting and use the questions above to bring your unconscious noticings into your conscious mind.

The challenge then is to enlarge our capacity by holding all those strands simultaneously; being aware of what is going for us, for others, and in the wider context, and being sensitive to interactions across those entangled domains. We deliberately broaden our action choices so that we may "act in different ways as appropriate to the situation" by flexing across a wide range of action (Cheung-Judge and Jamieson, 2018: 22).

Enhancing practical judgement

In complexity and continuous change, the situations we find ourselves in are always unique, always changing. We cannot simply follow recipes. So the art of leadership is enacting practical judgement in the unique situations we find ourselves in, amidst the continuous flow of activities (Stacey, 2012, Shotter and Tsoukas, 2014a).

We touched on practical judgement in Part II. While you may not have heard the term before that, practical judgement is not new. Indeed, its origins are extremely old.[5] We use practical judgement every day in negotiating the complexities of life, whether we are aware of it or not. So, the good news is that we are not starting from scratch.

Developing more skilful practice in the interactive world (see Figure 9.1) means broadening and deepening how we apply our practical judgement. We therefore need to understand more about what practical judgement means, so that we can *consciously* engage it in developing our leadership practice (rather like 'use of self' earlier). Let us start with a definition:

> Practical judgment is the experience-based ability to notice *more* of what is going on and intuit what is most important about a situation. It is the ability to cope with ambiguity and uncertainty, as well as the anxiety it generates. (Stacey, 2012: 108, emphasis added)

This should be familiar territory now because I have been talking about it throughout Part II. Practical judgement is hard to articulate and is exercised in ways that cannot easily be generalised (Stacey, 2012: 108). This complexity within practical judgement makes it a good match for outer-world complexity, but it also makes it difficult for managers to get to grips with.

I suspect that the difficulty in articulating practical judgement is one reason why it is often undervalued. Technical knowledge is so much easier to define because it has clear boundaries. Practical knowledge is more difficult because it crosses boundaries. It is found in the connections.

Some of the practical ideas that practical judgement has to offer often get lost in larger philosophical debates. Table 9.2 offers some much-needed clarity by using the complexity learning cycle from Part II to contextualise some useful ideas on what managers are actually doing. My aim is to bring practical judgement to life by incorporating some specifics, so Table 9.2 is rather lengthy. It is not an attempt to pin practical judgement down, but to stimulate your own thinking. In essence, what managers are doing here is noticing more of the patterns that they and others are co-creating, expressing those patterns, and learning through participation, particularly in conversation with others.

Table 9.2: Bringing practical judgement to life.

Focus	What managers are doing	Examples
Noticing	Developing awareness of dynamic patterning	– emerging themes in conversation – group, organisational, and societal patterns
	Paying attention to clues about deeper patterns	– power relations – ideologies that they and others are using to make choices – what is going on in the margins – clues about what people are not revealing (hidden transcripts) – anxiety and how it is defended against – the roles they play in organisational life
	Noticing what is changing in real time	– being perceptually alert to contextual uniqueness (Shotter and Tsoukas, 2014a) – sensing within situations (Shotter and Tsoukas, 2014b)

Table 9.2 (continued)

Focus	What managers are doing	Examples
Interpreting	Recognising patterns	– patterns of interaction that they and other people are creating – patterns of inclusion and exclusion – distinguishing between similarities with other circumstances and unique differences
	Articulating patterns	– expressing themes emerging in the local context – writing short narratives of troubling events to stimulate further enquiry
	Exploring alternative meanings	– imaginatively moving around in the situation at hand (Shotter and Tsoukas, 2014a) – bringing forth past experience to the present context (Shotter and Tsoukas, 2014a)
Responding	Getting actively involved	– engaging, with others, in the hurly-burly of organisational life – engaging in organisational politics in effective and persuasive ways – participating in conversation – learning by doing – improvising spontaneously – being exposed to a variety of experiences (Shotter and Tsoukas, 2014b: 392)
	Deepening conversation	– asking questions not jumping to solutions – grounding conversation in the present – widening and deepening communication to produce greater meaning
	Creating conversational spaces	– consciously creating opportunities for groups of colleagues to open up conversation – fostering the emergence of new knowledge by removing the blockages to free-flowing, flexible conversation – choosing when to temporarily close conversation to act
	Deepening reflection	– engaging in reflexive enquiry about (1) what they and others are doing and (2) why they are doing it the way they are – encouraging reflexive enquiry with groups of colleagues
	Engaging oneself	– coping with ambiguity, uncertainty, and the anxiety it creates – acting with courage and endurance in uncertainty (Shotter and Tsoukas, 2014a) – acting with emotional attunement (Shotter and Tsoukas, 2014a) – staying emotionally involved (Shotter and Tsoukas, 2014b)

Source: Examples extracted from Stacey (2012: 107–121), additions from Shotter and Tsoukas (2014a, 2014b).

Broadening and deepening practical judgement is an iterative process whereby "the capacity for practical judgment in some activity is gradually developed through actually performing the activity in question" (Stacey, 2012: 108). Therefore, deepening your sensitivity to picking up what is going on in the margins is acquired by doing that activity. The core skill for practical judgement is reflexive enquiry (Stacey, 2012, Cunliffe, 2003). It demands a learning orientation to leadership in complexity and change.

Developing complexity of mind

Engaging with the real-life complexity of the outer world (see Figure 9.1) demands a greater complexity of mind (Kegan, 1994, Kegan and Lahey, 2009, Garvey Berger, 2011). The good news is that adult development theory shows we can change our minds (Kegan, 1982). We can develop mental complexity.

Building on Kegan's (1982, 1994) work, Jennifer Garvey Berger (2011) identifies four forms of mind: self-sovereign, socialised, self-authoring, and self-transforming. She explains that, over time, we can develop an ever-increasing view of the world that enables us to grow our complexity of mind (Garvey Berger, 2019).

Developing complexity of mind

As we develop complexity of mind, the *self-sovereign* mind of our early adult lives, where other people's perspectives are unachievable (us or them), develops into a more *socialised* form of mind where we breathe in the perspectives of those around us. At that stage, our sense of self is imported without editing. As we develop a more *self-authored* form of mind, we become objects of our own reflection, so we can make more choices about our self and we write our own story. Developing a self-transforming form of mind entails holding our own and others' perspectives simultaneously (us and them).

Source: Garvey Berger (2018)[6]

Leadership development often focuses on a "self-authoring form of mind", for example, how to be our best self and how to bring that best self into leadership. In complexity, we are aiming to go one stage further by developing a "self-transforming form of mind" (Garvey Berger, 2011). Holding multiple perspectives simultaneously is like "being able to see a world with lots of greys and being able to operate in that world anyway"(Garvey Berger, 2018). It enables us to meet adaptive challenges adaptively, rather than technically (Kegan and Lahey, 2009: 31).

The question then, is how do we develop our complexity of mind? How do we ready ourselves to engage with the adaptive challenges of a complex world? Like 'use of self' and 'practical judgement', 'complexity of mind' is something we must cultivate from life experience. Learning to do that means overcoming our internal immunity to change (Kegan and Lahey, 2009) so that we learn from other people and from experience. Being too certain closes us off to learning.

Adopting a learning orientation means being curious and open to new experiences. Practically, it involves exposing oneself to new ideas, engaging with different people, seeking out different perspectives. The aim is to take in more of the world to help ourselves in developing a larger view that encompasses more diversity and therefore complexity. It is another way in which we can absorb complexity.

Yet early career success based on technical abilities can make it harder to change our minds. Letting go of the kind of thinking that made you successful in the past, especially if it has enabled you to climb the hierarchy, demands courage and a willingness to engage with your own anxiety. Involving others in our development can help us to get out of our own way. For example, engaging in coaching (Garvey Berger and Fitzgerald, 2002), mentoring, or more therapeutic processes (Cheung-Judge and Jamieson, 2018) may help us to take a wider perspective that encompasses me, you and us.

Stepping into our power

Complexity science offers a way of understanding the world. It explains some of the things that other theories and views leave out, such as constant motion, emergent novelty, and perpetual uncertainty. But it remains neutral on what we should do.

Despite growing interest in and understanding of complexity over the past 20 years, it remains an alternative view. However, leadership *in* complexity and change is too important to remain in the margins. We must get these ideas into the mainstream of leadership thinking and practice. That means stepping into our power.

We have not yet talked explicitly about our own power yet. We need to do so now because power is embedded in complexity. As Stacey puts it, "*power* is an aspect of *every act of human relating*" and it is rarely equal (Stacey, 2012: 28, emphasis in original). Power can be an emotive topic so in a leadership context, we often prefer to talk about influence. But we must be willing to acknowledge power dynamics and to step into our own power if we want to empower others (see Box 9.4).

> **Box 9.4 Stepping into power**
> Maggie is a specialist nurse practitioner in the National Health Service. She cares deeply about her patients and her colleagues. When she joined a leadership development programme I was running, Maggie felt frustrated and conflicted. The behaviours of some powerful colleagues were making it a difficult working environment and nurses were struggling to deliver the best possible patient care.
> Maggie wanted to change things but did not think she could. She was not the most senior person in the hierarchy, so did not have the formal power of authority. While very capable, she was not the most experienced person, so did not have the same power of expertise as others. Maggie is quiet and gentle, so she was concerned that she did not have the charismatic power of an extravert or forceful personality.

But one of Maggie's superpowers is her integrity. She returned to work determined to make a difference because it was the right thing to do. And she did.

Over the next weeks and months, Maggie began to step into her own power in her own way. Through many conversations, she gently raised some of the difficult issues and made it her business to get people talking in more respectful ways. She helped change the tone of the team and effectively brought people together to focus on delivering the best possible patient care.

Bringing complexity science into leadership is *not* a neutral position. It is a challenge to managerial orthodoxy. Those who have achieved personal success and climbed the hierarchies based on individualistic world views may feel they have a lot to lose. I say that we all have a lot to gain by engaging more fully with the complex challenges we face.

I acknowledge that this is a political statement. I understand that any change has the potential to upset the delicate power balances, and I recognise that those with vested interests may resist change. As we have learned to our cost, revolutions may be met with bloody backlashes. So, I am not advocating an uprising, or an overthrow of all that has come before. What I am suggesting is a deliberate expansion of leadership thinking and practice to incorporate more real-world complexity.

I invite you to join me in this evolution by spreading the thinking and practices of leadership *in* complexity and continuous change. Empower yourself to make small changes to incorporate these ideas into your normal everyday practice. Step into your own power by talking about complexity and continuous change and legitimising these ideas with others. Acknowledge everyday complexity in your everyday conversations. Make it OK to talk about. Wield your power and influence with skill to empower others to engage with complexity and change. Manage the stage and find ways to bring people in from the margins.

Let us empower ourselves and others to bring leadership *in* complexity and change into the mainstream of thinking and practice. If not now, when?

Key insights
- We use ourselves as the main instrument for leadership in complexity and change
- Being skilful in using our 'self' requires an ongoing commitment to self-work and to self-care
- Taking an ethical stance has value because it helps us judge what is good in action
- Being clear about our values helps us hold actions open to scrutiny and to modify our values
- Discussing undiscussables, acting into uncertainty and holding doubt demand inner courage
- Skilful practice requires deeper use of self, practical judgement and greater complexity of mind
- Engaging with complexity, talking about it, using our power to empower others will help us to expand mainstream leadership thinking and practice to incorporate more real-world complexity

being skilful **ethical stance**
inner courage **complexity of mind**
it's personal
self care **values** practical judgement
deeper use of self
power to empower

Noticing and noting

You have reached the end of this book, so I hope you are feeling energised and better equipped to engage with the dynamic patterning of the working world.

As you know, there are no end points in complexity and continuous changing, only loops. So, take a few minutes to loop back and revisit the key insights from each chapter to deepen your learning.

Now reflect on the following questions:
– What has most surprised or intrigued you?
– What new questions can you ask?
– What is now possible?
– What have you learned about yourself?

Notes

1 You can download key articles and the 2018 Use of Self research report from Quality-Equality: https://www.quality-equality.com/publications (accessed 08/01/21).
2 The shadow side comes from Jungian psychology, reflecting unconscious aspects of our personality that we may not want to admit to having.
3 This references a Keynote session entitled 'Naked consulting' by Bill Critchley, formerly of Ashridge Business School, at The Henley Forum Conference 06/03/2019.
4 For more on how to run a project premortem see https://hbr.org/2007/09/performing-a-project-premortem (accessed 07/01/2021).
5 The roots of practical judgement come from ancient Greek philosophy and Aristotle's ideas about a practical form of knowing (phronesis).
6 This useful podcast with Jennifer Garvey Berger is available on the Farnham Street blog https://fs.blog/knowledge-project/jennifer-garvey-berger/ (accessed 12/01/2021).

Glossary

Terms from complexity science in **bold**. Additional terms introduced in this book in ***bold italics***.

adaptive agent: The term given to the interacting elements in a complex adaptive system. In organisational systems, the adaptive agents are human beings. In a murmuration, the adaptive agents are starlings.

chaos theory: This branch of complexity science comes from mathematics and uses non-linear equations to model complex behaviour.

co-evolution: From biology, co-evolution highlights mutual dependence, specifically how two or more species reciprocally affect one another's evolution.

complex system: In complex systems, the many diverse, interacting elements are entangled, that is, they are interdependent.

complex adaptive systems (CAS): A CAS comprises many interacting elements, referred to as agents. As they interact, each agent adapts and responds to some other agents within the overall population; so, what each agent can do is shaped and affected by what other agents do. The behaviour of the whole system is dynamic and unpredictable because it is not a simple sum of the parts, that is, it arises non-linearly from the continuous iteration of interactions between interdependent adaptive agents.

    CAS takes a micro-level perspective on understanding complex and adaptive system behaviour. Its roots come from computer science and the work of John Holland (1995) and others at the Santa Fe Institute https://www.santafe.edu/ (accessed 06/02/21).

complex responsive processes (CRP): Drawing from CAS, Stacey's (2001) complex responsive processes of relating offers a theory of complexity that is particular to the human domain. CRP is a process view that sees iterative micro interactions between interdependent people as the source of both continuity and novelty. Importantly, the individual and social domains are entangled in interaction; human agency therefore resides in the *relationships* between people.

(The) Complexity Conundrum: My explanation of VUCA: Volatility + Complexity = Uncertainty + Ambiguity.

complexity learning cycle: A continuous cycle of noticing – interpreting – responding into the dynamic patterning of organisational life that enables learning informed leadership.

complicatedness: A term coined to describe the pervasive bureaucracy that often arises in organisational life.

deterministic: The behaviour of an entity over time can be understood from the initial conditions and subsequent external events.

dissipative structures: This branch of complexity science comes from thermodynamics, notably Ilya Prigogine's work (Prigogine and Stengers, 1984).

dynamic patterning: My term to describe the continuous changing of complex systems. It reminds us that organisational life is in constant motion; an ongoing process without beginning or end. The

https://doi.org/10.1515/9783110713343-010

patterning shapes and is shaped by interactions between people. Paying attention to the patterning offers clues about what is emerging in the here and now.

emergence: In emergence, something that was not there before comes into existence. In complexity science, emergence commonly refers to a qualitative change arising across a system which fundamentally changes the whole. Emergence is irreversible and unpredictable from the parts.

feedback loops: Outputs feed back into inputs. Feedback loops create non-linearity in a system.

far from equilibrium: When a thermodynamic system is pushed to a far-from-equilibrium state by external influences, it may create new structures.

Gaussian distribution: A Gaussian distribution (bell curve) assumes that data points are normally distributed around a stable mean.

heterogeneity: Complexity science assumes that individual agents are all different (heterogeneous), whereas the 'rational agent' of traditional economic theory assumes they are all the same (homogeneous).

increasing returns: That which is ahead tends to get further ahead through positive feedback.

interdependence: This highlights the relationship between the parts in a complex system and reminds us that they are not independent of one another. Entities and activities may be connected in non-linear ways whereby they are mutually dependent on one another (e.g., a social system).

irreducible: Something that only works as a whole, so it cannot be understood in terms of its parts. Examples include mayonnaise and a rainforest.

learning informed leadership: Using the complexity learning cycle to help inform our responses into the dynamic patterning; thus avoiding the automatic stimulus-response reaction of habit.

linear: The relationship between two factors is proportional, that is, it can be represented as a straight line. Linearity enables outputs (effects) to be described and predicted from inputs and interactions (causes).

local interaction: This refers to direct interaction between adaptive agents. Interaction is local because each agent only interacts directly with a subset of the overall population of agents. In a murmuration, each starling directly interacts with others in their immediate physical vicinity. In the working world, each individual directly interacts with the people they work with, albeit they may be geographically dispersed.

macro-level: In CAS, the macro-level relates to a collective of adaptive agents, for example, a brain, a team, a flock, an organisational system. When I talk about the macro-level, I am generally referring to human collectives.

mental aperture: A metaphor to describe varying degrees of open-mindedness related to engaging with real-world complexity.

micro-diversity: Small differences between adaptive agents of a particular type, for example, people. Micro-diversity matters in complex systems because it provides necessary conditions for macro-level adaptation in changing conditions.

micro-level: In CAS, the micro-level relates to the adaptive agents which comprise a complex adaptive system, for example, interacting neurons in a brain, interacting birds in a flock, interacting people in an organisational system. When I talk about the micro-level, I am generally referring to interacting people.

mutual causation: Recursive feedback loops create a causal relationship between the whole (system) and the parts (adaptive agents), as well as between the parts and the whole.

negative feedback: Negative feedback loops reduce the effect of inputs so that the system maintains a familiar pattern. This is also known as dampening or balancing feedback.

non-linear: Nonlinearity means that inputs are not neatly proportional to outputs. Large causes may have small effects, and vice versa.

Pareto distribution: A Pareto distribution is a skewed distribution that is characterised by a long, fat tail whereby much of the data is in the tail. It illustrates that many things are not distributed evenly around a stable mean.

path dependence: What emerges is sensitive to the precise details of the path traced.

perturbations: Outside influences that provoke a system to deviate from its regular state or path.

positive feedback: Positive feedback loops increase the effect of inputs so that the system is pushed away from familiar patterns of continuity, and towards patterns of novelty or change. This is also known as amplifying or reinforcing feedback.

power law: Plotted on a log-log scale, a power law demonstrates a linear relationship between variables, where one varies as a power of another.

reducible: A reducible system can be simplified and understood through its parts, for example, a clock or a sports car.

requisite complexity: A system's internal complexity must match the external complexity it confronts if it is to be sufficiently adaptive (Boisot and McKelvey, 2011a).

resilience: The ability to adapt to changing circumstances. Micro-level adaptations may produce a balance of negative feedback to help stay on course in changing conditions, or they may produce a balance of positive feedback to change the course (self-organisation).

self-organisation: In complex systems, the state of organisation arises spontaneously from iterative processes of local interaction. The system organises itself. Organisation is also referred to as 'order' or 'coherence'. I call it 'pattern'.

simple rules: Agent-based simulations have demonstrated how simple rules set by a programmer can create complex behaviour across the system.

small data: Qualitative behavioural data that is plentiful and freely available; a source of leading indicators about what is changing in the dynamic patterning of organisational life.

system: A system comprises multiple, interdependent elements. In a simple, or a complicated system, the elements that comprise that system interact linearly (see linear), so system level outcomes are knowable, even if they are not known. In a complex system, the elements that comprise that system interact non-linearly (see non-linear), so system level outcomes are unknowable.

tipping point: The point at which a system tips from one pattern of behaviour to another. Tipping points may only be evident with hindsight.

variable: Variables are elements, or parts of a system, that are liable to vary or change. Examples in an organisational context include physical and human resources.

vital signs of change: Affective, cognitive, and behavioural domains of emerging change. The four vital signs are the (1) patterning of events; (2) patterning of relations; (3) patterning of attention; and (4) patterning of emotion.

References

Allen, P. M. 2001. A complex systems approach to learning in adaptive networks. *International Journal of Innovation Management*, 5, 149.

Allen, P. M. 2010. What is the science of complexity? Knowledge of the limits to knowledge. *In:* Tait, A. & Richardson, K. A. (eds.), *Complexity and knowledge management: Understanding the role of knowledge in the management of social networks*. Charlotte, NC: Information Age Publishing.

Allen, P. M. 2014. Evolution: Complexity, uncertainty and innovation. *Journal of Evolutionary Economics*, 24, 265–289.

Allen, P. M. & Boulton, J. 2011. Complexity and limits to knowledge: The importance of uncertainty. *In:* Allen, P., Maguire, S. & McKelvey, B. (eds.), *The SAGE handbook of complexity and management*. London: SAGE Publications Ltd.

Andriani, P. & McKelvey, B. 2007. Beyond Gaussian averages: Redirecting international business and management research toward extreme events and power laws. *Journal of International Business Studies*, 38, 1212–1230.

Arden, P. 2006. *Whatever you think think the opposite*. London, Penguin.

Arena, M. & Uhl-Bien, M. 2016. Complexity leadership theory: Shifting from human capital to social capital. *People & Strategy*, 39, 22–27.

Argyris, C. 1977. Double loop learning in organizations. *Harvard Business Review*, 55, 115–125.

Argyris, C. 1980. Making the undiscussable and its undiscussability discussable. *Public Administration Review*, 40, 205–213.

Argyris, C. 2010. *Organizational traps: Leadership, culture, organizational design*. Oxford: Oxford University Press.

Argyris, C. & Schön, D. A. 1974. *Theory in practice: Increasing professional effectiveness*. Oxford: Jossey-Bass.

Arthur, W. B. 1996. Increasing returns and the new world of business. *Harvard Business Review*, 74, 100–109.

Ashkanasy, N. M., Humphrey, R. H. & Huy, Q. N. 2017. Integrating emotions and affect in theories of management. *Academy of Management Review*, 42, 175–189.

Bak, P. 1996. *How nature works: The science of self-organized criticality*. New York: Copernicus.

Balogun, J., Bartunek, J. M. & Do, B. 2015a. Senior managers' sensemaking and responses to strategic change. *Organization Science*, 26, 960–979.

Balogun, J., Hope Hailey, V. & Gustafsson, S. 2015b. *Exploring strategic change 4th ed*. London: Pearson Education Limited.

Balogun, J. & Johnson, G. 2005. From intended strategies to unintended outcomes: The impact of change recipient sensemaking. *Organization Studies*, 26, 1573–1601.

Bandura, A. 1977. Self-efficacy: Toward a unifying theory of behavioral change. *Psychological Review*, 84, 191–215.

Bandura, A. 2000. Exercise of human agency through collective efficacy. *Current Directions in Psychological Science*, 9, 75–78.

Barsade, S. G. 2002. The ripple effect: Emotional contagion and its influence on group behavior. *Administrative Science Quarterly*, 47, 644–675.

Bateson, G. 1972/2000. *Steps to an ecology of mind*. Chicago: The University of Chicago Press.

Bateson, G. 1979. *Mind and nature: A necessary unity*. New York: Dutton.

Bazerman, M. 2014. *The power of noticing: What the best leaders see*. New York: Simon & Schuster.

Beck, T. E. & Plowman, D. A. 2009. Experiencing rare and unusual events richly: The role of middle managers in animating and guiding organizational interpretation. *Organization Science*, 20, 909–924.

https://doi.org/10.1515/9783110713343-011

Bennett, N. & Lemoine, G. J. 2014. What VUCA really means for you. *Harvard Business Review*, 92, 27–27.

Berger, P. L. & Luckmann, T. 1969. *The social construction of reality: A treatise in the sociology of knowledge*. London: Allen Lane, The Penguin Press.

Berne, E. 1961. *Transactional analysis in psychotherapy: A systematic individual and social psychiatry*. London: Souvenir Press.

Birkinshaw, J., Bessant, J. & Delbridge, R. 2007. Finding, forming, and performing: Creating networks for discontinuous innovation. *California Management Review*, 49, 67–84.

Björneborn, L. 2020. Adjacent possible. *The Palgrave encyclopedia of the possible*. New York: Springer International Publishing.

Boal, K. B. & Schultz, P. L. 2007. Storytelling, time, and evolution: The role of strategic leadership in complex adaptive systems. *Leadership Quarterly*, 18, 411–428.

Bohm, D. 1996. *On dialogue*. London: Taylor & Francis.

Boisot, M. & McKelvey, B. 2010. Integrating modernist and postmodernist perspectives on organisations: A complexity science bridge. *Academy of Management Review*, 35, 415–433.

Boisot, M. & McKelvey, B. 2011a. Complexity and organization–environment relations: Revisiting Ashby's law of requisite variety. *In:* Allen, P., Maguire, S. & McKelvey, B. (ed.) *The SAGE handbook of complexity and management*. London: Sage Publications.

Boisot, M. & McKelvey, B. 2011b. Connectivity, extremes, and adaptation: A power-law perspective of organizational effectiveness. *Journal of Management Inquiry*, 20, 119–133.

Boje, D. M. 2008. *Storytelling organizations*. London: SAGE.

Boulton, J. G., Allen, P. M. & Bowman, C. 2015. *Embracing complexity: Strategic perspectives for an age of turbulence*. Oxford: Oxford University Press.

Bouquet, C. & Birkinshaw, J. 2008. Weight versus voice: How foreign subsidiaries gain attention from corporate headquarters. *The Academy of Management Journal*, 51, 577–601.

Bourdieu, P. 1998. *Practical reason: On the theory of action*. Stanford, CA: Stanford University Press.

Box, G. E. P. 1976. Science and statistics. *Journal of the American Statistical Association*, 71, 791–799.

Bradbury, H. & Lichtenstein, B. B. 2000. Relationality in organizational research: Exploring the space between. *Organization Science*, 11, 551–564.

Bridges, W. 2003. *Managing transitions: Making the most of change*. London: Nicholas Brearley Publishing.

Bromley, M. 2011. Working at the interface – pausing to talk. *e-Organisations & People, Winter 2011*, 18, 10–16.

Bruch, H. & Vogel, B. 2011. *Fully charged: How great leaders boost their organization's energy and ignite high performance*. Boston: Harvard Business Review Press.

Burke, W. W. & Litwin, G. H. 1992. A causal model of organizational performance and change. *Journal of Management*, 18, 523–545.

Burnes, B. 2005. Complexity theories and organizational change. *International Journal of Management Reviews*, 7, 73–90.

Burnes, B. 2009a. *Managing change, fifth edition*. Harlow, Essex: Pearson Education.

Burnes, B. 2009b. Reflections: Ethics and organizational change – time for a return to Lewinian values. *Journal of Change Management*, 9, 359–381.

Burnes, B. & By, R. 2012. Leadership and change: The case for greater ethical clarity. *Journal of Business Ethics*, 108, 239–252.

Burnes, B. & Cooke, B. 2012. Review article: The past, present and future of organization development: Taking the long view. *Human Relations*, 65, 1395–1429.

Bushe, G. R. 2011. Appreciative inquiry: Theory and critique. *In:* Boje, D., Burnes, B. & Hassard, J. (ed.) *The Routledge companion to organizational change*. Oxford: Routledge.

Bushe, G. R., Marshak, R. J. & Schein, E. H. 2015. *Dialogic organization development: The theory and practice of transformational change*. Oakland, CA: Berrett-Koehler.

Bushe, G. R. & Storch, J. 2015. Generative image. *In:* Bushe, G. R. & Marshak, R. J. (eds.) *Dialogic organization development: The theory and practice of transformational change*. Oakland, CA: Berrett-Koehler.

Carse, J. 2011. *Finite and infinite games*. New York: Free Press.

Cheung-Judge, M.-Y. 2012. The self as an instrument: A cornerstone for the future of OD. *OD Practitioner*, 44, 42–47.

Cheung-Judge, M.-Y. & Jamieson, D. W. 2018. Providing deeper understanding of the concept of use of self in OD practice. *OD PRACTITIONER*, 50, 22–32.

Chia, R. 2011. Complex thinking: Towards an oblique strategy for dealing with the complex. *In:* Allen, P., Maguire, S. & McKelvey, B. (eds.) *The SAGE handbook of complexity and management*. London: Sage Publications Ltd.

Chiles, T. H., Tuggle, C. S., McMullen, J. S., Bierman, L. & Greening, D. W. 2010. Dynamic creation: Extending the radical Austrian approach to entrepreneurship. *Organization Studies*, 31, 7–46.

Cilliers, P. 2002. Why we cannot know complex things completely. *Emergence*, 4, 77–84.

Cilliers, P. 2005. Complexity, deconstruction and relativism. *Theory, Culture & Society*, 22, 255–267.

Cilliers, P. 2006. On the importance of a certain slowness. *Emergence: Complexity & Organization*, 8, 105–112.

Cohen, M. 1999. Commentary on the Organization Science special issue on complexity. *Organization Science*, 10, 373–376.

Cohen, W. M. & Levinthal, D. A. 1990. Absorptive capacity: A new perspective on learning and innovation. *Administrative Science Quarterly*, 35, 128–152.

Cole, M. S., Bruch, H. & Vogel, B. 2012. Energy at work: A measurement validation and linkage to unit effectiveness. *Journal of Organizational Behavior*, 33, 445–467.

Colville, I., Brown, A. D. & Pye, A. 2012. Simplexity: Sensemaking, organizing and storytelling for our time. *Human Relations*, 65, 5–15.

Cooperrider, D. & Whitney, D. D. 2005. *Appreciative inquiry: A positive revolution in change*. Oakland, CA: Berrett-Koehler.

Cooperrider, D. L. & Srivastva, S. 1987. Appreciative inquiry in organizational life. *In:* Pasmore, W. & Woodman, R. (eds.) *Research in organizational change and development, (vol 1, pp 129–169)*. Greenwich: JAI Press Inc.

Cross, R., Ernst, C. & Pasmore, B. 2013. A bridge too far? How boundary spanning networks drive organizational change and effectiveness. *Organizational Dynamics*, 42, 81–91.

Csikszentmihalyi, M. 2014. *Applications of flow in human development and education: The collected works of Mihaly Csikszentmihalyi*. Netherlands: Springer.

Cunliffe, A. L. 2003. Reflexive inquiry in organizational research: Questions and possibilities. *Human Relations*, 56, 983–1003.

De Caluwe, L. & Vermaak, H. 2004. Change paradigms: An overview. *Organization Development Journal*, 22, 9–18.

Deal, T. E. & Kennedy, A. A. 1982. *Corporate cultures: The rites and rituals of corporate life*. Boston: Addison-Wesley Publishing Company.

Dewees, B. & Minson, J. A. 2018. The right way to use the wisdom of crowds. *Harvard Business Review*, December 2018.

Eoyang, G. 2011. Complexity and the dynamics of organizational change. *In:* Allen, P., Maguire, S. & McKelvey, B. M. (eds.) *The SAGE handbook of complexity and management*. London: Sage Publications Ltd.

Eoyang, G. H. & Holladay, R. J. 2013. *Adaptive action: Leveraging uncertainty in your organization.* Stanford, CA: Stanford University Press.

Fahy, K. M., Easterby-Smith, M. & Lervik, J. E. 2014. The power of spatial and temporal orderings in organizational learning. *Management Learning*, 45, 123–144.

Fleetwood, S. 2005. Ontology in organization and management studies: A critical realist perspective. *Organization*, 12, 197–222.

Galbraith, J. R. 1977. *Organization design*, Boston, Addison-Wesley Publishing Company.

Gamble, P. R. & Blackwell, J. 2001. *Knowledge management: A state of the art guide.* London: Kogan Page.

Garrow, V. & Varney, S. 2011. Learning to swim, learning to fly? A career in organisational development. Brighton: Institute for Employment Studies.

Garrow, V. & Varney, S. 2013. The palace: Perspectives on organisation design. Brighton: Institute for Employment Studies.

Garrow, V., Varney, S. & Lloyd, C. 2009. Fish or bird? Perspectives on organisational development. Brighton: Institute for Employment Studies.

Garvey Berger, J. 2011. *Changing on the job: Developing leaders for a complex world.* Stanford: Stanford University Press.

Garvey Berger, J. 2018. The mental habits of effective leaders *In:* Parrish, S. (ed.) *The Knowledge Project Podcast #43.* Farnham Street.

Garvey Berger, J. 2019. *Unlocking leadership mindtraps: How to thrive in complexity.* Stanford: Stanford University Press.

Garvey Berger, J. & Fitzgerald, C. 2002. Leadership and complexity of mind: The role of executive coaching. *In:* Fitzgerald, C. & Garvey Berger, J. (eds.) *Executive coaching: Practices & perspectives.* Boston: Davies-Black Publishing.

Geertz, C. 1973. *The interpretation of cultures: Selected essays.* New York: Basic Books.

Gioia, D. A. & Chittipeddi, K. 1991. Sensemaking and sensegiving in strategic change initiation. *Strategic Management Journal*, 12, 433–448.

Goffee, R. & Jones, G. 2006. *Why should anyone be led by you?: What it takes to be an authentic leader.* Boston: Harvard Business Review Press.

Goldspink, C. & Kay, R. 2010. Emergence in organizations: The reflexive turn. *Emergence: Complexity & Organization*, 12, 47–63.

Goldstein, J. 2000. Emergence: A construct amid a thicket of conceptual snares. *Emergence*, 2, 5–22.

Goldstein, J. 2013. Re-imagining emergence: Part 1. *Emergence: Complexity & Organization*, 15, 78–104.

Goleman, D. 2009. *Working with emotional intelligence.* London: Bloomsbury Publishing.

Goodwin, D. K. 2006. *Team of rivals: The political genius of Abraham Lincoln.* New York: Simon & Schuster.

Granovetter, M. S. 1973. The strength of weak ties. *American Journal of Sociology*, 78, 1360–1380.

Grint, K. 2005. Problems, problems, problems: The social construction of 'leadership'. *Human Relations*, 58, 1467–1494.

Heifetz, R., Grashow, A. & Linsky, M. 2009a. Leadership in a (permanent) crisis. *Harvard Business Review*, 87, 62–69.

Heifetz, R., Grashow, A. & Linsky, M. 2009b. *The practice of adaptive leadership: Tools and tactics for changing your organization and the world.* Boston: Harvard Business Press.

Heifetz, R. & Laurie, D. L. 2001. The work of leadership. *Harvard Business Review*, December 2001, 37–47.

Higgs, M. & Rowland, D. 2005. All changes great and small: Exploring approaches to change and its leadership. *Journal of Change Management*, 5, 121–151.

Hodgson, G. M. 2011. Organizational evolution versus the cult of change. *Corporate Finance Review*, January/February 2011.

Holland, J. 1995. *Hidden order: How adaptation builds complexity*. Cambridge, MA: Perseus Books.

Houchin, K. & MacLean, D. 2005. Complexity theory and strategic change: An empirically informed critique. *British Journal of Management*, 16, 149–166.

Howard-Grenville, J., Golden-Biddle, K., Irwin, J. & Mao, J. 2011. Liminality as cultural process for cultural change. *Organization Science*, 22, 522–539.

Huy, Q. N., Corley, K. G. & Kraatz, M. S. 2014. From support to mutiny: Shifting legitimacy judgments and emotional reactions impacting the implementation of radical change. *Academy of Management Journal*, 57, 1650–1680.

Ibarra, H., Kilduff, M. & Wenpin, T. 2005. Zooming in and out: Connecting individuals and collectivities at the frontiers of organizational network research. *Organization Science*, 16, 359–371.

Isaacs, W. 2008. *Dialogue: The art of thinking together*. New York: Crown.

James, W. 2012. *A pluralistic universe: Hibbert lectures at Manchester College on the present situation in philosophy*. Aukland: Floating Press.

Jamieson, D. W., Auron, M. & Shechtman, D. 2010. Managing use of self for masterful professional practice. *OD PRACTITIONER*, 42, 4–11.

Janis, I. L. 1972. *Victims of groupthink: A psychological study of foreign-policy decisions and fiascoes*. Boston: Houghton Mifflin.

Joines, V. & Stewart, I. 1987. *TA today: A new introduction to transactional analysis*. Nottingham: Lifespace Publishing.

Juarrero, A. 2011. Causality and explanation. *In:* Allen, P. M., Maguire, S. & McKelvey, B. (ed.) *The SAGE handbook of complexity and management*. London: Sage Publications.

Kahneman, D. 2012. *Thinking, fast and slow*. London: Penguin Books.

Kan, M. M. & Parry, K. W. 2004. Identifying paradox: A grounded theory of leadership in overcoming resistance to change. *The Leadership Quarterly*, 15, 467–491.

Kauffman, S. 1993. *The origins of order: Self-organization and selection in evolution*. New York: Oxford University Press.

Kauffman, S. 1995. *At home in the universe: The search for laws of self-organization and complexity*. Oxford: Oxford University Press.

Kegan, R. 1982. *The evolving self*. Cambridge, MA: Harvard University Press.

Kegan, R. 1994. *In over our heads: The mental demands of modern life*. Cambridge, MA: Harvard University Press.

Kegan, R. & Lahey, L. L. 2009. *Immunity to change: How to overcome it and unlock potential in yourself and your organization*. Boston MA: Harvard Business Press.

King, B. G., Felin, T. & Whetten, D. A. 2010. Finding the organization in organizational theory: A meta-theory of the organization as a social actor. *Organization Science*, 21, 290–305.

Klein, G. 2007. Performing a project premortem. *Harvard Business Review*, September 2007.

Klein, G. 2013. *Seeing what others don't: The remarkable ways we gain insights*. London: Nicholas Brearley Publishing.

Knight, E. & Paroutis, S. 2017. Becoming salient: The TMT leader's role in shaping the interpretive context of paradoxical tensions. *Organization Studies*, 38, 403–432.

Knight, F. H. 1921. *Risk, uncertainty and profit*. Boston MA: Houghton Mifflin.

Kotter, J. 1995. Leading change: Why transformation efforts fail. *Harvard Business Review*, March-April, 58–67.

Kotter, J. P. 2001. What leaders really do. *Harvard Business Review*, 79, 85–96.

Kotter, J. P. 2012. Accelerate! *Harvard Business Review*, 90, 43–58.

Kübler-Ross, E. 1997. *On death and dying*. New York: Scribner.

Lave, J. & Wenger, E. 1991. *Situated learning. Legitimate peripheral participation.* Cambridge: University of Cambridge Press.

Letiche, H., Lissack, M. & Schultz, R. 2011. *Coherence in the midst of complexity: Advances in social complexity theory.* London: Palgrave Macmillan.

Lewin, K. 1947a. Frontiers in group dynamics: Concept, method and reality in social science; social equilibria and social change. *Human Relations*, 1, 5–41.

Lewin, K. 1947b. Frontiers in group dynamics: II. Channels of group life; social planning and action research. *Human Relations*, 1, 143–153.

Lewin, K. 1947/2009. Quasi-stationary social equilibria and the problem of permanent change. *In:* Burke, W., Lake, D. & Paine, J. W. (ed.) *Organization change: A comprehensive reader.* San Francisco: Jossey-Bass.

Lewin, K. 1951. *Field theory in social science.* New York: Harper & Row.

Lewis, M. W. & Smith, W. K. 2014. Paradox as a metatheoretical perspective: Sharpening the focus and widening the scope. *The Journal of Applied Behavioral Science*, 50, 127–149.

Lichtenstein, B. B. 2000. Self-organized transitions: A pattern amid the chaos of transformative change. *Academy of Management Executive*, 14, 128–141.

Lichtenstein, B. B. 2009. Moving far from far-from-equilibrium: Opportunity tension as the catalyst of emergence. *Emergence: Complexity & Organization*, 11, 15–25.

Lichtenstein, B. B. 2014. *Generative emergence: A new discipline of organizational, entrepreneurial, and social innovation.* New York: Oxford University Press.

Lichtenstein, B. B. & Plowman, D. A. 2009. The leadership of emergence: A complex systems leadership theory of emergence at successive organizational levels. *Leadership Quarterly*, 20, 617–630.

Lindblom, C. E. 1959. The science of "muddling through". *Public Administration Review*, 19, 79–88.

Livne-Tarandach, R. & Bartunek, J. M. 2009. A new horizon for organizational change and development scholarship: Connecting planned and emergent change. *Research in organizational change and development, volume 17.* Bingley: Emerald Group Publishing.

Lorenz, E. 1972/2000. The butterfly effect. *In:* Abraham, R. & Ueda, Y. (ed.) *The chaos avant-garde: Memories of the early days of chaos theory.* Singapore: World Scientific.

Mack, A. & Rock, I. 1998. *Inattentional blindness.* Cambridge, MA: Bradford.

Mackay, R. B. & Chia, R. 2013. Choice, change, and unintended consequences in strategic change: A process understanding of the rise and fall of northco automotive. *Academy of Management Journal*, 56, 208–230.

Maguire, S. & McKelvey, B. 1999. Complexity and management: Moving from fad to firm foundations. *Emergence*, 1, 19.

Mantel, H. 2010. *Wolf hall.* New York: Fourth Estate.

March, J. G. 1991. Exploration and exploitation in organizational learning. *Organization Science*, 2, 71–87.

Marshall, J. 1999. Living life as inquiry. *Systemic Practice and Action Research*, 12, 155–171.

Marshall, J. 2016. *First person action research: Living life as inquiry.* Thousand Oaks, CA: SAGE Publications.

Mayton, S. M. 2011. Survivor coping: A fresh look at resiliency in the wake of downsizing. *OD PRACTITIONER*, 43, 42–47.

McKelvey, B. 2013. Reflections on Max Boisot's Ashby space applied to complexity management. *In:* Child, J. & Ihrig, M. (ed.) *Knowledge, organization, and management: Building on the work of Max Boisot.* Oxford: Oxford University Press.

McKenzie, J. 1996. *Paradox: The next strategic dimension.* Maidenhead, Berkshire: McGraw Hill.

McKenzie, J. & Van Winkelen, C. 2004. *Understanding the knowledgeable organization: Nurturing knowledge competence.* London: Thomson.

McKenzie, J. & Van Winkelen, C. 2011. Beyond words: Visual metaphors that can demonstrate comprehension of KM as a paradoxical activity system. *Systems Research & Behavioral Science*, 28, 138–149.

McKenzie, J. & Varney, S. 2018. Energizing middle managers' practice in organizational learning. *The Learning Organization*, 25, 383–398.

Meadows, D. H. 2008. *Thinking in systems: A primer*. Chelsea, VT: Chelsea Green Publishing.

Merali, Y. & Allen, P. M. 2011. Complexity and systems thinking. *In*: Allen, P., Maguire, S. & McKelvey, B. (ed.) *The SAGE handbook of complexity and management*. London: Sage Publications Ltd.

Mikkelsen, K. & Martin, R. 2016. *The neo-generalist: Where you go is who you are*. London: LID publishing.

Mitchell, M. 2019. *Artificial intelligence: A guide for thinking humans*. London: Penguin Books Limited.

Mitchell, S. A. & Aron, L. 2013. *Relational psychoanalysis, volume 14: The emergence of a tradition*. Abingdon, Oxon: Taylor & Francis.

Mitleton-Kelly, E. 2003. Ten principles of complexity & enabling infrastructures. *In*: Mitleton-Kelly, E. (ed.) *Complex systems and evolutionary perspectives of organisations: The application of complexity theory to organisations*. Oxford: Elsevier.

Mitleton-Kelly, E. 2006. A complexity approach to co-creating an innovative environment. *World Futures*, 62, 223–239.

Morgan, G. 1997. *Images of organization*. Thousand Oaks, CA: Sage Publications.

Morrison, K. 2010. Complexity theory, school leadership and management: Questions for theory and practice. *Educational Management Administration & Leadership*, 38, 374–393.

Nonaka, I. 1994. A dynamic theory of organizational knowledge creation. *Organization Science*, 5, 14–37.

Nonaka, I. & Konno, N. 1998. The concept of "Ba": Building a foundation for knowledge creation. *California Management Review*, 40, 40–54.

Norman, G. 2011. Chaos, complexity and complicatedness: Lessons from rocket science. *Medical Education*, 45, 549–559.

Ocasio, W. 2011. Attention to attention. *Organization Science*, 22, 1286–1296.

Oettingen, G. 2014. *Rethinking positive thinking: Inside the new science of motivation*. London: Penguin Publishing Group.

Oliver, D. & Roos, J. 2000. *Striking a balance: Complexity and knowledge landscapes*. New York: McGraw-Hill.

Oreg, S., Bartunek, J. M., Lee, G. & Do, B. 2018. An affect-based model of recipients' responses to organizational change events. *Academy of Management Review*, 43, 65–86.

Orlikowski, W. J. 1996. Improvising organizational transformation over time: A situated change perspective. *Information Systems Research*, 7, 63–92.

Orlikowski, W. J. 2007. Sociomaterial practices: Exploring technology at work. *Organization Studies*, 28, 1435–1448.

Osborn, R. N., Hunt, J. G. & Jauch, L. R. 2002. Toward a contextual theory of leadership. *Leadership Quarterly*, 13, 797–837.

Pawson, R. & Tilley, N. 1997. *Realistic evaluation*. London: Sage Publications.

Perls, F. S., Goodman, P. & Hefferline, R. F. 1994. *Gestalt therapy: Excitement and growth in the human personality*. United Kingdom: Souvenir.

Peters, T. & Waterman, R. 1988. *In search of excellence*. New York: Harper & Row.

Pettigrew, A. M. 1992. The character and significance of strategy process research. *Strategic Management Journal*, 13, 5–16.

Plowman, D. A., Baker, L. T., Beck, T. E., Kulkarni, M., Solansky, S. T. & Travis, D. V. 2007. Radical change accidentally: The emergence and amplification of small change. *Academy of Management Journal*, 50, 515–543.

Polanyi, M. 1958. *Personal knowledge: Towards a post-critical philosophy*. Abingdon, Oxon: Taylor & Francis.

Poole, M. S. & Van De Ven, A. H. 1989. Using paradox to build management and organization theories. *Academy of Management Review*, 14, 562–578.

Price, I. 2004. Complexity, complicatedness and complexity: A new science behind organizational intervention? *Emergence: Complexity & Organization*, 6, 40–48.

Prigogine, I. & Stengers, I. 1984. *Order out of chaos: Man's new dialogue with nature*. New York: Bantam Books.

Rerup, C. 2009. Attentional triangulation: Learning from unexpected rare crises. *Organization Science*, 20, 876–893.

Reynolds, C. W. 1987. Flocks, herds and schools: A distributed behavioral model. *Proceedings of the 14th annual conference on computer graphics and interactive techniques*. New York: ACM.

Richardson, K. A. 2008. Managing complex organizations: Complexity thinking and the science and art of management. *Emergence: Complexity & Organization*, 10, 13–26.

Richardson, K. A. 2010. *Thinking about complexity: Grasping the continuum through criticism and pluralism*. Litchfield Park, AZ: Emergent Publications.

Rodgers, C. 2021. *The wiggly world of organization*. Abingdon, Oxon: Routledge.

Romanelli, E. & Tushman, M. L. 1994. Organizational transformation as punctuated equilibrium: An empirical test. *Academy of Management Journal*, 37, 1141–1666.

Rothman, N. B. & Melwani, S. 2017. Feeling mixed, ambivalent, and in flux: The social functions of emotional complexity for leaders. *Academy of Management Review*, 42, 259–282.

Russell, J. A. 1980. A circumplex model of affect. *Journal of Personality and Social Psychology*, 39, 1161–1178.

Sanchez-Burks, J. & Huy, Q. N. 2009. Emotional aperture and strategic change: The accurate recognition of collective emotions. *Organization Science*, 20, 22–34.

Sargut, G. & McGrath, R. G. 2011. Learning to live with complexity. *Harvard Business Review*, 89, 68–76.

Schein, E. H. 1997. The concept of "client" from a process consultation perspective: A guide for change agents. *Journal of Organizational Change Management*, 10, 202–216.

Schneider, M. & Somers, M. 2006. Organizations as complex adaptive systems: Implications of complexity theory for leadership research. *Leadership Quarterly*, 17, 351–365.

Schoemaker, P. J. H. & Day, G. S. 2009. How to make sense of weak signals. *MIT Sloan Management Review*, 50, 81–89.

Schön, D. 1983. *The reflective practitioner*. Aldershot: Ashgate Publishing.

Schreiber, C. & Carley, K. M. 2006. Leadership style as an enabler of organizational complex functioning. *Emergence: Complexity & Organization*, 8, 61–76.

Shaw, P. 1997. Intervening in the shadow systems of organizations: Consulting from a complexity perspective. *Journal of Organizational Change Management*, 10, 235–250.

Shaw, P. & Stacey, R. D. 2006. *Experiencing risk, spontaneity and improvisation in organizational change: Working live*. Abingdon, Oxon: Routledge.

Shepard, H. 1975. Rules of thumb for change agents. *OD Practitioner*, 7, 1–5.

Shotter, J. & Tsoukas, H. 2014a. In search of phronesis: Leadership and the art of judgment. *Academy of Management Learning & Education*, 13, 224–243.

Shotter, J. & Tsoukas, H. 2014b. Performing phronesis: On the way to engaged judgment. *Management Learning*, 45, 377–396.

Simons, D. J. & Chabris, C. F. 1999. Gorillas in our midst: Sustained inattentional blindness for dynamic events. *Perception*, 28, 1059–1074.

Simpson, P. 2007. Organizing in the mist: A case study in leadership and complexity. *Leadership & Organization Development Journal*, 28, 465–482.

Smith, T. W. 2015. *The book of human emotions: An encyclopedia of feeling from anger to wanderlust*. London: Profile.

Smith, W. K. & Lewis, M. W. 2011. Toward a theory of paradox: A dynamic equilibrium model of organizing. *Academy of Management Review*, 36, 381–403.

Snowden, D. 2002. Complex acts of knowing: Paradox and descriptive self-awareness. *Journal of Knowledge Management*, 6, 100–111.

Snowden, D. J. & Boone, M. E. 2007. A leader's framework for decision making. *Harvard Business Review*, 85, 68–76.

Stacey, R. D. 1992. *Managing the unknowable: Strategic boundaries between order and chaos in organizations*. San Francisco: Jossey-Bass.

Stacey, R. D. 1995. The science of complexity: An alternative perspective for strategic change processes. *Strategic Management Journal*, 16, 477–495.

Stacey, R. D. 1996. *Strategic management and organisational dynamics: The challenge of complexity*. London: Pitman.

Stacey, R. D. 2001. *Complex responsive processes in organizations: Learning and knowledge creation*. Abingdon, Oxon: Routledge.

Stacey, R. D. 2010. *Complexity and organizational reality*. Abingdon, Oxon: Routledge.

Stacey, R. D. 2012. *Tools and techniques of leadership and management: Meeting the challenge of complexity*. Abingdon, Oxon: Routledge.

Stacey, R. D. & Griffin, D. 2005. *A complexity perspective on researching organizations: Taking experience seriously*. Abingdon, Oxon: Routledge.

Stacey, R. D. & Mowles, C. 2016. *Strategic management and organisational dynamics: The challenge of complexity to ways of thinking about organisations*. London: Pearson Education.

Stake, R. E. 2010. *Qualitative research: Studying how things work*. New York,:The Guilford Press.

Starbuck, W. H. & Hedberg, B. 2003. How organizations learn from success and failure. *In:* Dierkes, M., Antal, A. B., Child, J. & Nonaka, I. (eds.) *Handbook of organizational learning and knowledge*. Oxford: Oxford University Press.

Starbuck, W. H. & Milliken, F. J. 1988. Executives' perceptual filters: What they notice and how they make sense. *In:* Hambrick, D. C. (ed.) *The executive effect: Concepts and methods for studying top managers*. Greenwich: JAI Press.

Sterling, J. 2019. How leadership teams can face and fix their "undiscussable" dysfunctions. *Strategy & Leadership*, 48, 12–20.

Streatfield, P. J. 2001. *The paradox of control in organizations*. London: Routledge.

Sullivan, T. 2011. Embracing complexity. *Harvard Business Review*, 89, 89–92.

Swan, J., Scarbrough, H. & Ziebro, M. 2016. Liminal roles as a source of creative agency in management: The case of knowledge-sharing communities. *Human Relations*, 69, 781–811.

Taleb, N. N. 2010. *The black swan: The impact of the highly improbable fragility*. New York: Random House Publishing Group.

Tichy, N. M. 1983. *Managing strategic change: Technical, political, and cultural dynamics*. New York: Wiley.

Toegel, G. & Barsoux, J. 2019. It's time to tackle your team's undiscussables. *MIT Sloan management review*, 61, 37–46.

Tourish, D. 2019. Is complexity leadership theory complex enough? A critical appraisal, some modifications and suggestions for further research. *Organization Studies*, 40, 219–238.

Tsoukas, H. & Chia, R. 2002. On organizational becoming: Rethinking organizational change. *Organization Science*, 13, 567–582.

Tushman, M. L. 1977. Special boundary roles in the innovation process. *Administrative Science Quarterly*, 22, 587–605.

Uhl-Bien, M. & Arena, M. 2018. Leadership for organizational adaptability: A theoretical synthesis and integrative framework. *Leadership Quarterly*, 29, 89–104.

Uhl-Bien, M. & Marion, R. 2009. Complexity leadership in bureaucratic forms of organizing: A meso model. *The Leadership Quarterly*, 20, 631–650.

Uhl-Bien, M., Marion, R. & McKelvey, B. 2007. Complexity leadership theory: Shifting leadership from the industrial age to the knowledge era. *The Leadership Quarterly*, 18, 298–318.

Uhl-Bien, M., Meyer, D. & Smith, J. 2020. Complexity leadership in the nursing context. *Nursing Administration Quarterly*, 44, 109–116.

Varney, S. 2007. *Learning in complex organisations: Uncovering the secrets of success*, Horsham, Roffey Park Institute.

Varney, S. 2013. *A complexity perspective on organisational change: Making sense of emerging patterns in self-organising systems*. Unpublished doctoral thesis, Henley Business School, University of Reading.

Varney, S. 2015. Change – why "small data" is HR's best friend. *Croner-i Human Resources* [Online].

Varney, S. 2019. An OD-based framework for advancing change practice. *e-ORGANISATIONS & PEOPLE*, VOL. 26, 63–71.

Vuori, T. O. & Huy, Q. N. 2016. Distributed attention and shared emotions in the innovation process: How Nokia lost the smartphone battle. *Administrative Science Quarterly*, 61, 9–51.

Vygotsky, L. 1978. *Mind in society*. Cambridge, MA: Harvard University Press.

Watts, D. J. 2012. *Everything is obvious: How common sense fails*. London: Atlantic Books.

Weick, K. E. 1995. *Sensemaking in organizations*. Thousand Oaks, CA: Sage Publications.

Weick, K. E. 2000. Emergent change as a universal in organizations. *In:* Beer, M. & Nohria, N. (eds.) *Breaking the code of change*. Boston: Harvard Business School Press.

Weick, K. E. 2011. Reflections: Change agents as change poets – on reconnecting flux and hunches. *Journal of Change Management*, 11, 7–20.

Weick, K. E. 2012. *Making sense of the organization, volume 2: The impermanent organization*. Chichester: Wiley.

Weick, K. E. & Quinn, R. E. 1999. Organizational change and development. *Annual Review of Psychology*, 50, 361–386.

Wheatley, M. 1999. *Leadership and the new science*. San Francisco: Berrett-Koehler.

Wheatley, M. J. & Frieze, D. 2011. *Walk out walk on: A learning journey into communities daring to live the future now*. Oakland, CA: Berrett-Koehler Publishers.

Yukl, G. 2008. How leaders influence organizational effectiveness. *Leadership Quarterly*, 19, 708–722.

List of figures

https://doi.org/10.1515/9783110713343-012

List of tables

https://doi.org/10.1515/9783110713343-013

About the author

Sharon Varney is a scholar-practitioner who specialises in developing people and organisations.

Sharon developed her deep expertise in leadership and change working in large, complex organisations. She was Vice President for international learning and development at a US bank, before joining a global engineering and construction company in the offshore oil and gas industry as their group head of learning and communications.

In the early 2000s, Sharon was bitten by the complexity bug. This changed the trajectory of her career and she left the offshore business to take a deep dive into academia. Her award-winning doctoral research, which has a very practical edge, explored the complex dynamics of organisational change and the role of change leaders within it.

Sharon now effectively bridges academia and practice. Working across a wide variety of business settings, she applies complexity science insights in her leadership and organisational development (OD) work. This includes bringing thought and practice leadership to The Henley Forum, an applied research centre at Henley Business School, and to Masters' programmes at Henley and beyond.

https://doi.org/10.1515/9783110713343-014

About the series editor

Bernd Vogel is a Professor in Leadership and Founding Director of the Henley Centre for Leadership at Henley Business School, UK.

Bernd has more than 20 years of global experience in research, educating, speaking, and consulting with outstanding companies, business schools and universities. He supports organisations and people in life-long learning journeys that transform lives, organisations, and society. He bridges academia with practice and is an executive coach.

His expertise is in leadership and leadership development; future of work and leadership; strategic leadership to mobilise and sustain healthy energy and performance; developing leadership and followership capability; healthy and performing senior management teams; change, transformation and culture; leadership development architectures.

Bernd features regularly in media. He publishes in top-tier global academic journals and has written and edited several books, case studies and industry reports.

Throughout his career Bernd has had academic roles at the Leibniz University Hannover, Germany, and University of St. Gallen, Switzerland. He has held global visiting positions at Claremont Graduate University, USA; IESE Business School, Spain; and Marshall School of Business, USC, USA.

https://doi.org/10.1515/9783110713343-015

Index

Bold page numbers indicate figures; *italics* indicate tables.

https://doi.org/10.1515/9783110713343-016

www.ingramcontent.com/pod-product-compliance
Lightning Source LLC
Chambersburg PA
CBHW061809210326
41599CB00034B/6933